IN THE WOODS
BEFORE DAWN

In the WOODS BEFORE DAWN

The Samuel Richey Collection of the Southern Confederacy

Jerry Frey

THOMAS PUBLICATIONS
Gettysburg **PA 17325**

Copyright © 1994 Jerry Frey

Printed and bound in the United States of America

Published by THOMAS PUBLICATIONS
P.O. Box 3031
Gettysburg, Pa. 17325

ISBN-0-939631-73-3

Cover design by Ryan C. Stouch

Dedicated to the memory of Rose Frey

Maj Milligan
    Maj

In the Woods, Thursday before
dawn April 14th '64

John, Ed, Wright & I have
just returned from over the river, the
whole beach is closely picketed, we made sever
al attempts but did not succeed in landing
untill last night, & then we had to risk it
between the pickets, there are 50 sentinels from
Caskins to Mrs Mansfields besides a number
patroling the roads, Whilst we were crossing
3 G.B. went up the river (something unusual
in 2 hours one came back, I think they landed
something (not men) at Sleepy-Hole whf.

Burnsides Corps was arriving at Portsmouth
on Monday, they are Camping near the City, their
destination from their account is Weldon and
Goldsboro; Bunting reports that tis thought that
Spiers is there, I could learn nothing of him,
Some foward movement by the way of Suffk is
on foot,

Will apprise you of anything that
occurs

Very truly yrs &c
Jo C Wordsworthy

Maj Milligan

Maj

John, Ed, Wright & I have just from returned from over the river, the whole beach is picketed, we made several attempts but did not succeed in landing untill last night, & then had to risk it between the pickets, there are 50 sentinels from Gaskins to Mrs. Mansfields besides a number patroling the roads, Whilst we were crossing 3 G B. went up the river (something unusual) in 2 hours one came back, I think they landed something (not men) at Sleepy Hole whf.

Burnsides Corp's was arriving at Portsmouth on Monday, they are Camping near the City, their destination from their account is Weldon and Goldsboro, Bunting reports tis thought that Spiers is there, I could learn nothing of him, Some forward movement by the way of Suffo[lk] is on foot,

Will apprise you of anything that occurs

Very truly yrs &c
JosC Norsworthy

CONTENTS

LIST OF MAPS

PREFACE

On February 24, 1911, Daniel Buchwalter, a veteran of Company A, 120th Ohio Volunteer Infantry, began writing his recollections of service during the Civil War. Seventy-nine years later I obtained his reminiscence from Alan Hoeweler, past president of the Cincinnati Civil War Round Table. I edited Buchwalter's words and wrote a parallel account of the 120th Ohio's service. An obscure outfit, the 120th Ohio raised the first Union flag over Arkansas Post on January 11, 1863, after the Confederate garrison surrendered. The regiment participated in the Vicksburg Campaign and suffered sixty percent casualties during the Red River Campaign. In November 1864, the survivors were consolidated with the 114th Ohio. Daniel Buchwalter served with the 114th until the end of the war and fought in the last battle of the war at Fort Blakely, Alabama, on April 9, 1865. Upon completion of the manuscript, I sought another project.

I had a hunch that nearby Miami University might possess source material from Union soldiers. On March 30, 1992, I travelled to Oxford, Ohio, to the King Library. Located in the Special Collections section of the library, I discovered that a great deal of interesting material was available for examination. A collection of letters from a member of the 83rd Ohio captured my attention because the author of them had served in the same brigade as Daniel Buchwalter during the assault on Fort Blakely.

As I read the letters, I came across a booklet entitled "The Samuel Richey Collection Of The Southern Confederacy." I then discovered that Jefferson Davis had written or received all of the letters listed in the booklet. There were also many other infamous Confederate officers such as Jubal Early, Braxton Bragg, D.H. Hill, and Ben L. Posey mentioned as Davis' correspondents.

Later that same night, I examined the booklet more closely and noted a letter written by Jefferson Davis that described the circumstances of his capture in 1865. Daniel Buchwalter had mentioned "the capture of Jeff Davis the arch traitor" and I knew that details of Davis' capture were controversial. I then concluded that the material deserved a thorough investigation.

The next day I again returned to the library and was overwhelmed with the information that I was uncovering. Throughout the booklet were numerous controversies and disputes between Confederate leaders. The people involved were of the utmost importance to the Confederacy and included men such as Beauregard, Johnston, Jackson, and Stuart.

There are hundreds of documents in this collection; most of them written by staff officers or clerks during the war. Others came from people unknown to historians, and dozens were written by civilians. There are also some which were written by junior and senior Confederate officers both during and after the conflict.

During the weeks that followed I did a close examination of a large portion of the documents. At one point, I discovered that I was looking at a page written by John Bell Hood which described his feelings toward Leonidas Polk, who had been killed just two days before. The emotion and details were extraordinary.

By mid-April I began to see that the material in the collection covered much of the war. It then became my personal goal to place several of the more informative letters into their correct historical context in a book form so they may be enjoyed by anyone with an interest in the Civil War. Because most Civil War buffs have no reason to read the entire collection of the *Official Records of the War of the Rebellion*, I have noted any instances where the letters from the Richey Collection appear in the *OR*. Many historians quote bits and pieces from reports and letters, but I have strived to reproduce complete documents, which sometimes differ from the *OR*. For example, during the Atlanta Campaign, President Davis sent General Bragg to Georgia in July. The disgraced former commander of the Army of Tennessee forwarded a long letter to Davis dated July 15, 1864, that described the situation. Bragg's letter included a suggestion to replace General Joseph E. Johnston as commander of the Army of Tennessee. This letter is often quoted in part, but the entire document is worth reading.

Two of the most interesting letters contained in the Richey Collection were written by D.H. Hill to Jefferson Davis in 1867. They concern Hill's removal as a corps commander in the Army of Tennessee in October 1863. One of them reveals the hitherto unknown reason for Hill's removal by General Bragg. It was this kind of information that I found the most inspirational for taking on a project of this size.

Sutton C. Richey, an 1855 graduate of Miami University, began the collection. An admirer of General Lee, he discovered that autographed letters of the Virginian were more difficult to acquire than autographed letters from President Davis. His son, Samuel W. Richey (1874-1973; Miami University 1894) continued to collect Civil War documents during business trips in the South. Most of the collection was donated to Miami University in 1960, while the remainder was obtained later. My profound thanks are extended to Miami University for sharing the documents collected by Samuel Richey and his father. The perusal of their collection was a continuous delight.

There are many others whom I wish to acknowledge and thank for their support and assistance. First and foremost are my family and Alan Hoeweler; without them this book could not have been attempted or completed. I would also like to thank three members of the Cincinnati Civil War Round Table, Tom Breiner, Dan Reigle, and Dave Smith, who provided me with many books and encouragement. Jack Friend provided valuable assistance when I visited

Mobile. And, finally, I must acknowledge the professionalism and kindness of the Special Collections staff at the King Library: Mr. C. Martin Miller, Head Special collections and Archives; Frances McClure, assistant to Mr. Miller; Elizabeth Brice, and Jim Bricker. Thank you all very much.

Jerry Frey
Cincinnati, Ohio
December 8, 1993

FOREWORD

The ongoing fascination of the American public with the Civil War continues unabated. We continue to be held spellbound by the battles, personalities, facts, and figures about a conflict that occurred over 130 years ago, and our appetite for more shows no signs of diminishing.

Much of what is read in Civil War literature comes from first hand material which was written in the form of diaries, letters, and reports from men and women who may well have been our direct ancestors. The Civil War was the first war in which the literacy of the common soldier allowed us to have first-hand accounts of the conflict itself.

In spite of all this, much of the flavor and personality of primary material is severely diluted by the time it is published. Writers tend to use a only a small part of the material at hand which is relevant to a specific topic. The rest is usually overlooked. When this happens, many comments and anecdotes which contain valuable details remain hidden within the pages of history.

In the Woods Before Dawn is not about a particular subject concerning the Civil War. It revolves around the Samuel Richey Collection of documents located at the Miami University in Oxford, Ohio. Frey has taken a large portion of these documents and used them to link together several aspects of the Civil War. Most importantly, the reader has the opportunity to read entire documents, and in many cases, actually see the reproduced letter itself. This brings an immediacy to the work that is often not seen in historical literature of this type.

For example, the text enables the reader to follow the letters of Jubal Early to Jefferson Davis regarding Joseph E. Johnston and the First Manassas Campaign. Johnston and Davis were engaged in the 1870s in a bitter series of personal attacks on each other. Early found himself caught in the middle; having already responded to Johnston, he became the recipient of a similar request from his former president. The letters illustrate the almost desperate attempt of Early to find a way of covering himself without giving Davis any reason to believe that he had aided the camp of his enemy.

Having spent many hours helping Frey decipher the writing of several of the correspondents in this book, the result has provided me with a greater appreciation for all the historical figures involved. Because many of the letters have never before been seen in print, there is sure to be something of interest for everyone interested in the Civil War.

Dave Smith
Past President,
Cincinnati Civil War Round Table
Cincinnati, Ohio
May 6, 1994

1

THE ARMY OF NORTHERN VIRGINIA

War between the United States and the Confederate States erupted at 4:30 A.M., April 12, 1861, at Charleston, South Carolina, when Rebel artillerymen opened fire on Fort Sumter. Major John Anderson surrendered the next day to Brigadier General Pierre G.T. Beauregard (1818-1893; West Point 1838). In response to the outbreak of hostilites, President Abraham Lincoln called for 75,000 volunteers on April 15. Two days later, Virginia seceded from the Union. Governor John Letcher called out the militia on April 20 to defend his state from Northern invaders.

Many companies rendezvoused at Harpers Ferry. Located at the northern end of the Shenandoah Valley, the town commanded the entrance to Virginia's breadbasket. Control of the agricultural area was crucial to the defense of Virginia. An eccentric and energetic instructor from the Virginia Military Institute, Colonel Thomas J. Jackson, arrived at Harpers Ferry at the end of April to oversee training of the raw companies and organize them into regiments.

Two weeks after he took charge of the troops at Harpers Ferry, Colonel Jackson was superseded by Brigadier General Joseph E. Johnston (1807-1891; West Point 1829). Prior to the war, Johnston had served as quartermaster of the U.S. Army with the staff rank of brigadier general. With the bureaucratic tendency to avoid making decisions that made him look bad, Johnston's "fundamental gift was his accuracy in appraising the enemy's intentions

1

against him, and he could always move his army out of harm's way. As this skill in evasion was not accompanied by any purpose to inflict injury on the enemy, he could never lose a battle."[1]

General Johnston considered Harpers Ferry to be indefensible. When Brigadier General Robert Patterson (1792-1881; Mexican War) advanced from Harrisburg, Pennsylvania, toward the Potomac River in mid-June, Johnston fell back toward Winchester to await developments. A report that the enemy intended to cross the Potomac caused General Johnston to reinforce his cavalry patrol with an infantry brigade under Colonel Jackson. The following three documents sent to Adjutant and Inspector General Samuel Cooper (1798-1876; West Point 1815) relate Johnston's assessment of the situation and the organization of his army.

Hd Qrs Winchester

June 24 1861

General,

I was informed yesterday by a person just from Baltimore, and strongly recommended to me by a friend in that place for his principles and means of information that Gen'l Patterson's troops are still occupying Hagerstown & Williamsport [Maryland], the main body being in the former place, and six or eight thousand men under Gen'l Cadwallader[2] in the latter. He says that Gen'l Patterson has been corresponding with the authorities of the B&O R.R. in relation to repairing the road, and talks of occupying Harpers Ferry. Should he do so with less than ten or twelve thousand men, an equal force attacking him would have the advantage of ground.

Col. Jackson who is in the neighborhood of Martinsburg to support the Cavalry, which is observing the enemy, has according to his instructions, destroyed all the "rolling stock" of the road within his reach. I have directed him to have such of the large stock of coal as the inhabitants require, sold to them, and accounts to be kept of the sales, and the proceeds to be used in purchasing provisions in the neighborhood. I have had the pleasure to receive the order for Capt. W. E. James to report to me with his company of Cavalry. We require three or four more companies of that arm, from the great extent of the country to be observed.

Another officer capable of commanding a Brigade and four or five competent to the duties of Quarter Masters and Commissaries are greatly needed. In this connection I recommend the appointment of Lieutenants Davis & Morgan as assistant Quarter Masters. They have proved themselves competent to the discharge of the duties of that position.

very respectfully
your obt servt.
(signed) J.E. Johnston
Brig Genl C.S.A

Genl S. Cooper
Adjt & Inspct Genl
Richmond Va.
[*OR* II Series I pp. 948, 949]

General Pierre Gustave Toutant Beauregard

General Joseph Eggleston Johnston

Hd. Qrs. Winchester Va

June 29th 1861

General,

I have just had the pleasure to read Brig. Gen E. K. Smith's appointment to that grade.

I have divided these troops into four brigades. Two more such officers as Brig Genl's Bee & Smith would add greatly to the efficiency of this force.

Gen'l Smith has been acting as Adjt Gen'l. If Col. Pemberton can be spared do send him immediately for that post. If he cannot, Major [Thomas B.] Rhett, now at Manassas Junction, would like to join me. If Col. Pemberton is in the position of Lt. Col. I am sure that he would gladly serve with me.

I hear of no movements of the enemy.

Most respectfully,
Yr. Obt. Servt.
[Signed] J. E. Johnston
Brig. Gen. C. S. A.

Gen'l S. Cooper

Hd. Qrs. Winchester
July 9th 1861; 7 P.M.

General:

I have just been informed by Lt. Col. Stuart, Commd'g our Cavalry, that he has no reason to believe that the enemy intends to advance upon us to night (the distance is but 22 miles) the evidences are, that it is the belief of the people living near the town, ascertained by his pickets, and that three days' provisions were issued today, & that a U. S. Lt. had mentioned it.

We are not prepared beyond the readiness of our men to fight. The field works have not been progressed with far enough to make them useful, & the militia is not provided with fixed ammunition, having received but powder & Lead.

Gen'l S. Cooper   Most respectfully &c
A.& I. Gen.   (Signed)   Jos. E. Johnston
[*OR* II Series I p. 969]

General Beauregard emerged as the Confederacy's first hero after Fort Sumter fell. In May, he reported to Richmond and received orders to take command of the army being organized around Manassas Junction in northern Virginia. The Manassas Gap Railroad, which served the Shenandoah Valley, joined the Orange and Alexandria Railroad at Manassas. The Virginia Central Railroad connected with the Orange and Alexandria Railroad east of the Valley at Gordonsville. Should a Federal force threaten northern Virginia, Gen. Johnston could rush troops via the railroad to Gen. Beauregard. If Johnston was threatened, Beauregard could reinforce the army defending the Valley. Therefore it was vital for the Confederates to hold Manassas Junction.

The Federals were also aware of the importance of the railroad junction at Manassas and planned to pin General Johnston with General Patterson's force, then advance toward Manassas from Washington. On July 16, Brigadier General Irvin McDowell (1818-1885; West Point 1838) marched from the capital with great reluctance in command of a green army of more than 30,000 men. General Beauregard, who opposed McDowell with 20,000 equally inexperienced troops, fell back before McDowell's divisions.

General Beauregard's volunteers were positioned behind a creek called Bull Run. Most of his brigades waited in the center of the line about two miles from Manassas Junction. Brigadier General Daniel Tyler's (1799-1882; West Point 1819) Union division entered Centreville on the morning of July 18. Tyler sent a brigade to probe enemy strength along the creek. A skirmish broke out at Blackburn's Ford, but neither side suffered significant losses and the Yankees withdrew.

For the next two days, General McDowell prepared his army for battle and developed his strategy. He decided to sweep around the enemy's left with three divisions while one of Tyler's brigades demonstrated to prevent Beauregard from reinforcing the threatened flank. The Southern line was eight miles long; the left flank was weak. McDowell's plan was well-conceived but the two-day delay ruined his opportunity to win the first major battle of the war because Patterson failed to carry out his part of the plan. His lack of aggression allowed General Johnston to reinforce Beauregard's Army of the Potomac. When the Richmond government learned of McDowell's advance, General Johnston was ordered to General Beauregard's aid. The first troops to detrain at Manassas Junction on July 20 were commanded by Brigadier General T.J. Jackson (1824-1863; West Point 1846).[3] Four brigades arrived from the Valley along with the Hampton Legion from Richmond; four companies of the 1st Virginia Cavalry cantered cross country and camped on the evening of July 20 in the vicinity of a stone bridge on the Warrenton Turnpike.

Forward elements of General Tyler's division approached Stone Bridge around dawn. Here a tiny brigade under Colonel N.G. "Shanks" Evans, backed by two cannon, covered the extreme left of the Confederate line. Evans refrained from bringing on a general engagement in order to conceal the weakness of his position. This decision was critical to the outcome of the battle for upstream, two Union divisions under Brigadier Generals Samuel P. Heintzelman (1805-1880; West Point 1826) and David Hunter (1802-1886; West Point 1822) were fording Bull Run at Sudley Springs. When he learned that the enemy was on his left flank as well as his front, Evans left four companies to confront Tyler, then marched northwest to meet the new threat. The Rebels occupied Matthews Hill a mile from the ford and the Battle of Bull Run began in earnest around 9:30 A.M.

General Thomas Jonathan Jackson

Meanwhile, General Beauregard prepared to launch an attack toward Centreville. Around 10:00 A.M., when informed of the situation on his left, Beauregard revised his plan; three brigades were sent to support Evans.

General Hunter, who was wounded in the fighting, could not drive the Confederates from Matthews Hill. A counterattack by the 1st Louisiana Special Battalion gained time for the defenders until the brigades of Brigadier General Barnard E. Bee (1824-1861; West Point 1845) and Colonel Francis S. Bartow reached the field. Even though the Southerners remained badly outnumbered, they surged forward again. Three brigades advanced against the Union line but they did not get far. The 4th Alabama gained the most ground but lost its field officers. The untried Rebel soldiers could not endure the Union volleys and artillery fire. They retreated as General Heintzelman's regiments prepared to enter the battle.

Colonel William T. Sherman's Brigade of Tyler's Division forded Bull Run above Stone Bridge around 11:30 A.M. His appearance on the field along with pressure from Heintzelman caused the Confederates to abandon Matthews Hill. Sherman's Brigade joined Hunter's line, now commanded by Brigadier General Andrew Porter (1820-1872; Mexican War) and the Union advance resumed. With most of his army across Bull Run by noon, General McDowell sensed victory was at hand. General Jackson's Brigade, however, had not seen action.

General Beauregard recognized the extreme peril on his left flank and sent additional units to build up his defense. The Hampton Legion joined the disorganized Rebel regiments on Henry Hill and then moved toward Matthews Hill to resist Heintzelman. For an hour, the line of South Carolinians held as the Confederate generals established a new defensive line.

Colonel Wade Hampton's men were forced to retreat to Henry Hill where Jackson's stalwart Virginians waited. General Bee rallied the 4th Alabama and cried: "There is Jackson standing like a stone wall. Let us determine to die here and we will conquer. Follow me."[4] Bee led the Alabamians against the batteries of Captains J.B. Ricketts and Charles Griffin, but his soldiers broke and the general was mortally wounded.

Generals Beauregard and Johnston rode among the disorganized units to rally the tired men. Their presence encouraged the troops and Johnston personally brought the 4th Alabama into line on Jackson's right. Other fragmented regiments responded to the appeals and formed to the right of the Alabamians. Around 1:00 P.M., General Beauregard assumed tactical control of the battle while General Johnston departed to direct additional brigades toward the critical flank.

General McDowell renewed his attack and directed the batteries of Griffin and Ricketts to take position near the crest of Henry Hill. Supported by several regiments and a battalion of marines, the Union cannoneers fired at Jackson's Brigade. Around 2:00 P.M., the 33rd Virginia left the woods and headed for the guns. Captain Griffin observed their advance, but was ordered not to fire. Throughout the battle, friendly units fired on each other due to confusion caused by similar uniforms. The advancing soldiers revealed their identity with a withering volley that crippled both batteries. Captain Griffin managed to save one gun but the fire power of two strong batteries was lost. Volleys from a brigade of Heintzelman's Division drove off the 33rd Virginia.

For the next two hours Americans fought to control the Henry Hill plateau. As Confederate numbers gradually increased, General McDowell committed a tactical error. He allowed his regiments to enter the battle one by one which allowed the Rebels to concentrate their fire on a single target. Sherman's brigade suffered the highest number of casualties in McDowell's army by attacking in piecemeal fashion. Colonel Oliver O. Howard's command was an exception. His brigade reached the crest of Henry Hill only to fall back before Confederate musketry.

The last of the brigades from the Shenandoah Valley, under the command of Brigadier General E. Kirby Smith (1824-1893; West Point 1845), arrived on the field and quickly went into action. General Smith was seriously wounded and Colonel Arnold Elzey took command of the regiments which swept toward Colonel Howard's bruised brigade. By this time, about 4:00 P.M., much of the Union army was disheartened and disorganized. Pushed by Elzey and Colonel Jubal A. Early's Brigade, General McDowell's right flank crumbled. General Beauregard, who witnessed the attack, realized the decisive moment had arrived. He ordered the entire line forward. The Federals offered little resistance and fell back. Retreat degenerated into rout but the Confederate pursuit was ineffectual. A false report that Union troops were attacking at Union Mills Ford, southeast of the battlefield, caused Beauregard to recall his infantry. J.E.B. Stuart chased the invaders many miles but the cavalry arm was too weak to inflict much damage on the enemy. "Little was accomplished."[5] With the fighting over, the victorious army began to police the battlefield.

Late in the afternoon President Davis arrived from Richmond. He surveyed the battlefield and then returned to Manassas with General Johnston. General Beauregard joined them late that night.

> Parish of Plaquemines _ La
> Magnolia Plantation _ May 4/78

My Dear Sir,

Your favor of the 27th ulto. was received by me as I was making my preparations to leave the City for the country, in the hope of recuperating my health. I have reflected over the matter referred to in your letter, but cannot recollect any definite Order given by you, at my Hd. Qrtrs. on the night of the 21st of July 1861 _ to or for Gov. Bonham[6] to pursue the Federals on their retreat or flight to Washington, except the order referred to by Genl. Thos. Jordan[7] in the letter of the 18th ulto., which order was not finally issued for the reason stated by him. The question of pursuing was lengthily discussed by yourself, Genl. Johnston & myself but my present recollection is that no order was issued to pursue with greater vigor than was actually done. Moreover, no such order is to be found in my Order Book.

With regard to the time of arrival of yourself & Genl. Johnston to my Hd. Qrtrs. that night, I am confident it was before 10 h. P.M. instead of between 11 & 12 h. P.M. as you believe, for I reached the vicinity of Union Mills, from the pursuit on the Warrenton Turnpike, about sundown. I staid [*sic*] there about a half hour to ascertain the true state of affairs, I then returned toward the Lewis House as far as my jaded horse (the 2d horse I had mounted that day) could travel. When near there I was informed by one of my Staff officers whom I met on the road, that you & Genl. Johnston had left for my Hd. Qrtrs. at Manassas, where you expected to see me. I started immediately across the country for that point. The storm was then gathering rapidly & the night was dark. When I reached Manassas, at about 10 h., the rain had commenced falling with considerable force. I was told there that you & Genl. J had preceded me about half an hour. I joined you at once in my office & not long after, possibly about 11h., Capt. Hill of Genl. J.'s command, reported that he had been to Centreville & that the Federals had left there, retiring in great confusion &c. as stated by Gen. Jordan in his letter.

I am, Resply & truly Yours
G.T. Beauregard
362 S. Claude Str
Prest. Jeff. Davis   N.O.
Beauvoir
near Miss. City _ Miss.

The victorious triumvirate were discussing the possibility of pursuing McDowell's men when Captain Edward Porter Alexander of Beauregard's staff intruded. He was accompanied by a pre-war friend, Captain Robert C. Hill, who reported (falsely) that he had been to Centreville and found no Yankees there. Davis began to write out an order for Brigadier General Milledge L. Bonham (1813-1890; lawyer) to begin the pursuit that night. When Davis learned that his informant had been nicknamed "Crazy Hill" at West Point, he reconsidered the order. The next morning General Bonham conducted a reconnaissance in force toward Centreville but his movements were hampered by mud. No further advance was attempted.

Failure to advance on Washington by the disorganized Confederate army became a source of bitter controversy between Joseph Johnston and Jefferson Davis after the war. As the following letter to Davis suggests, one of the reasons for the lost opportunity to threaten the Capital of the United States was a lack of wagons to transport supplies. John S. Preston, a colonel on Beauregard's staff during the battle and related by marriage to Wade Hampton, remained unreconstructed after the war.

Columbia Dec 12th 1877

My dear Sir

Only three days ago I received your letter of the 3rd. I regret extremely that we differ so widely in our recollections concerning events at the first battle of Manassas.

I am perfectly certain I did not see until you came into my tent at Manassas. I ["do" lined out] am not sure of the hour. It was after dark, may have been nine _ ten _ or eleven. I sat up all night with Hampton who was suffering from a wound on the head. I had heard of your arrival, and you being on the battle field on my way to Manassas or on my reaching there about sun set.

I left the Generals Johnston & Beauregard about 5 P M. with orders to hasten to Manassas, by Mitchells Ford and McLeans [Ford], for the purpose of hurrying up Rations and other Supplies. Beauregards words in giving me the order were, "hurry up every-thing.—the army will camp on the field of victory"____ I took with me one orderly. At Mitchells I heard firing toward Centreville, or below that point. I sent the orderly back to Lewis to inform the Generals. I dont think they ever received the message. Hence I went to McLeans in search of the supply waggons __ & found none. On my way from McLeans, or at Manassas I first heard of your being on the battle field ___ then nearly dark.

I assure you, positively, this statement is correct. I left at Lewis's Colonels [John L.] Manning, [James] Chestnut [William P.] Miles and others of the Staff. May it not have been one of these officers with whom you rode and conversed. Where they and the Generals went after that I do not know.

I delivered the orders for the sending the Supplies to Lewis's (the battle field) __ before dark, about Sunset. Why they were not instantly forwarded __ was, as I heard afterwards, that transportation could not be had. Colo [R.B.] Lee (Commissary) expressed a fear of this when I gave him the order. These matters were above my sphere of duty, which was simply to extend the order, and I have no recollections of the details. My belief is that no field transportation was sent to the field, during the battle.

I presume upon a friendship with which you have honored me, and which was the chief pride of my humble official life to express my regret concerning these unhappy controversies among our compatriots, the martyrs of a holy Cause. Cannot they be hushed, for the remnant of our lives? You are great and high, your name precious & untarnished. The privilege of greatness is to be magnanimous. Silence is magnaminity. When we are all in the grave, History, cooled and impartial, by Time, will consecrate our cause, and embalm our name in the approval and admiration of those who live after us. You are safe on her record.

> Faithfully & truly Yrs
> John Preston

Another letter, written to General Bonham, shortly after the battle, indicates that the Confederate War Department was ill-prepared to supply the army's needs. The following letter indicates that individuals should not have been assigned blame for the failure to follow McDowell's army to Washington.

> Manassas Junction
> 30th July 1861

My dear Bonham,

I have just had an interesting visit with Gen. Beauregard, after waiting two hours on him until he roused himself from his nap. In regard to the information as to [Neitch?] he said nothing, but I think his silence on that point is explained by what I am now about to transmit.

As to Cash he says, he desires that the most earnest representations should be made to him, twice a week, which he will forward with earnest requests on his part, to the Department in Richmond. He told me to say, as coming from him, to the President, Sec. of War, & Mr [Secretary of the Treasury Christopher G.] Memminger, that, but for the destitute condition of the troops, as to transportation, subsistence, and clothing, this army would now be in Washington. That he has twenty thousand troops sent to him at this place, with not a horse, or a wagon to transport them. He says the Head of Departments at Richmond, seem to think we must fight the enemy at the end of Rail Road lines, & if the enemy appears off the line, no means of transporting the army are afforded. I understood him to say that but for the great cause in which we are engaged, he would not hold his commission a day. He seems to be much dissatisfied, & says he has again & again made the most earnest representations as to the conditions of our troops__ [illegible] he has written to Richmond to say that our army is anchored here for the want of food, transportation & clothing, that the winter is coming on, & if things go on as heretofore, we will have the army in the field, without the first provision for its comfort, which will not only destroy its efficiency but ruin the cause.

Good bye & God bless you

As ever your friend

(Signed) A P Aldrich

Genl. Bonham

On the plains of Manassas both sides were inexperienced. Superior military prowess brought victory to the Confederates; they did not have the easier task as defenders since their opponents held the initiative. If "Shanks" Evans had not disputed the advance of McDowell's flanking column, Beauregard could not have bolstered his weak left flank. Had General McDowell's strategy succeeded, the Confederates would have been forced to retreat and General Tyler's Division could have crossed Bull Run at Stone Bridge much sooner. As would be expected, the attackers lost more men[8] than the defenders, but only 17,000 Confederates were engaged from a force of 32,000 men; they were opposed by 28,000 soldiers in blue. Nine Union brigades (out of thirteen present) were engaged in the battle; seven suffered severe losses.

Before his arrival at Manassas Junction, General Johnston had telegraphed Richmond to clarify that he outranked General Beauregard. Johnston was senior to Beauregard, and in the following letter to Adjutant General Cooper, he demonstrates his extreme sensitivity toward his own authority, another bureaucratic trait.

Hd. Qrs. Manassas

July 29th 1861.

General,

I had the honor to write to you on the 24th inst. on the subject of my rank compared with that of other officers of the C.S. Army. Since then, I have recd daily, orders purporting to come from the "Hd. Qrs. of the forces"[9] some of them in relation to the internal affairs of this Army. Such orders, I cannot regard, because they are illegal.

Permit me to suggest, that orders to me, should come from your Office.

Most respectily

Yr. obt. Servt.

J.E. Johnston

Genl. C.S.A.

Genl. S. Cooper

A & I. Genl.

[*OR* II Series I p. 1007]

64

Hd. Qrs. Manassas.
July 29th 1861.

General,

I had the honor to write to you
on the 24th inst. on the subject of my rank
compared with that of other officers of the
C. S. Army. Since then, I have rec'd daily, orders purporting to come from the "Hd. Qrs. of
the forces"– some of them, in relation to the internal affairs of this army. Such orders, I
cannot regard, because they are illegal.

Permit me to suggest, that
orders to me, should come from your office.

Most respectfully
Y. obt. Servt.
J. E. Johnston
Genl. C. S. A.

Genl. S. Cooper.
A & I. Genl.

A letter from General Joseph E. Johnston to General Cooper

General Johnston endured another blow to his prestige the following month. Based on an act passed by the Confederate Congress on May 16, President Davis nominated five West Point graduates to the rank of full general. According to the legislation, the relative rank of the generals would be determined by their seniority in the U.S. Army. Generals Cooper, Albert S. Johnston (1803-1862; West Point 1826), Robert E. Lee (1807-1870; West Point 1829), Johnston, and Beauregard comprised this group. As the only pre-war general to resign among the five, Johnston anticipated being named senior officer of the Confederate army; he already considered himself so. President Davis placed General Cooper at the head of the list, even though his rank before the war had been colonel, because General Johnston had been a staff officer. Johnston regarded Davis' action to be a personal attack and responded by writing an unrestrained letter to the president, who reacted as though his own honor was at stake. The dispute damaged their relationship, and by 1863 Johnston and Davis were embroiled in a feud that lasted until 1889.

Colonel Richard "Dick" Taylor of the 9th Louisiana wrote in his memoirs: "I am persuaded that General Johnston's mind was so jaundiced by the unfortunate disagreement with President Davis...as to seriously cloud his judgment and impair his usefulness...I feel confident that his great abilities under happier conditions would have distinctly modified, if not changed, the current events. Destiny willed that Davis and Johnston should be brought into collision, and the breach, once made, was never repaired. Each misjudged the other to the end."[10]

On October 1, President Davis arrived at Fairfax Court House, a suburb of Washington, to discuss future strategy with Johnston, Beauregard, and Major General Gustavus W. Smith (1821-1896; West Point 1842). General Johnston commanded the reorganized regiments now called the Army of the Potomac. Generals Beauregard and Smith commanded the 1st and 2nd Corps respectively. Davis learned that his generals favored an offensive across the Potomac River but required 20,000 additional men to conduct the operation. Johnston suggested that the necessary reinforcements could come from the Georgia and the Carolinas, but because of political considerations, the president was reluctant to strip these states of troops. Moreover, thousands of volunteers remained unarmed.[11] Without Davis' backing, the planned offensive could not take place, and the Army of the Potomac withdrew to a defensive line around Centreville.

Secretary of War Judah P. Benjamin irritated Generals Beauregard and Johnston. Before the war, Benjamin had served in the U.S. Senate from Louisiana, but he had no prior acquaintance with military affairs. Secretary Benjamin combined affability with intelligence and devotion to President Davis. He served in the cabinet as the president's lackey. In the following letter to President Davis, General Beauregard expresses his frustration with Secretary Benjamin's style of management.

Head Quarters 1st Corps Army of the Potomac
Near Centreville
October 21st 1861

Sir

I have again to refer for your consideration a communication addressed to me by the present incumbent of the War office characterized, as your excellency will perceive, by that unwarrantable tone which he has chosen to assume in his cor[r]espondence with me.

What possible public interest is to be served by these communications with me at this time, I am utterly at a loss to perceive. At such a crisis however with the enemy's guns sounding in my ears as I write, his masses gathering in their mighty numbers within a few miles of us and the destiny of the Confederacy hanging most probably on the events of the next 48 hours, I shall not halt to discuss the subject matter of his last letter. I shall only say that I am willing that in the future, my Countrymen shall adjudge whether or not I have "studied" aright [torn] legislation of Congress in relation to Army organizations: whether, as the honorable secretary courteously advises. I have taken the "pains" to read the laws of Congress made "to provide for the public defence;" or whether in my ignorance of that legislation, I require enlightenment after the manner of the communication enclosed.

Meantime, I am here as a soldier of the cause, ready to the best of my ability, to execute the orders of the Government, either with regard to organization of this army or its operations, asking only for definite orders from the proper source, and expressed in proper terms. I am ready to act in any capacity demanded of me.

With this, I shall leave it to your excellency, an educated soldier, keenly alive to all the sensibilities which our profession and association engender, to shield me for the present from these ill timed unaccountable annoyances.

Respectfully Your Obt Servt
G.T. Beauregard
Genl. Comdg.

To his Excellency
President Jeff. Davis
Richmond Va.

As a result of the army's reorganization, brigades were composed of regiments from the same state. President Davis also wanted state divisions to be created, but as General Beauregard explained, this was inadvisable. Beauregard also disliked serving as second in command to Johnston and considered his corps to be separate from Johnston's overall command.

To Prest Davis

Centreville Va. Oct 22nd. 1861

My dear Sir,

Your letter of the 16th inst. has been received with its enclosures. Similar information had reached us from other sources; it would seem probable that McClellan under the pressure of public impatience has determined on a move & an attack of our army, which was thwarted by our falling back to our present very strong position, the right resting on Union Mills ford _ the centre at Centreville (the salient of the triangle) & the left on or near the Stone bridge; a position which I feel confident, he will not dare attack; but which unfortunately he may be able to turn, like all other positions in this neighborhood. If however the odds were only two to one against us, I am certain he will meet with a terrible defeat; for our troops are eager for the fray & have confidence in themselves & in their officers. I have read very carefully your observations touching the organization of this Army into state Brigades _ my preceding letter enclosing a copy of the Brigade organization of my Corps or Army must have shown you that not only the So. Ca. Brigade but all the others under my command were organized as desired by you, as far back as the 25th July last, four days after the Battle of Manassas & they were placed as far as practicable under the command of officers of the same or contiguous States _ the latter arrangement, however, is still to be tested more fully before being endorsed by me, for reasons already communicated to you in my last letter _ But I am decidedly of the opinion that the State organization ought not to go beyond the Brigades, for if in Battle a Division were cut to pieces or taken prisoner the loss would fall too heavily on one single state.

With regard to the organization of the two corps of this Army into one single Army, of course we stand ready to obey your orders relative thereto _ but as I suppose you deserve hearing my views on the subject I will give them to you freely. I believe that this system of absorption of one Army by another will naturally produce two very bad results.

1st the commander of the contiguous armies will always delay as long as possible coming to the assistance of a Senior commanding officer whose army may be in a critical position _ often losing also the chance of great achievements by a rapid combination of forces. 2nd When three or four armies shall have come together for a great object, 2 or 3 of the highest officers in the Service will be virtually thrown out of active employment at the very time their services would be most needed _ for instance if the Armies of Va & Holmes [in North Carolina] were united to this Army for a march on Washington, their forces, like mine, would be absorbed anaconda like by the army of the Potomac & Johnston, myself & Holmes would be de facto mere "lookers on in Vienna for like Othello our occupations would be gone" _ Arrange it as we will (notwithstanding the sophistry of the Hon Actg Secty of War) without seperate [*sic*] corps, an army in the field, can only be commanded by one officer-in-chief at a time _____

But the Armies of the Potomac & the Shenandoah, were never merged into one by any order of the War Dept; they were called 1st & 2nd Corps on or about the 21st July last by Genl. Johnston & my self for the sake of ab[b]reviation & convenience _ but they were always considered by us (as well as yourself I have understood) as two distinct Armies, acting together under the command of Genl. J. the senior officer present_ I beg, however, again to call your attention to the present inauspicious moment for making any change in the organization of this Army _ when we are hourly expecting an attack from an Enemy 3 or 4 times our number & far better equipped in every respect than we are _ the consequences of such a change at this time, might be most disastrous to our cause & country; far better would it be if, the word Corps be illegal, to resume the designation of armies of the Potomac & the Shenandoah __ But rest assured that whatever you shall order in that respect will be cheerfully carried into effect to the best of my ability. I thank you for the high appreciation you seem to place in my services _ which in the hour of need will always belong to my country, regardless of position _ & by always doing faithfully & truly my duty I feel convinced I will obtain the confidence of my troop & the respect of my enemies.

I remain, Dear Sir,
Respctly & truly your friend.

To his Excelly
President Jeff Davis
Richmond Va

(signed)   G.T. Beauregard

General Beauregard, who was regarded by Southerners as the hero of the Battle of Bull Run, soon fell out of favor with President Davis. Upon reading Beauregard's report of the battle which was fought on July 21, Davis thought the flamboyant Creole presented a claim to have won the battle himself. On November 7, the *Richmond Whig* published a self-serving letter from General Beauregard that brought the dispute out into the open. The Confederate Congress became involved and the legislators published the report which ended the quarrel between the president and general. Beauregard continued to question Johnston's authority over him. Late in January he was transferred west to serve under Albert Sidney Johnston, who was mortally wounded at Shiloh.

Throughout the winter of 1861, Joseph Johnston's army remained inactive. His department was divided into three districts and General Jackson, who had been assigned to the Shenandoah Valley, established his headquarters at Winchester. Jackson, following the theories of Napoleon I, believed that

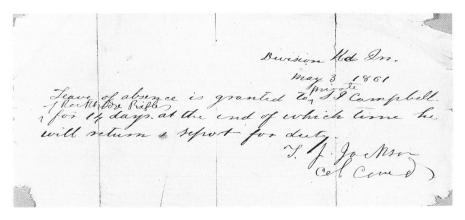

A pass signed by "Stonewall" Jackson

soldiers should remain active during the winter to reduce the incidence of disease. On January 1, "Stonewall" Jackson's small army marched for Romney (now West Virginia) to cut communications between Federal forces in western Virginia and the corps commanded by Major General Nathaniel P. Banks (1816-1894; governor of Massachusetts) which was scattered along the Potomac River.

On January 10, Jackson's forces occupied Romney and he detached the Army of the Northwest under Brigadier General William W. Loring (1818-1886; Mexican War) to garrison the isolated spot. The "Stonewall Brigade" returned to Winchester and General Loring complained to Richmond that Jackson practiced favoritism. On January 30, Secretary Benjamin telegraphed Jackson and directed him to order Loring's men back to Winchester because the government feared the Federals were moving against Loring.

General Jackson, angered over the interference with his authority, requested duty at the Virginia Military Institute. "Should this application not be granted, I respectfully request that the President will accept my resignation from the army."[12] Governor Letcher and influential friends persuaded Jackson to withdraw the letter of resignation, and meanwhile, General Loring was promoted to major general on February 15 and sent west; Jackson retained command of the Valley district. President Davis received the following letter from General Johnston that included an enclosure.

Hd Qrs Centreville
February 25th 1862

Mr President,

I respectfully enclose for your information a copy of a report by Major General Jackson.

Brigr Genl Whiting informs me that brigr Genl French & Capt: [Frederick] Chatard think the desired removal impracticable by water. I submit Genl French's letter on the subject. The land transportation, it seems to me, would require too much time & labor even were the roads tolerable. Now, they are not practicable for our field artillery with its teams of four horses. The accumulation of subsistence stores at Manassas is a great evil. The Commissary General was requested more than once to suspend the forwarding of those stores. A very extensive meat-packing establishment at Thoro[ugh]fare [Gap] is also a great incumbrance. It was made without my knowledge. The great quantity of personal property in our camps is a still greater one. Much of both property must be sacrificed in the contemplated movement.

The army is crippled, & its discipline is greatly impaired for want of General officers. The four regiments observing the fords of the lower Occopuan [Creek], are commanded by a Lieut: Colonel _ & besides, a division & five brigades are without generals _ & at least half of our field officers [are] absent _ & at least half of our field officers [are] absent _ generally sick.

17

At this point the letter ends and is unsigned. The last two paragraphs are inverted in the *OR* V Series I p. 1081. General Jackson's report, found in the *OR* V Series I pp. 1075-1076, is as follows.

Hd. Qrs. Valley District
Winchester February 17th 1862

General
    Your letter of the 14th instant respecting the disposition of Genl. Loring's command has been received, availing myself of your permission, I will retain [Captain M.L.] Shumaker's battery. The other Troops will for their respective destinations via the Rail Road except for those directed to proceed to Manassas, they will march via Snicker's Gap.
    The enemy under Genl. Lander[13] after taking possession of Bloomery Gap on the morning of the 14th instant fell back with the exception of some cavalry to Paw Paw [now West Virginia]. I have reason to believe he commands about 12000 troops, scattered along the frontier of the District and West of Williamsport, his main force being at Paw Paw. As long as the communications by R.R. with the West remain unbroken he can supply himself from that direction. From information received he is constructing the R.R. bridge over the Big Capen. From last accounts the federal forces had left New Creek & the mouth of Patterson creek: their movements are towards Morgan County. Things are quiet along the frontier of Berkley & Jeffersone [*sic*] Counties. I have no satisfactory means of estimating the number of the enemy between Hancock and the Blue Ridge.
    There should be not less than nine thousand Troops under my command: for Lander may concentrate all his command at Paw Paw, seize Blooming Pass, and by a graded road advance on this place. You know how Banks could cooperate in such a movement from Williamsport and even by Harpers Ferry.

Respectfully Your obt servant
(Signed) T.J. Jackson
Maj. Genl.

In August, following his defeat at Bull Run, General McDowell was replaced by Major General George B. McClellan (1826-1885; West Point 1846). McDowell's army was subsequently renamed the Army of the Potomac.[14] McClellan proved to be an able strategist and an outstanding administrator, but a poor combat general, like Braxton Bragg of North Carolina. His efforts to train, discipline and organize the volunteers produced an army that endured defeat after defeat.

Despite political pressure, General McClellan refused to advance against the Rebel concentration at Centreville. On November 1, he was designated general-in-chief of the U.S. Armies and by February 1862, McClellan had devised a new plan to capture Richmond. Instead of marching south from Washington, the engineer decided to use Union naval superiority to his advantage. In mid-March, a dozen divisions left their camps and sailed down the Potomac River for the Chesapeake Bay and Fort Monroe, Virginia. On April 4, the vast army began to advance up the Yorktown Peninsula, but stopped the next day. McClellan's men were blocked by a defensive line on the Warwick River manned by troops under the command of Major General John B. "Prince John" Magruder (1807-1871; West Point 1830).

As the season for campaigning approached, General Johnston had watched for signs of enemy activity on his front. Reports from cavalry patrols convinced Johnston that the long-awaited Union offensive was about to begin. His army fell back and by March 11 had crossed the Rappahannock River. Wary of security leaks,[15] General Johnston did not inform the president of his movement. As a consequence of his retreat, Johnston was forced to abandon many tons of cured meat as well as heavy cannon in position along the lower Potomac River.

The following letter is a description of the events which occurred in early 1862 written by Brigadier General Jubal A. Early (1816-1894; West Point 1837). Originally opposed to secession, he led a brigade in Richard S. Ewell's (1817-1872; West Point 1840) Division. After the war, General Early corresponded regularly with Jefferson Davis.

General Jubal Anderson Early

General Richard Stoddard Ewell

Lynchburg Va. Sept 22nd 1877

My Dear Sir:

I arrived here on the 11th, and have copied, as soon as I could, the narrative for which you asked in your last letter to me, which I received at Allegheny Springs. While in Canada in 1867 & 68, I wrote out my fully my [*sic*] recollections of the war as they came within my knowledge or observation. __ What I now send you is from the manuscript so written.

When General Johnston was engaged in writing his book he requested me to furnish him a narrative fixing the dates &c of the movement back from Manassas, and from the Peninsula __ After some delay I copied & sent him my narrative of events within the period covering the two evacuations. What I now send you is the same, except that I began the copy for you, a little further back than that sent General Johnston, and I have, in copying, made some changes in a few instances so as to improve & correct the phraseology, but without changing the facts or the sense. I left out what I said about the presence of officers' wives in camp, in the copy sent Gen. J., as that was not important for the use he wished to make of the narrative, and might be construed as a reflection on him for having his own wife in camp occasionally. _ The statements in regard to the stores, supplies &c, lost at Manassas & Yorktown, are in the exact words contained in the copy sent him, for I have that now before me. You will see that I have expressed myself quite freely in regard to the wisdom of the movements back from Manassas & Yorktown, and so far as the movements themselves are concerned my narrative will sustain General Johnston. __ The fact is, that as soon as we heard of the movement in Kentucky & Tennessee, by which Forts Henry & Donaldson [Donelson][16] were captured & the position at Bowling Green [Kentucky] turned, I began to reflect on our position on the line running from Aquia Creek up the Potomac, & Bull Run, and by Leesburg in Loudon to the Valley, and it was very evident to me that the same operation of flanking us out of our position, by the way of the Potomac & Cheasapeake Bay, could be performed under greater advantages for an enemy in Virginia, than had attended the movement in Kentucky and Tennessee, and I came to the conclusion that we must fall back before General Johnston gave us any intimation of his purposes __ So strong was my conviction on this point, that I assembled the colonels of my own brigade and told them I was satisfied such must be the results, and advised them to have all their surplus baggage sent to the rear _ I, in fact, anticipated the movement by having the baggage of myself & staff sent to the rear before General Johnston opened his mouth on the subject to me _ As soon as I arrived on the Peninsula, where I was shown at Magruder's head quarters, the map of the Peninsula, containing on it the sketch of the line of Yorktown & Warwick Rivers, I told Genl McLaws, who asked my opinion as to what I thought of the line, that we could not hold it. That it must be inevitably broken, sooner or later, & in that event our whole force there gobbled up _ I pointed out to him the narrowness of the Peninsula at Williamsburg, and the character of the country north of the York River, where the movement of a column up the River could turn our position, and I then expressed the opinion that we should run back to the line of the Chickahominy, so as to cover Richmond and have room to maneuver in. _ I subsequently wrote a private letter to General Randolph, then Secretary of War,[17] urging the same views, and suggesting to him to send some officers high in rank down to view the situation _ I think I suggested General Lee or Genl Johnston _ When General Johnston came down on his tour of observation, I went with him riding out of Yorktown, and I endeavored to give same views to him, but he did not seem disposed to discuss the matter, and I desisted. My views, therefore, on these questions, did not result from afterthought __ I have stated the facts in regard to the loss of supplies, at both places without undertaking to fix the responsibility for their loss _ I believe that all might have been carried off from Manassas if the railroad had been energetically operated. The rolling stock, of the Orange & Alexandria, Manassas Gap, & Virginia Central roads might to[o] have been sufficient for the transfer, of recovering everything in the two weeks allowed, if properly used._ I know that General Johnston sent General Trimble,[18] an old railroad man, to Manassas Junction to superintend the transportation of the stores &c. to the rear, and there was some complaint that he took care to send all the baggage of his own brigade to the rear, while valuable public stores were lost. __ Gen'l Johnston's chief Quarter Master, Maj. Bonham, was not energetic or efficient. Two or three steamers of reasonable capacity ought to have carried off the most valuable of the stores &c lost at Yorktown.

Perhaps the narrative I have given is more voluminous than you desired, but I thought it better to send it as I have done, in order that you might see the context in which I have made my statements: and perhaps I may give you the facts in regard to the two evacuations more fully than you have before seen them.

The personal issues that have been made since the war, have been painful to me; and I have read General Johnston's Narrative with great regret that he ever wrote it. I think it has done his cause no good.

I trust you will not think me impertinent if I remind you that you are the representative of our cause, and caution you against the danger of entering into a more personal controversy with General Johnston about the questions he has raised, and the issues he has made with you, and other officials holding positions under you. __ I know that your provocation is great, but a calm and lucid statement of facts, with dignified comment on the difficulties attending all the questions you were called upon to deal with, will have far greater weight with the enlightened world, than bitter or [illegible] strictures on the querrelousness [*sic*] of a subordinate who always seemed to think more of his own rank and position, than of the public cause. You can afford to be liberal and generous to the infirmities of temper and disposition which always gave a personal aspect to all the questions which there was a difference of opinion between their position and those above him.

I trust you will understand well enough the personal regard and respect I have for you, and the deep interest I feel in our cause though we failed, to know that these suggestions result solely from my anxiety that your presentation of the history of our struggle and the part you bore in it, in your private and official capacity, shall be such as to command the respect of all enlightened men and defy the carpings of your enemies and revilers. __ Pardon the liberty I have taken and believe me

Most sincerely & truly
Your friend
JA Early

Hon. Jefferson Davis __.

After surveying General Magruder's line of defense, General McClellan chose to employ siege tactics instead of assaulting the enemy position. McClellan's delay permitted the Confederates to rush reinforcements to the threatened point. General Johnston hoped to hold back the Federals in order to concentrate Confederate manpower for Richmond's defense. He knew that the weight of metal which could be thrown by McClellan's numerous siege guns would eventually force a withdrawal.

By the evening of May 4, McClellan was prepared to bombard the Confederate line. The previous night, however, Johnston's army began retreating up the Peninsula toward the capital of the Confederacy. On May 5, the Rebels fought a rear guard action at Williamsburg and checked their pursuers. General Johnston neglected to inform his superiors of this sharp action and did not communicate with Richmond for nearly a week.

When Johnston resumed correspondence with President Davis' military advisor, Robert E. Lee, he expressed no optimism. Advanced elements of his worn out army reached the outskirts of Richmond on May 17 and encamped. The president rode out to ask his secretive subordinate to reveal his plans for the defense of the city. Johnston refused to make a commitment. Events in the Shenandoah Valley, as the following letter indicates, brightened Confederate prospects at Richmond.

Richmond, Va. June 4th, 1862
Gen'l T.J. Jackson,
Comdg. in the Valley of Va.

Gen'l:

I return to you my congratulations for the brilliant campaign you have conducted against the enemy in the Valley of Virginia. Where it practicable to send you reinforcements it should be done, and your past success shows how surely you would with adequate force destroy the wicked designs of the invader of our homes and assailer of our political rights. From the honorable Mr. Bottelen [Col. A.R. Boteler] I have learned something of your probable movements. At this distance it is not possible to obtain such exact information as would justify a conclusion, but I hope you will not find at Front Royal a force which you cannot overcome. The only aid which seemed to be in reach was such as could be collected at Staunton. The comdg. officer at that place has been directed to gather all he could and move down the valley to communicate with you. Such a movement may have the effect on the enemy beyond its real value, but it is on your skill and daring that reliance is to be placed. The army under your command encourages me to hope for all which men can achieve.

Very Respectfully & truly yours
(signed)   Jeffn. Davis.

[*OR* XII Series I Pt.3 p. 905]

Less than three months before, "Stonewall" Jackson had suffered a tactical defeat when he attacked a numerically superior force at Kernstown. His aggressive posture, however, alarmed President Lincoln, who believed Jackson must have been reinforced. Lincoln detached a corps under Banks from McClellan's control and directed an additional division under Major General John C. Fremont (1813-1890; direct appointment 1838) to contain Jackson, who reorganized his small command. General Lee believed a massive concentration against Johnston could be prevented if General Jackson maneuvered against the Union columns and defeated them in detail. Without General Johnston's knowledge, Lee reinforced the Army of the Valley in mid-April. When Major General Richard S. Ewell's Division united with Jackson, the former military instructor commanded 16,000 men of all arms. Dick Taylor (1826-1879; planter), promoted to brigadier general the previous October, led the Louisiana Tigers in Ewell's Division. General Taylor recounted his initial encounter with "Stonewall" Jackson.

Approaching, I saluted and declared my name and rank, then waited for a response. Before this came I had time to see a pair of cavalry boots covering feet of gigantic size, a mangy cap with visor drawn low, a heavy, dark beard and weary eyes_ eyes I afterward saw filled with intense but never brilliant light. A low, gentle voice inquired the road and distance marched that day. "Keazletown road, six and twenty miles." "You seem to have no stragglers." "Never allow straggling." "You must teach my people; they straggle badly." A bow in reply. Just then my creoles started their band and a waltz. After a contemplative suck on a lemon, "Thoughtless fellows for serious work" came forth. I expressed a hope that the work would not be less well done because of the gayety. A return to the lemon gave me the opportunity to retire....[19]

Success for General Jackson depended on celerity. The ability of Jackson's "foot cavalry" to outmarch the Yankees became the deciding factor in the Valley Campaign. On May 8, Jackson defeated a portion of Fremont's force, west of the Valley, and the Federals retreated. Two weeks later the Rebels appeared unexpectedly in the northern end of the Shenandoah Valley. An outpost of 1,000 men was captured at Front Royal on May 23. Jackson's audacious maneuver menaced Banks who retreated to Winchester.

General Banks believed he was secure from attack at Winchester. On the morning of May 25, Jackson's army massed south of Winchester. The Rebels hit the Yankees early and hit them hard. By 8:00 A.M. Banks' army was routed, outflanked on the right and the left. The Federals fled in panic from their foe and General Banks attempted to rally his men. He shouted to the 3rd Wisconsin: "Stop, men! Don't you love your country?" A scampering soldier replied: "Yes, by God, and I'm trying to get back to it just as fast as I can."[20]

General Jackson's execution of Lee's strategy had borne bountiful fruit. His victories frightened the Lincoln administration. General McDowell's Army of the Rappahannock, advancing from central Virginia to unite with the Army of the Potomac, was recalled to protect Washington city. General McClellan's own army, however, was exposed to attack. Most of his divisions were north of the Chickahominy River waiting for McDowell's arrival. General Johnston, who sensed the unease of his own government, finally attacked on May 31.

The Federal 4th Corps, commanded by Brigadier General Erasmus D. Keyes (1810-1895; West Point 1832), occupied positions between the Williamsburg Road and Nine Mile Road, south of the Chickahominy River. General Heintzelman's 3rd Corps was in support several miles to the rear. The two roads intersected at Seven Pines. A track branched off from Nine Mile Road at Old Tavern and led to the bridges that linked the wings of McClellan's army. The hamlet of Fair Oaks was located between Old Tavern and Seven Pines.

If Johnston could concentrate a strong force, then launch a powerful blow against Keyes, the 4th Corps might be wrecked. The key element of Johnston's operation would be to control Nine Mile Road on the Union right flank. By cutting off General Keyes from the river, reinforcements would be unable to assist the Union soldiers before they were overwhelmed.

General Johnston planned to send Major General Daniel H. Hill (1821-1889; West Point 1842) against the Federals on the Williamsburg Road. Major

General James Longstreet (1821-1904; West Point 1842) would march to Old Tavern and wait for Hill to begin the battle. General Hill's orders were to attack when a supporting division under Major General Benjamin Huger (1805-1877; West Point 1825) made contact with his command. Longstreet discussed the details of the impending action at Johnston's headquarters on May 30. "The things Johnston failed to make clear or Longstreet failed to understand were the objective of the assault, Longstreet's area of responsibility, and the road on which Longstreet was to attack."[21] As a consequence, on the morning of May 31, when General Huger's men marched to reach their assigned position on General Hill's flank, they found Longstreet's large division on the Williamsburg Road, blocking their advance.

The mix up on the Williamsburg Road delayed D.H. Hill's deployment to attack. Hill, one of the Confederacy's hardest fighters, hurled his brigades against Brigadier General Silas Casey's (1807-1882; West Point 1826) division at 1:00 P.M. and forced it to give ground. Reinforcements aided Casey, and by mid-afternoon Hill's single division was fighting almost the entire Union wing south of the Chickahominy. General Longstreet, who had assumed command

General James Longstreet

of Johnston's right wing "might as well have not been on the field."[22] Though he sent two brigades to Hill's support, General Longstreet never exercised control of General Huger's Division, which did not actively engaged the enemy. Moreover, only one of Longstreet's own brigades joined the fight. Half of his division spent the day marching and countermarching to no purpose.

The day had begun badly for General Johnston. He did not learn until 10:00 A.M. that Longstreet occupied the wrong road. Momentarily stunned, Johnston decided to proceed with his plan and assumed direct control of Smith's Division, temporarily commanded by Brigadier General William W.C. Whiting (1824-1865; West Point 1845) on Nine Mile Road. Hour after hour he waited nervously for the sound of battle that signalled General Hill had engaged the enemy. An atmospheric anomaly, however, prevented the clash of arms from being audible. With no word from Longstreet, Johnston's agitation increased. Around 3:00 P.M., Lee arrived at Johnston's headquarters. Lee could not elicit any information from Johnston concerning the progress of the battle.

Reconnaissance would have revealed to Johnston that no enemy troops were on his front which made the Union flank near Fair Oaks vulnerable. Johnston, a lazy general, allowed the opportunity to win a splendid victory slip away. His inactivity allowed the division (2nd Corps) of Brigadier General John Sedgwick (1813-1864; West Point 1837) to cross the Chickahominy undetected.

At 4:00 P.M., Johnston received a message from Longstreet that requested support for Hill's left flank. The note energized Johnston, but without adequate intelligence, his units could only grope for friendly lines. In his haste to exploit the perceived opportunity, Johnston failed to send artillery forward to accompany the infantry. The leading brigade under Colonel Evander M. Law ran into a fragment of the 4th Corps that had been cut off near Fair Oaks. Union cannon smashed Colonel Law's attacks and compelled his regiments to retire. Three other Rebel brigades encountered Sedgwick's Division. The grayclads suffered severe losses and a native of Ohio, Brigadier Robert H. Hatton (1826-1862; lawyer), was killed as he led his Tennessee regiments against the blueclads. A fifth brigade, under the direction of Brigadier General John Bell Hood (1831-1879; West Point 1853), suffered minor losses as it searched for Longstreet's lines.

The most significant Confederate casualty of the day was General Johnston. At sunset, a shell exploded near him and he was knocked off his horse with a severe chest wound. President Davis, who arrived on the battlefield, comforted Johnston as he was carried from the field. General Smith attempted to revive the battle the next day but accomplished nothing. McClellan's men quickly recovered the ground they had lost at Seven Pines.

Despite overwhelming numerical superiority, Johnston failed to crush the 4th Corps. Johnston's sortie achieved nothing because the assaults were uncoordinated (a common occurence during the Civil War). Yet Porter Alexander, who had been promoted to major and served on Johnston's staff, concluded in his memoirs: "The responsibility for the blunder seems to me to rest solely upon Johnston. He evidently failed to make Longstreet understand fully & exactly what to do, & he failed to keep an eye on the doing."[23] General Johnston's inexcusable lack of diligence voided the best opportunity he ever enjoyed during the war to win a major battle, and merit the prestige he craved.

Illness described as "paralysis" rendered General Smith unfit for field duty. General Lee, who had rendered rather undistinguished service to the Confederacy, assumed command of the army before Richmond on June 1. In accordance with his aggressive nature, Lee renamed his command the Army of Northern Virginia. He had no intention of holding a line of earthworks around the capital against McClellan's superior numbers and fire power. General McClellan, known in the North as the "Young Napoleon," wanted to advance toward Richmond in stages and then scorch the city with artillery fire, but McClellan believed his army was outnumbered. He constantly appealed to Washington for reinforcements, and by doing so handed the initiative over to his opponent, Robert E. Lee, the most dangerous general of the war.

General Lee contemplated an attack on the wing of General McClellan's army north of the Chickahominy River. To formulate his plan, Lee needed to establish the location of McClellan's right flank. He summoned Brigadier General James Ewell Brown "J.E.B." Stuart (1833-1864; West Point 1854)[24] to his headquarters and discussed the details of the mission with the eager cavalryman. Stuart was ordered to conduct an expedition that would determine the exact position of the Federal army north of the river. The next day, Stuart received his instructions and prepared for what would become an epic ride around McClellan's entire army.

Early on the morning of June 12, General Stuart set out from Richmond and headed north with 1,200 troopers and two pieces of artillery. His route over the next two days carried his brigade east, and then south, roughly parallel to the Pamunkey River. The Confederate troopers found themselves deep behind enemy lines, but no body of Union troops appeared to dispute their presence. Stuart's reconnaissance became a raid as his men burned wagons and captured horses. On June 14, the worn out cavalrymen crossed the Chickahominy River and the next day were within their own lines. General Stuart rode ahead of his column to deliver his report to General Lee.

General Stuart's reputation soared as a result of his well-reported exploit. Governor Letcher rewarded him with a sword. More importantly, Lee now knew where to strike McClellan's divided army. As Lee's grip tightened around the Army of Northern Virginia and he developed the strategy that would save the Confederacy's capital, "Stonewall" Jackson had defeated two more Yankee

General James Ewell Brown Stuart

generals. At the Battle of Cross Keys, a force under General Fremont's command was trounced on June 8. The following morning at Port Republic the Louisiana Tigers saved the day as a division commanded by Brigadier General James Shields (1810-1879; Mexican War) was routed.

General Jackson's success and reputation removed any threat to the Valley. General Lee therefore ordered the South's most successful general to cross the Blue Ridge Mountains with his army and march for Richmond to participate in the counteroffensive. On June 23, Jackson, Longstreet, D.H. Hill, and Major General Ambrose P. Hill (1825-1865; West Point 1847) conferred with Lee at his headquarters to learn details of the forthcoming operation. General Lee believed that a thrust against McClellan's northern wing would cause his opponent to retreat to protect his supply base at the White House on the Pamunkey River. While Generals Huger and Magruder held the lines south of the Chickahominy, Longstreet, D.H. Hill, and A.P. Hill would hit the Federals from the west. General Jackson, attacking from the north, would complete the pincer movement against the 5th Corps commanded by Brigadier General Fitz-John Porter (1822-1901; West Point 1845). Lee's design depended on timing and coordination between his generals; the arrival of Jackson's army was crucial to maximize success. In

General Ambrose Powell Hill

the series of battles that developed, known as the Seven Days, "Stonewall" did not live up to his reputation.

According to Lee's orders, Jackson was supposed to link up with A.P. Hill on June 26 before the attack on the 5th Corps could begin; however, Jackson failed to keep the schedule that Lee had established. General Hill, who grew impatient, desired to give battle, and in mid-afternoon he threw his division against the enemy position at Beaver Dam Creek. Although he was supported by a brigade from D.H. Hill, his division was repulsed with a loss of approximately 1,400 men. During the battle at Mechanicsville, the leading elements of Jackson's army rested less than three miles from A.P. Hill's left flank. In unfamiliar country and without adequate information about the unauthorized battle brought on by the impetuous Hill, Jackson did nothing.

General McClellan, acutely aware of the threat posed by General Jackson's force, decided to abandon his base at the White House and establish a new base on the James River. General Porter was ordered to make a stand while the army shifted its position south of the Chickahominy River. The 5th Corps took up a defensive line which was stronger than the position at Beaver Dam Creek. Following an afternoon of hard fighting and slaughter, the Battle of

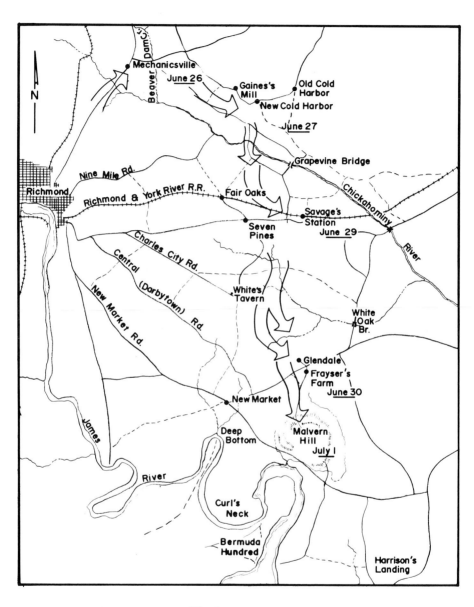

The Seven Days
June 25 - July 1, 1862

Gaines Mill concluded with a Rebel breakthrough. Darkness prevented effective pursuit by the victors and Porter skillfully withdrew his corps across the Chickahominy on a single bridge.

General Lee believed that General McClellan intended to establish a new base on the James River. General Stuart confirmed this belief on June 29 when he reported to his chief that the huge supply base at the White House had been burned. Aware that the large number of slow-moving wagons would hamper the enemy withdrawal, Lee hoped to trap the Army of the Potomac before it reached the sanctuary provided by the fearsome gunboats prowling the James River. Lee transferred his divisions north of the Chickahominy to the opposite side of the river hoping that McClellan's rear guard would be forced to fight. General Magruder marched from Seven Pines with orders to press the Union army's left flank in concert with General Huger.

On June 29, General Magruder's troops caught up with the enemy at Savage's Station. He attacked, expecting support from Jackson, as Lee had ordered. Magruder's division was too weak to drive the foe and the Federals continued their withdrawal. Again, Jackson failed to play his part in the sanguinary drama assigned to him by Lee, and the three divisions under his command did not reach Savage's Station until 3:00 A.M. There has been much speculation regarding "Stonewall" Jackson's state of mind during the Seven Days. Fatigue, illness, and an unwillingness to cooperate because he had experienced independent command in the Valley, have been advanced for his behavior. The last days of June 1862 constitute a low point in an otherwise outstanding career.[25]

During the night, Union reserve artillery and the wagon trains continued their trek to Harrison's Landing on the James. The next day the 2nd Corps (Brigadier General Edwin V. Sumner 1797-1863; direct commission 1819) and the 6th Corps (Brigadier General William B. Franklin 1823-1903; West Point 1843) were south of White Oak Swamp. Seven divisions were posted in an arc to block pursuit from the north and west. Generals Huger and Magruder marched toward the Federals on separate roads, while the divisions of A.P. Hill and Longstreet marched farther south on the Long Bridge Road. The divisions commanded by General Jackson approached from the north. Three Confederate columns were converging on half of McClellan's army; if McClellan's men did not hold their ground, the Army of the Potomac would be cut in half.

General Huger's Division approached the center of the Union line very cautiously. His brigades advanced two miles in six hours. At 2:30 P.M., Huger's artillery opened fire but his delay in deployment allowed McClellan's trains to pass the crossroads at Glendale. According to Lee's plan, Huger's Division was to lead the attack against the Federals at White Oak Swamp. Beyond long range artillery bombardment, however, Huger's Division did nothing more for the rest of the day. General Jackson also accomplished little on June 30, as his divisions were stopped by the destruction of Grapevine Bridge. Instead of fording the creek farther up from the bridge, Jackson again remained passive, and General Magruder's Division spent a weary day marching to no purpose.

With no word from Jackson, Lee ordered Longstreet forward at 4:30 P.M. to take Glendale. The Pennsylvania Reserves, 5th Corps, a division commanded by Brigadier General George A. McCall (1802-1868; West Point 1822) was roughly handled and a brigade routed. McCall was captured by the 47th Virginia late in the day. Reinforcements from the fronts of Huger and Jackson entered the battle. Federal counterattacks forced Longstreet to commit A.P. Hill's Division at sunset to retain captured ground. The Army of Northern Virginia failed to take the coveted crossroads because senior generals could not, or would not, coordinate the efforts of their columns. General McClellan's Divisions marched away from White Oak Swamp and reunited with the rest of the army on July 1 at Malvern Hill.

The next morning when he met his generals at Glendale, Lee could not conceal his disappointment. The Northern army had escaped without enduring the punishment he had expected. General McClellan, on the contrary, exuded confidence and desired to confront his adversary from the defensive advantages offered by Malvern Hill. Dozens of cannon, backed by long lines of infantry, covered the slope of Malvern Hill, which dominated the road leading to the James River.

Though McClellan's army had been forced to withdraw from Richmond, Lee desired a more complete victory and ordered an assault against the formidable position. This inadvisable decision tarnished his otherwise spectacular performance during the campaign. As D.H. Hill observed after the war: "It was not war—it was murder."[26] The array of Union artillery smothered Confederate counterbattery fire and even though his artillery had been neutralized by mid-afternoon, Lee chose to attack. Ten brigades belonging to the divisions of Generals Hill, Huger, and Magruder braved the musketry and canister that shattered their formations. Three isolated fights developed and some Southern regiments advanced far enough to shoot down opposing artillerymen and horses, but Lee's last attempt to gain a decisive victory over McClellan failed. "Lee never before nor since that action delivered a battle so ill-judged in conception, or so faulty in its details of execution. It was as bad as the worst blunders ever committed on the Union side."[27] Union casualties during the Seven Days were about 16,000 while the Confederates lost 20,000 soldiers.

The Army of the Potomac completed its withdrawal to Harrison's Landing during the night. The new location of McClellan's army, farther south of Richmond on the James River, represented a potentially greater threat to the capital of the Confederacy. Instead of attacking Richmond directly, General McClellan could now cross the river and move against Petersburg to threaten the city's communications with the deep south. This sound strategy was not carried out: he needed reinforcements. On August 3, McClellan received orders to relocate the Army of the Potomac to Aquia Creek in order to cooperate with the Army of Virginia, commanded by Major General John Pope (1822-1892; West Point 1842). Pope had enjoyed success in the west and crossed the Allegheny Mountains to whip the Rebels. Several of McClellan's Divisions were transferred to Pope's control.

General Lee, who knew that McClellan's army was being transferred, determined to strike Pope before he could be reinforced. In mid-August he united the Army of Northern Virginia behind the Rappahannock River and created an opportunity to defeat the Army of Virginia. General Jackson's Divisions crossed the upper Rappahannock on August 25 and the next day captured supply depots at Bristoe Station and Manassas Junction in Pope's rear. General Longstreet's Divisions were two marches distant from Jackson's force. General Pope's army concentrated to smash General Jackson's isolated command.

"Stonewall" Jackson's movements confused Pope and allowed the Confederates time to establish a strong defensive position behind the embankment of an unfinfinished railroad near Groveton in the vicinity of the Bull Run battlefield. On August 29, with around 60,000 available men, Pope attacked Jackson's force of 23,000. The morning's action achieved nothing since the Union attacks were uncoordinated. In the afternoon a brigade led by Brigadier General Cuvier Grover (1828-1885; West Point 1850), 3rd Corps, crossed the railroad embankment and penetrated the left center of Jackson's line. Grover's five regiments fought magnificently but received no support; a savage counterattack drove them back with severe losses. A second brigade attacked with the same result. A one-armed general, Philip Kearney (1815-1862; direct commission 1837), organized another assault around 5:00 P.M. His troops penetrated Jackson's left center and threatened to compel A.P. Hill's Division to retreat. General Early's oversized brigade of Virginians counterattacked and routed the Federals in ten minutes. General Porter[28] received orders to advance against Jackson's right flank but darkness and the arrival of Longstreet precluded any attempt to prolong the day's combat.

The following day, though aware of Longstreet's presence, Pope renewed the battle because he believed that Jackson was in retreat. Several regiments of the 5th Corps reached the railroad embankment. The Federals reformed their lines repeatedly to sustain their effort but accurate artillery fire from a battalion commanded by Colonel Stephen D. Lee disrupted the advance of Porter's reserves. General Lee wisely allowed Pope to become heavily engaged against

Jackson before he committed Longstreet. At 3:00 P.M., Longstreet ordered four tested divisions forward and much of Pope's army fled the field.

The Pennsylvania Reserves, along with several battalions of regulars, held Henry Hill which permitted Pope's battered army to retreat across Stone Bridge to Centreville. Confederate pursuit was checked as the defeated divisions withdrew toward the defenses of Washington. The Second Battle of Bull Run represented a stunning Southern victory that added renown to "Stonewall" Jackson's reputation and cost Lee slightly more than 9,000 men. Defeat for Pope ruined his reputation and resulted in the loss of 16,000 soldiers, nearly 6,000 of whom were prisoners. Pope spent most of the remainder of the war in command of the Department of the Northwest. General McClellan was restored to overall command.

Determined to retain the initiative and to carry the war away from ravaged northern Virginia, Lee invaded Maryland. He hoped to rally the state for the Confederate cause and to feed his army. Lee divided his depleted army and sent Jackson to capture Harpers Ferry while Longstreet marched for Hagerstown. On September 13, an Indiana soldier discovered a copy of Lee's orders addressed to D.H. Hill. With this intelligence, McClellan had the opportunity to defeat the Army of Northern Virginia in detail. It was a golden opportunity that soldiers dream about but McClellan failed to take advantage of it because of his cautious and deliberate nature. General D.H. Hill delayed the Army of the Potomac's advance at South Mountain on September 14 which allowed Longstreet to fall back to Sharpsburg on the Potomac River. Harpers Ferry surrendered to General Jackson on September 15 and Lee decided to make a stand at Sharpsburg.

General Jackson left A.P. Hill's Division at Harpers Ferry to parole prisoners while the remainder of his command marched for Sharpsburg. McClellan, who moved slowly, retained a great numerical superiority but had lost his initial advantage by the time he attacked Lee's reunited army at dawn on September 17. Names such as the "West Woods," "The Cornfield," and "Bloody Lane" became part of American military history as the Army of Northern Virginia resisted wave after wave of attackers. Throughout the day McClellan threw his divisions at Lee's depleted brigades in a series of uncoordinated charges. Several Rebel brigades entered the battle at regimental strength.

In mid-afternoon, the 9th Corps, under the command of Major General Ambrose E. Burnside (1824-1881; West Point 1847) crossed Antietam Creek on Lee's right flank. Burnside's fresh brigades were poised to pound Lee's depleted flank when A.P. Hill's Division appeared at the right place at the right time. The "Light Division" counterattacked savagely and the 9th Corps was driven back to Antietam Creek. The next day Lee's generals persuaded him not to risk his worn out army in an attack. Despite 24,000 available unused troops, McClellan remained inactive. On the night of September18, the Army of Northern Virginia retreated toward the Shenandoah Valley and was reorganized into two corps commanded by Jackson and Longstreet.

The Battle of Antietam must be regarded as a great victory for Lee. Like the Duke of Wellington at Waterloo, who won because of the timely arrival of the Prussians, Lee endured a terrific beating until A.P. Hill reached the field to save the Army of Northern Virginia from sure destruction. Yet, it was certainly Lee's most senseless battle since he achieved nothing of strategic consequence. Perhaps he calculated, correctly, that McClellan could not defeat him, but Lee could have avoided the nearly 11,500 men (out of approximately 40,000) it cost him to prove his point. McClellan could have avoided the loss of 12,410 men but his method of campaigning left him unable to wrest the initiative from General Lee.

Following the bloodiest day in American history (D-Day pales in comparison) both armies rested and reorganized. President Lincoln grew increasingly frustrated with General McClellan's inaction, who seemed determined to avoid combat with the Army of Northern Virginia. Not until the beginning of November did the Army of the Potomac march back into Virginia. General McClellan directed his divisions toward Warrenton, some fifteen miles west of Manassas. By the time his army arrived there on November 9, McClellan had been relieved and replaced by Burnside, who reorganized his six corps into three Grand Divisions. The Right Grand Division (2nd and 9th Corps) was commanded by General Sumner, while General Franklin led the Left Grand Division (1st and 6th Corps). Major General Joseph Hooker (1814-1879; West Point 1837) commanded the Center Grand Division (3rd and 5th Corps).

General Burnside did not conspire to become the commander of the Army of the Potomac. He accepted his new responsibility with great reluctance and his appointment was unfortunate. Instead of maneuvering against Lee's divided army (Jackson's 2nd Corps remained in the Valley), Burnside chose to advance on Richmond by using Fredericksburg on the Rappahannock River as his base. On November 15, the Right Grand Division departed Warrenton and reached the Rappahannock two days later. General Burnside denied General Sumner permission to ford the river to occupy Fredericksburg which allowed Longstreet's 1st Corps to concentrate behind the Rappahannock. By the end of November, the Army of Northern Virginia was prepared to dispute an advance toward Richmond from Fredericksburg.

Lee made no serious attempt to resist his adversary's effort to bridge the river and occupy Fredericksburg. Instead he deployed his army beyond the town on a ridge some six miles long. On December 12, Burnside maneuvered his army onto a plain below the ridge. General Franklin, with his two corps along with part of the 3rd Corps, formed on the left while the 2nd Corps and the 9th Corps under

General Sumner held the right. General Hooker remained across the river with the 5th Corps and the rest of the 3rd Corps. The Army of the Potomac attacked the following day and at first it went well. The Pennsylvania Reserves (1st Corps), now commanded by Major General George G. Meade (1815-1872; West Point 1835), pushed through the "Light Division" on Lee's right flank, commanded by A.P. Hill. Confederate reserves contained the penetration and the Pennsylvanians were thrown back upon their supports with severe losses.

General Sumner ordered two divisions of the 2nd Corps forward on the Federal right but they too were repulsed with heavy casualties. A third assault by a division of the 2nd Corps along with two from the 9th Corps likewise failed to carry Marye's Heights. General Burnside became desperate and ordered General Hooker to cross the river and carry the high ground. Upon examining the ground, "Fightin' Joe" Hooker protested that an assault would be hopeless. Burnside insisted that the attack be carried out and Hooker complied. Hundreds of gallant Yankees fell short of the stone wall on Marye's Heights defended by Longstreet's men.

The following day, Burnside declared that he would personally lead the 9th Corps in an assault against the heights. At the last minute General Sumner persuaded Burnside to call off the attack. The next night, the Army of the Potomac recrossed the Rappahannock River after losing nearly 13,000 men; the Army of Northern Virginia had lost 5,300 soldiers.

Following the disaster at Fredericksburg, Burnside groped for a plan that promised success and would restore the confidence of his officers and men. The beleaguered general decided to cross the Rappahannock above Fredericksburg in order to outflank Lee. Burnside ordered feints to be made above and below the town to mask his intent. On January 19, Burnside set his columns in motion. A terrible rainstorm struck the area the next night and once firm roads turned into a muddy mess, thus allowing the operation to become known as the "Mud March." General Burnside was compelled to abandon his effort to transfer his army across the river and his disgusted soldiers returned to their camps.

Burnside believed that a lack of support from many generals contributed to the failure of his operation. He prepared a list of officers that he wanted removed from their commands, and travelled to Washington to deliver it to the president. He asked President Lincoln to approve his proposal or accept his resignation. Joseph Hooker, at the top of the hit list, replaced the hapless Ambrose Burnside.

General Hooker assumed command of the Army of the Potomac on January 26. His most immediate problem was to restore the morale and efficiency of the army. Under Hooker's discipline, desertion was curtailed and he did away with the cumbersome arrangement of Grand Divisions. General Hooker also instituted a system of distinctive badges that identified each corps. Soldiers of the 1st Corps, for example, sewed a piece of cloth shaped like a disc on their caps, while members of the 3rd Corps wore a diamond on their kepis.

During the winter, the Army of the Potomac recovered its pride and vigor. By the end of April, General Hooker's host numbered 134,000 men. Due to the fact that Longstreet and two of his divisions were detached in February for service in North Carolina, Lee's army numbered 60,000.

Using his great numerical advantage, Hooker divided his army into three groups for another campaign to take Richmond. General Sedgwick remained before Fredericksburg with the 1st and 6th Corps to threaten a crossing of the Rappahannock at that point. The 2nd and 3rd Corps remained in the center while the 5th, 11th, and 12th Corps crossed the river on April 28 at Kelly's Ford, twenty-seven miles above Fredericksburg. By April 30, the 2nd, 5th, 11th, and 12th Corps had concentrated on Lee's left rear at Chancellorsville, a crossroads in an area known as The Wilderness.

When Lee learned that a strong column of enemy infantry was pushing toward his rear, he split his army. The bulk of the Army of Northern Virginia marched to confront Hooker, while Jubal Early, who had received his promotion to major general in January, remained at Fredericksburg to observe the enemy because Sedgwick had bridged the river. Meanwhile, Hooker and the 3rd Corps had reached Chancellorsville. General Hooker boasted: "The rebel army is now the legitimate property of the Army of the Potomac. They may as well pack up their haversacks and make for Richmond...."[29] But Hooker's five corps had assumed a defensive posture which handed the initiative to Lee.

General Stuart informed Lee that Hooker's right flank was "in the air," unsupported by a terrain feature or troops and vulnerable to attack. This oversight led to Lee's greatest victory and resulted in the death of his most able lieutenant. Lee ordered General Jackson to assail the exposed flank with three divisions. As Jackson's men marched a dozen miles to the Plank Road for their attack, the remainder of Lee's force demonstrated against Hooker's troops. By 6:00 P.M. on May 2, the division of Robert E. Rodes (1829-1864; Virginia Military Institue 1848) was in position, ready to strike the unprepared soldiers of Major General Oliver O. Howard's (1830-1909: West Point 1854) 11th Corps. Less than an hour later, the 11th Corps had been brushed aside and a torrent of fugitives spread over the Plank Road, running for the Rappahannock fords.

"Stonewall" Jackson directed the attack from the front. Brigadier General Raleigh E. Colston (1825-1896; Virginia Military Institue 1846) extended his divisional line to cut off retreat to United States Ford and A.P. Hill was ordered to press the attack. Around 9:00 P.M., the "Light Division" stepped out into a clearing called Hazel Grove where Brigadier General Alfred Pleasanton (1824-1897; West Point 1840) and twenty-two cannon awaited. The Butternut infantry fired without effect. "Had it been daylight, at that close range a single volley would have left the guns, without men or horses, to be captured & turned on their former owners in a few minutes. But musketry fire requires daylight to make it effective, especially at artillery...So the volley of our infantry was comparatively harmless...."[30] The ominous cannon belched a broadside and then began to fire rapidly, driving the Rebels away from the key to the Union army's position.

On the Plank Road, a company of North Carolinians fired on horsemen whom they thought to be enemy cavalry. General Jackson, with his left arm shattered (later amputated) and struck in both hands, was about to hit the ground when a staff officer caught him. The following two letters written by Mrs. Anna Jackson relate details concerning her husband, who died from pneumonia on May 10, 1863, at Guinea Station.

306 W. Trade st. Charlotte, N.C.
Oct. 23d 1908

Mr. H.C. Ezekiel
Cincinnati, Ohio,

Dear Sir,

Your letters & also that of Mrs. Wiggins of Nashville have been received, & I hope you will pardon the delay in answering, as I am somewhat disabled from writing by a break of my right arm a few months since. I also have a large correspondence getting letters from many quarters asking information about my dear husband.

With regard to what you desire for your brother's work in his model for the statue, I'm afraid I will not be able to give you much assistance. I have a splendid life like portrait painted by Wm Garle Brown, in Confederate uniform, & I've had some cabinet sized photo's taken from it here that I consider good. The photographers are Seay & Enstler, N. Tryon st. I would not copy the death mask made by Volk, as the face was too emaciated. I think the English statue at Richmond, Va the best that has been made yet. I have no suit to send, but I shouldn't think he would have any difficulty copying one, as they are seen in many pictures. Seay & Entsler can furnish you with a copy of Gen. Jackson's sword, as I know it was photographed there.

yours truly
Mrs. T. J. Jackson

306 W. Trade st. Charlotte, N.C.
Oct. 29th 1908

Mr. H. C. Ezekiel
Cincinnati, Ohio,

My dear Sir,

Yours of the 26th just received, and in reply I would say that I am unable to supply any of the articles you wish, or even photo's of them. I have not in my possession any suit of Confederate uniform. The coat that my husband wore at the time he was wounded was badly cut up by the officers who tried to get to his wounds to staunch the blood before a

Surgeon arrived, and afterwards his staff officers (seeing the handsome new coat was ruined) cut it all to pieces and took a piece each man for himself, as relics, so in this way the coat was lost.

His cap, spurs, sashes and many other articles are in the Confederate Museum at Richmond, Va. I was requested to loan all of the most valuable to the Museum, and they were placed in a glass case all to themselves   Like cases are there of the relics of Gen. Lee and other officers. Mine are simply loans, and I have been asked to let them be taken out and copied, but the anchorites there object to this. I should think the uniform could be copied from any Confederate general's portrait. Is this statue that your brother is modeling to be placed at Charleston, W. Va? I have had a letter from Mrs. S.S. Green of that place, asking for the same information which you desire, and I replied that I had written you all the information That I could give. I am sorry not to be able to do more.

> With kind regards, I am
> Yours truly,
> Mrs. T. J. Jackson

General Stuart, in command of the army's cavalry, assumed temporary command of the 2nd Corps.[31] Stuart attacked at dawn on May 3 and through his inspirational leadership, the Confederate infantry captured Hazel Grove early in the morning. After hours of bitter combat, General Stuart's corps connected with the rest of the army on the field. At Hazel Grove, Porter Alexander, now a colonel in command of an artillery battalion, directed the fire of the Confederate cannon in battery there. A cannonball from one of his guns hit a pillar of the Chancellor House. A brick struck General Hooker, who was incapacitated briefly. "Till he met the enemy, Hooker showed a master-grasp of the elements of war, but the moment he confronted his antagonist, he seemed to suffer collapse of all his powers and after this his conduct...was marked by an incomprehensible feebleness and faultiness...the general whose first stride had been that of a giant, shrunk to the proportions of a dwarf."[32] At 10:00 A.M., the Confederates captured the Chancellorsville crossroads and Hooker withdrew his army to protect his line of retreat.

Back at Fredericksburg, General Sedgwick had carried Marye's Heights. His advance threatened to push past General Early and cut communications with Richmond. Early managed to delay Sedgwick's column at Salem Church and at 5:00 P.M., a division of the 1st Corps under Major General Lafayette McLaws (1821-1897; West Point 1842) came up to check his forward move-ment. The next day, Lee arrived accompanied by an additional division. General Early recaptured Mayre's Heights which cut the 6th Corps off from Fredericksburg. Confronted on three sides by Confederates, Sedgwick extricated his command by bridging the Rappahannock to gain safety. On the night of May 5, the remainder of Hooker's army recrossed the river, "without the consciousness have having been beaten."[33]

At a cost of 12,500 men, the Army of Northern Virginia had again prevailed against overwhelming odds and inflicted 17,300 casualties on the Army of the Potomac. Lee's army seemed to be invincible and capable of any feat. The loss of "Stonewall" Jackson, however, would be felt in the next battle.

J.E.B. Stuart's career reached its zenith in the spring of 1863. He revelled in the image of a dashing cavalier and yearned for glory. "His natural inclination was to reduce complex matters to their simplest terms. He wanted to perceive this war as combat between individuals; at base his orientation was personal, not corporate or institutional."[34] On June 5, near Culpeper Court Horse, Stuart displayed his horsemen, almost 10,000 strong, in a memorable grand review. Three days later, the paladin of the Confederacy repeated the egotistical exercise for Lee. Union cavalry, backed by six batteries and two brigades of infantry, crossed the Rappahannock River the next morning and attacked Stuart. The unexpected movement by the enemy caught the gray knight by surprise and for the first time in the war, Union horsemen fought their Confederate counterparts on equal terms.

One blue column threatened to take Fleetwood Hill, which would have forced Stuart to yield the field. The commander of Lee's cavalry reacted slowly to the situation but a staff officer managed to hold the hill with a scratch force until reinforcements arrived. After hours of charge and countercharge the Federals retired unmolested back across the Rappahannock. Though the Northerners suffered nearly twice as many casualties as the Southerners at Fleetwood Hill (Brandy Station), J.E.B. Stuart had clearly been humiliated. Lee praised him, but the Southern press criticized the hero; his image had become tarnished.

Before Stuart's embarrassment, Lee had begun to shift to his army toward the Shenandoah Valley to invade Pennsylvania. Conscious of the difficulties his nation faced in the west, Lee expected his strategic movement to relieve pressure on the Confederate armies defending Vicksburg and Chattanooga. Victories in Virginia over the Army of the Potomac had not improved the outlook for Southern independence. Lee believed that a decisive victory on enemy soil would convince the Northerners to accept a political solution that would end the war.

The Army of Northern Virginia was now organized into three corps. A.P. Hill led the newly created 3rd Corps while Longstreet and Ewell commanded the 1st and 2nd Corps respectively. On June 12, the 2nd Corps tramped into the Valley. Two days later General Ewell intercepted a column commanded by Major General Robert H. Milroy (1816-1890; Mexican War) fleeing Winchester. Richard Ewell crushed Milroy and on June 22, Robert Rodes marched proudly into Pennsylvania after disposing of small Federal garrisons at Berryville and Martinsburg. Lee entered the Keystone State five days later.

Upon learning of Ewell's presence in the Valley, Hooker left the line of the Rappahannock and deployed the Army of the Potomac to protect Washington. On June 25 and 26, Hooker's army crossed the Potomac River to concentrate around Frederick, Maryland. He also intended to evacuate the garrison at Harpers Ferry and unite those troops with his own force. This proposal was unacceptable to the government; Hooker asked to be relieved. The Lincoln administration, anxious to find a reason to replace Hooker, complied with his request. General Meade was appointed commander of the Eastern Army on June 28. The historian of the Army of the Potomac, William Swinton, believed that "it was fortunate for the Union cause at this crisis, that the choice of the Government for the commander of the Army of the Potomac fell upon one who proved fitted for the high trust; and fortunate, too, that that oft-displayed steadfastness of the army, unshaked of fortune and committed to the death to a duty self-imposed, rendered such transitions, elsewhere dangerous, here safe and easy."[35]

While Lee's infantry and artillery moved down the Valley toward Pennsylvania, Stuart's cavalry covered the passes of the Blue Ridge Mountains. When Hooker's army marched to catch up with Lee's army, Stuart detached two brigades to protect the passes and the army's rear. Stuart then set out with his three remaining brigades to make contact with Ewell's Corps. Lee had given Stuart instructions which allowed him to choose his own route to follow. Instead of interposing his force between the two armies to gather intelligence for his chief, he decided to ride east around Hooker's right flank, and then crossed the Potomac River. Vanity overcame military common sense as Stuart effectively removed himself from the beginning of the campaign.

Stuart's cavalry began the passage of the Potomac on June 27 and reached Rockville, a northern suburb of Washington, the next day. The cavalrymen captured a large wagon train and continued north into Pennsylvania cutting telegraph lines along the way. At Hanover on June 30, the Rebel horsemen encountered enemy cavalry, and during the ensuing clash, Stuart narrowly avoided capture or death. The wagons slowed the Confederate column and Stuart, unable to locate Ewell, sent two staff officers to search for the army.

On July 1, Stuart led his weary and hungry troopers first to Dover, and then to Carlisle, where he hoped to find provisions and part of the army. To his dismay he discovered hundreds of Pennsylvania militia men. The cavalrymen skirmished with the Cornstalk Soldiers, burned down a barracks, and shelled the town. That night Stuart learned that Lee and the army was thirty-three miles south at Gettysburg, a strategic crossroads in Adams County. Around midnight the Southerners started for Gettysburg with 125 wagons.

Earlier that day, at 5:00 A.M., Brigadier General Henry Heth's (1825-1899; West Point 1847) Division of Hill's Corps broke camp and marched for

Gettysburg to investigate a report that enemy cavalry had been observed there the day before. Around 8:00 A.M., General Heth's advance began to skirmish with Union cavalry and pushed them back slowly. Major General John F. Reynolds (1820-1863; West Point 1841), who commanded General Meade's vanguard, the 1st Corps, received word of the Confederate activity from the cavalry commander, Brigadier General John Buford (1826-1863; West Point 1848). Reynolds galloped to Gettysburg to investigate and arrived on the scene at 10:00 A.M. After conferring with Buford, Reynolds decided to bring up his infantry and make a stand on McPherson's Ridge northwest of town. Reynolds sent a messenger to inform General Meade of his decision. As he brought the Iron Brigade into action, Reynolds was killed by a sharpshooter.

The 1st Corps punished Heth's Division, which was forced to withdraw. Brigadier General James J. Archer (1817-1864; Mexican War) became the first general officer to be captured since Lee assumed command of the army. Meanwhile, reinforcements from both sides rushed to reach Gettysburg. The 11th Corps arrived to extend the Union line north and east while Rodes deployed his division to attack the right flank of the 1st Corps. Around 2:30 P.M., Rodes ordered two brigades to advance, but his success at Chancellorsville was not repeated.

Due to miscommunication, only three regiments of Colonel Edward A. O'Neal's Brigade charged. The 3rd and 5th Alabama Regiments remained in the rear, as did Col. O'Neal. Four companies of the 45th New York (11th Corps) and a battery from Cincinnati, the Army of the Potomac's best, Captain Hubert Dilger's Battery I, 1st Ohio Artillery (11th Corps) repulsed the Alabamians who suffered heavy casualties. The withdrawal of O'Neal's men exposed the left flank of a North Carolina brigade led by Brigadier General Alfred Iverson (1829-1911; Mexican War). Taking advantage of the tactical opportunity, a brigade commanded by Brigadier General Henry Baxter (1821-1873; commissioned captain 7th Michigan in 1861) mowed down the Tar Heels who fell in company lines, and then captured most of the survivors. Iverson's losses reduced the strength of his brigade to that of a regiment.

General Early's division delivered the next Rebel blow around 4:00 P.M. While part of Rodes' Division hit the front of the 11th Corps, Early's brigades enveloped the right flank and the two Union divisions collapsed into a disorganized mob. This development produced an advance by the entire Rebel line. Most of the 1st Corps withdrew to Seminary Ridge to make a stand but sustained attacks forced them to flee. Survivors scurried into Gettysburg to mingle with fugitives of the 11th Corps. The defense of McPherson's Ridge by the Iron Brigade and the performance of Lieutenant Colonel Rufus R. Dawes, 6th Wisconsin, also of the Iron Brigade, was overlooked by many early historians. Consequently, the general public is aware of Little Round Top and

Devil's Den, but knows nothing about the defenders of McPherson's Ridge. The Westerners bought both time and space for the Army of the Potomac to concentrate at Gettysburg and defeat the Army of Northern Virginia. Casualties in the 19th Indiana, which lost 210 men out of 288 engaged, testify to the Iron Brigade's tenacity and sacrifice.

The Rebels followed the Yankees closely and captured hundreds of prisoners. Those who were lucky or swift escaped the disaster and made their way to Cemetery Hill, south of town. A fresh brigade from the 11th Corps occupied the high ground and formed a nucleus of resistance which enabled the refugees of two corps to rally.

Lee, who had reached the field around 2:00 P.M., suggested to Ewell that it might be "practicable" to seize Cemetery Hill. Ewell made no effort to take the initiative. Had "Stonewall" Jackson commanded the 2nd Corps that day, he would have attempted to carry Cemetery Hill. Excuses that have been offered to explain Ewell's inaction would have presented no obstacle to Jackson. The poor judgment exercised by senior Confederate officers on July 1 reflect their overall performance during the rest of the battle, as well as the campaign.

On the afternoon of July 2, the Army of Northern Virginia's cavalry commander reported to Lee. "Lee reddened at the sight of Stuart and raised his right arm as if he would strike him. 'General Stuart, where have you been?' Stuart seemed to wilt, and explained his movements to Lee. 'I have not heard a word from you for days,' Lee said, 'and you the eyes and ears of my army.' 'I have brought you 125 wagons and teams, general,' Stuart said."[36]

Concerning the wagons, a recent biographer of J.E.B. Stuart concluded: "He was greedy. He clearly underestimated the need for speed, and he gravely miscalculated the effect of his tardiness on the campaign. And as he rode through enemy country, he seemed to see only the road on which he was, when he should have been seeing a map of Pennsylvania."[37]

General Stuart defended his actions during the Gettysburg Campaign in a fantastic report that amounted to an apology of more than 14,000 words. Following the war, many bitter Southerners explained the failure at Gettysburg by using J.E.B. Stuart (or James Longstreet) as a scapegoat. A fellow cavalryman, Major General Thomas Rosser (1836-1910; resigned from West Point 1861) blamed the defeat on Stuart's absence, whereas John S. Mosby, the "Gray Ghost," defended his deceased friend.

In May 1864, the Army of the Potomac, still commanded by General Meade but directed by Lieutenant General Ulysses S. Grant (1822-1885; West Point 1843), began a campaign, which was designed to destroy the Army of Northern Virginia. J.E.B. Stuart and his horsemen became the personal target of Major General Philip H. Sheridan (1831-1888; West Point 1853).[38] While the veteran armies clashed at Spotsylvania Court House (May 7-20), General Sheridan took 10,000 troopers on a raid toward Richmond. Sheridan set out on May 9 and the next day his men captured a major supply base at Beaver Dam Station. Stuart collected three brigades, some 4,500 men, to oppose Sheridan.

Richmond May 10 1864

General R E Lee

Guinea's Depot   The following dispatch just received from General Stuart

General: While pursuing the Enemy from Beaver Dam on the Richmond Road the barricading was So Serious an Obstruction that a Road parallel to their line of March was taken by my Command and the Head of the Column will rest near Taylorsvile tonight A Small party was Sent to discover his position, Should he attack Richmond I will certainly move to his Rear and do what I can at the Same time I hope to be able to Strike him if he endeavors to escape

His force is large and if attack is made on Richmond it will be principally as dismounted Cavalry which fights better than Enemy's Infantry

JEB Stuart

Maj Genl

On the morning of May 11, 1864, General Stuart waited at a crossroads called Yellow Tavern with two brigades as his remaining brigade operated against General Sheridan's rear. Before noon the Federals appeared and the Confederates fought off two attacks. At 4:00 P.M., the blue cavalrymen launched a heavy assault against the Rebel right. Stuart shouted encouragement to the 1st Virginia Cavalry as he shot his Le Mat revolver at the swarming enemy. A countercharge drove back the Yankees and in the melee a dismounted Union trooper, Sergeant John A. Huff, Co. E., 5th Michigan Cavalry, aimed his pistol at a conspicuous officer. Huff's bullet tore into Stuart's abdomen at a distance of less than fifteen yards. Stuart remained in the saddle but soon dismounted with aid from his men. An ambulance pulled up to remove the stricken knight from his last tourney. J.E.B. Stuart died at Richmond on May 12, just after 7:30 P.M.

On the night of June 1, Grant attempted to outflank Lee from Spotsylvania Court House by marching south, but the Rebels outmarched the Yankees. The antagonists collided again at Cold Harbor on June 3. The Federals attacked at dawn and continued throughout the morning but they made little headway against their entrenched foe. At 1:30 P.M. "General Meade sent instructions to each corps-commander to renew the attack...but no man stirred, and the immobile lines pronounced a verdict, silent, yet, emphatic, against further slaughter."[39] In three hard fought battles, the Army of Northern Virginia and the Army of the Potomac nearly bled to death as Lee lost 32,000 irreplaceable veterans; Grant's loss was more than 50,000.

The destruction of Lee's army remained Grant's primary objective, but the fighting spirit of the Eastern Army had been crippled. Grant adjusted his strategy of attrition, and in order to defeat the Army of Northern Virginia, he resolved to cross the James River and break up the railroads running to Petersburg, which would cripple Lee's supply line. By June 16, the Army of the Potomac had passed over the James on a pontoon bridge more than two thousand feet long, but Petersburg did not fall until April 3, 1865.

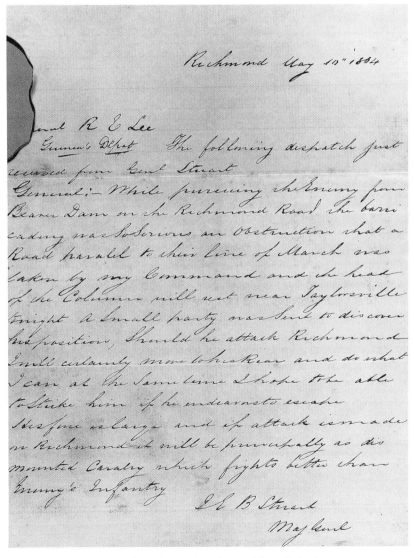

One of the last dispatches dictated by J.E.B. Stuart

2

THE ARMY OF TENNESSEE

In December 1862, veterans of Shiloh, known as the Army of the Mississippi, were reorganized into two corps. Renamed the Army of Tennessee, the "Army of the Heartland" defended Tennessee and Georgia from 1862 to 1864 and North Carolina in 1865. Misfortune camped with the divisions of the South's saddest army. Hard fighting followed by retreat described the career of its first commander, Braxton Bragg. Joseph Johnston, who replaced Bragg, corroborated his own reputation as the master of retreat. John Bell Hood, who replaced "Old Joe" Johnston, saw the survivors of Fishing Creek (January 19, 1862) and Shiloh (April 7 and 8, 1862) slaughtered in Tennessee.

From the beginning of the Civil War, Confederate units raised in the West suffered from a lack of officers with military experience to train them. In 1861, 304 officers resigned from the U.S. Army to fight with the South. These men, with few exceptions returned to serve in their home states. Less than 20 percent of this number were from Texas, Tennessee, Alabama, Mississippi, Arkansas, or Louisiana. "Extensive study of the history and records of both of the two major Southern armies leads inexorably to the conclusion that the Virginia army was better managed than was the Army of Tennessee. The organization of the eastern army was tighter and more efficient, its administration was thorough and more sound, and—above all—its discipline was better than that of the Army of Tennessee."[1]

Leadership, more so than superior numbers or luck, is the most essential element for the successful prosecution of war. Both Southern armies operated under a system whereby the commanding general issued an order and allowed subordinates the discretion to carry it out. With able subordinates like "Stonewall" Jackson, A.P. Hill, and Longstreet, General Lee was victorious until Gettysburg. Personality conflicts, as between Jackson and A.P. Hill for example, complicated Lee's task, but never contributed to defeat. The principal personality clash in the Army of Tennessee eventually damaged its effectiveness. Before the war, Lieutenant General Leonidas Polk (1806-1864; West Point 1827) had been a bishop in the Episcopal Church. An insubordinate officer, Polk disobeyed orders when it suited him, which was frequently. In his autobiography written after the war, Major General Samuel G. French (1818-1910; West Point 1843) said of the courtly prelate: "As a soldier he was more theoretical than practical."[2]

When General Johnston returned to duty in November 1862, President Davis ordered him West to oversee the operations of two forces, the Army of Tennessee, commanded by General Braxton Bragg (1817-1876; West Point 1837) and the 1st and 2nd Corps of the Department of Eastern Louisiana and Mississippi commanded by Major General John C. Pemberton (1814-1881; West Point 1837). In north central Mississippi, General Pemberton opposed the Army of the Tennessee which was directed by General Grant. General Bragg confronted the Army of the Cumberland under Major General William S. Rosecrans (1819-1898; West Point 1842) in central Tennessee. The following two letters were written by General Johnston to General Cooper in regard to reinforcing Pemberton, who faced the most immediate threat, with troops from Arkansas.

Chattanooga, Tenn.
Dec. 4th 1862

Genl. S. Cooper.
A&I Genl.

Sir

    I have received this evening your telegram of yesterday informing me that Lieut. Genl. Pemberton is falling back before very superior force– that Lieut. Genl. Holmes had been peremptorily ordered to reinforce him but as Genl. Holmes' troops may be too late the President urged on me the importance of sending a sufficient force from Genl. Bragg's command to the aid of Lieut. Genl. Pemberton.

    Three Rail Road accidents delayed my journey so much so that I did not reach this place until two oclock [*sic*] last night consequently your dispatch was delivered to day too late for communication with Genl. Bragg– before tomorrow when I shall visit his Hed. Qrs. I do not know Genl. Pemberton's position– His march I suppose will be towards Vicksburg when Genl. Holmes' troops must cross the River– His movements therefore are facilitating the junction while they daily under that of Genl. Bragg with him more difficult. The enemy too is exactly between the latter and himself. It seems to me consequently that the aid of Genl. Holmes can better be relied on than that of Genl. Bragg– I therefore respectfully suggest that Officer be urged to the utmost expedition should the enemy get possession of Vicksburg we cannot dislodge him. The Tennessee river, is a formidable obstacle to the expeditious march of Genl. Bragg's troops into Mississippi– He may besides be compelled to take a circuitous route– of this however I am not fully informed nor have I learned the enemy's attitude in Tennessee. It is to be presumed that all such information can be acquired at Genl. Bragg's Hed. Qrs. which I shall reach tomorrow.

Most respectfully
Your obedient servant
J.E. Johnston

[*OR* XX Series I Pt.2 p.436]

Murfreesboro Tenn.
Gen'l S. Cooper   Dec. 6th 1862
Adjt.&I. Genl
Richmond

Sir

Gen'l Rosencranz [*sic*] has an army of about sixty five thousand men in and around Nashville, and some thirty five thousand distributed along the Rail Road to Louisville, & in Kentucky_ Gen'l Bragg has about forty two thousand men besides irregular Cavalry, which in a few days will occupy Reedyville, this place & Eagleville_ We can cross the Tennessee only by ferrying, a very slow process which Rosencranz would certainly interrupt. The movement to join Gen'l Pemberton would, by any route, require at least a month. From the information given here, I believe that the Country between the Tennessee & Gen'l Pemberton, could not support the trains our troops would require for a march through it. If I am right in this estimate, the President's object, speedy reinforcement of the Army in Mississippi, cannot be accomplished by sending troops from Tennessee_ To send a strong force would be to give up Tennessee, and would, the principal officials think here, disorganize this army. Rosencra[n]z could then move into Virginia or join Grant before our troops could reach Pemberton's position, for the Transfer is no obstacle to him. The passage of the Tennessee is so difficult, and slow, that we shall be unable to use the same troops on both sides of the river, until next summer.

Two thousand (2000) Cavalry will be sent to break up the Louisville & Nashville Rail Road, and four thousand will be employed in the same way in West Tennessee and Northern Mississippi. The latter may delay Gen'l. Grant.

Very respectfully
Your Obt. Svt.
(Signed) J.E. Johnston
General.

[*OR* XX Series I Pt. 2 p.441]

General Leonidas Polk

General Braxton Bragg

General Johnston was unfamiliar with the condition of affairs in his new area of responsibility. His letters to Richmond, however, are correct in their conclusion regarding the advisability of reinforcing General Pemberton's army from Arkansas; the Confederates there faced no immediate threat. In response to the crisis in his home state, President Davis left Richmond on December 10 and journeyed to Tennessee. The next day Davis reached Chattanooga to find Johnston ill from the effects of his earlier wound. The president soon departed for Murfreesboro to confer with Bragg and his generals. Davis reached army headquarters on December 12, accompanied by Colonel G.W.C. Lee, son of Robert E. Lee. The following day President Davis reviewed three divisions commanded by General Polk. Bragg disliked the well-connected cleric and considered him unfit for high command; Polk had become "the chief source of the backbiting and criticism that would eventually undermine Bragg's effectiveness."[3]

While on his way home to Louisiana earlier that year, Richard Taylor, who had been promoted to major general in July, stopped at Chattanooga. At dinner with Bragg and his staff, General Taylor heard the commanding general describe General Polk as "an old woman, utterly worthless." Taylor was astonished that such a remark would be made in public since it would certainly be repeated. The son of President Zachary Taylor offered this opinion of Bragg in his post war autobiography.

> Possessing experience and talent for war, he was the most laborious of commanders, devoting every moment to the discharge of his duties. As a disciplinarian he far surpassed any of the senior Confederate generals; but his method and manner were harsh, and he could have won the affections of his troops only by leading them to victory. He furnished a striking illustration of the necessity of a healthy body for a sound intellect. Many years of dyspepsia [indigestion] had made his temper sour and petulant; and he was intolerant to a degree of neglect of duty, or what he esteemed to be such, by his officers.[4]

To be fair, it is important to note that General Bragg truly cared about his soldiers. He visited hospitals to inspire the wounded and sought to improve the welfare of his men by inspecting their camps and asking questions. Easily excited when engaged with the enemy, Bragg seemed to lose his nerve. He was an adequate strategist but had difficulty executing his plans, never learned from his mistakes on the battlefield, and blamed others for his failures.

By the time Davis arrived at army headquarters in December 1862, Bragg had lost the confidence of many senior generals. They criticized him for the way he had handled the army during the fall campaign in Kentucky. The occupation of Munfordville in September had threatened Louisville, but Bragg had discarded the opportunity, advanced into central Kentucky, scattered his army and installed a Confederate governor at Lexington. He believed, incorrectly, that the Union army which opposed him had received reinforcements. When General Bragg began to concentrate his army, Polk disobeyed orders which brought on the Battle of Perryville in early October. Though a tactical victory for the Confederates, it brought them no strategic advantage. Short on results, long on promise and expectations, the most lasting effect of the Perryville Campaign was the damage it brought to General Bragg's military reputation. Even though northern Alabama and Middle Tennessee had been recovered for the Confederacy, the withdrawal from Kentucky had disheartened Bragg's troops. General Bragg became a target of criticism from both civilians and military men.

General Polk, along with an important ally, Lieutenant General William J. Hardee (1815-1873; West Point 1838) started to campaign to replace General Bragg. Hardee, a former commandant of the military academy, tried to turn the officer corps against Bragg while Polk used his connections with influential friends, including the president, to bring down Bragg. Shortly after his army returned to Tennessee, General Bragg was called to Richmond. In a week of interviews with President Davis and Secretary of War George W. Randolph, Bragg successfully defended his actions during the late campaign and attempted to assign Polk the blame for its disappointing outcome.

General William Joseph Hardee

President Davis summoned General Polk to the capital on November 3. Davis' West Point classmate explained that Bragg alone was responsible for the failure in Kentucky. Polk suggested that General Johnston be named to replace Bragg, but Davis declined to act. His confidence in Bragg remained undiminished. Following the meeting, General Polk went home on leave; General Bragg went back to his command.

Despite manifest friction between General Bragg and many of his subordinates, the president believed that all was well with the Army of Tennessee. Conversation with senior officers convinced him that the army was willing to fight and he expected Rosecrans' army to remain in camp for the winter. Davis solved the problem of reinforcements for General Pemberton by ordering General Johnston to detach the division of Major General Carter L. Stevenson (1817-1888; West Point 1838) from the Army of Tennessee. Davis left Tennessee on December 15 to inspect the fortifications at Vicksburg. On December 26, he addressed the Mississippi legislature in session at Jackson, then returned to Richmond. Major General William T. Sherman (1820-1891; West Point 1840) commanded four divisions that boarded transports at Memphis and disembarked north of Vicksburg on December 26. After skirmishing with the Confederates and probing their defenses, Sherman launched a major assault at Chickasaw Bayou on December 29. Part of General Stevenson's Division reached Vicksburg in time to participate in the battle. The Yankees were repulsed with heavy casualties and they retreated three days later. On January 11, 1863, the four Midwestern divisions, now led by an Illinois politician, Major General John A. McClernand (1812-1890), captured several thousand Rebels at Arkansas Post.

Sherman's attempt to capture Vicksburg was designed to cooperate with Grant, who had penetrated into central Mississippi. Confederate cavalry captured and burned his forward base at Holly Springs on December 20. This disaster combined with the effect of a Rebel raid into West Tennessee caused General Grant to retreat from Mississippi, before General Sherman ever landed at Vicksburg. Meanwhile, General Rosecrans, under pressure from Washington, advanced from Nashville.

By December 30, two great American armies faced each other two miles northwest of Murfreesboro. Nightfall ended skirmishing and regimental bands from the opposing sides dueled with tunes. Union musicians played "Yankee Doodle" while their adversaries countered with "Dixie." Both sides ended the bloodless contest with "Home Sweet Home," the most favorite song of Civil War soldiers. That night, both Rosecrans and Bragg decided to attack their opponent's right flank the next morning. A bend in Stones River divided the Confederate army. Major General John C. Breckinridge's (1821-1875; Vice President of the United States) large division of Hardee's Corps crossed the

General John Cabell Breckinridge

river to cover General Bragg's right flank. This deployment became the decisive factor in the outcome of the battle as Rosecrans' entire army opposed Bragg's four remaining divisions. At daybreak, as the Federals ate breakfast, the Confederates struck. Major General John P. McCown's (1815-1879; West Point 1840) Division, Hardee's Corps, tore apart Brigadier General Richard W. Johnson's (1827-1897; West Point 1849) Division of Major General Alexander M. McCooks' (1831-1903; West Point 1852) right wing. More than a thousand prisoners were taken by McCown's men. When they ran low on ammunition, Hardee's other division, led by Major General Patrick R. Cleburne (1828-1864; lawyer) sustained the attack. Cleburne's Brigades tangled with Brigadier General Jefferson C. Davis' (1828-1879; Mexican War) Division, now on the Army of the Cumberland's right flank.

To the left of Davis, Brigadier General Philip H. Sheridan's Division of three brigades, repelled the attacks of divisions led by Major General Benjamin F. Cheatham (1820-1886; Mexican War) and Major General Jones M. Withers (1814-1890; West Point 1835) of Polk's Corps. He counterattacked at 9:30 A.M., but Cleburne enveloped the Union line on his front, Sheridan's right, and the Federals were compelled to fall back. From the center, commanded by Major General George H. Thomas (1816-1870; West Point 1840), a division

General Patrick Ronayne Cleburne

commanded by Major General Lovell H. Rousseau (1818-1869; Mexican War) came up to support Sheridan. In the center of the heavily wooded battlefield, General Withers' Division drove back Brigadier General James S. Negley's (1826-1901; Mexican War) Division, which fought under Thomas' command. By noon, much of the battered Army of the Cumberland had reformed near the Nashville Turnpike. General Rosecrans' right wing now faced northwest on a line perpendicular to its original position.

Two fresh divisions from the left wing, Major General Thomas L. Crittenden (1819-1893; Mexican War), which had been designated to lead General Rosecrans' original attack, reinforced the Union line defending the turnpike. Brigadier General Horatio P. Van Cleve's Division (1809-1891; West Point 1831) opposed McCown while Sheridan, Rousseau, and fragments of Davis' Division confronted Cleburne's exhausted brigades. Brigadier General Thomas J. Wood's Division (1823-1906; West Point 1845) extended back from the turnpike toward the river. On its right flank, the line of Brigadier General John M. Palmer's (1817-1900; politician) Division, ran across the turnpike. These two divisions faced Polk's Corps. General Hardee required additional troops to swing past General Rosecrans' extreme right flank, gain control of the

Nashville Turnpike, and cut the Ohioan's avenue of retreat. Stanley Horn, who produced the first study of the Army of Tennessee wrote: "One more push, it seemed, and the rout of the right wing would be complete. If Stevenson's absent division could have been thrown into action at this juncture it would probably have pulverized the Federal defense...."[5]

General Breckinridge's Division formed the strategic reserve and the Kentuckian believed, erroneously, that enemy infantry was on his front. He delayed compliance with an order from General Bragg to send reinforcements across the river. Historian Peter Cozzens, author of the definitive work on the battle, speculates that General Breckinridge, who had lost confidence in General Bragg, feared his troops would be mishandled. If this was his assumption, it proved correct. When two of Breckinridge's Brigades approached the field at about 2:00 P.M., General Polk sent them into the fight.

At the point in the Federal defensive line where it angled northwest and northeast, a salient known after the battle as the "Round Forest," had become the focus of repeated assaults. General Cheatham's Division, which had disrupted Hardee's initial attack by entering the battle late, had been attacking the strong point since before noon. One of Cheatham's Brigades had achieved a short-lived success to the right of the Round Forest, but the Union units remained resolute. General Polk had permitted General Cheatham to feed his brigades into the fight piecemeal and repeated the same mistake when Breckinridge's first two brigades arrived.

Each brigade attacked alone with valiant effort; both were thrown back with heavy losses. An hour later when General Breckinridge reached the area with ten more regiments, General Polk modified his tactics. Breckinridge's last two brigades (one remained across the river) advanced together and were repulsed with ease by the Yankees.

General Bragg's obsession with taking the Round Forest may have cost him the battle. Instead of reinforcing Hardee, who was more competent, Bragg gave his reserves to Polk. "Although Bragg had ordained the attack, he had left its timing and execution to the bishop; certainly Polk could have waited the hour necessary to muster all four brigades, rather than commit them individually to almost certain defeat."[6]

Both armies remained in position New Year's Day. The Army of Tennessee hoped their adversaries would retreat while the Army of the Cumberland awaited events. When Bragg did not renew the battle, his men began to think their hard won victory on the last day of the year was slipping away. Polk occupied the Round Forest when the Federals withdrew and Breckinridge recrossed Stones River. As darkness settled over Tennessee, the Union soldiers became optimistic. With faith in "Old Rosey," they believed Bragg was played out.

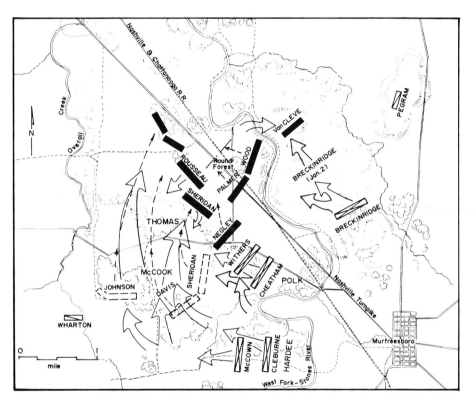

The Battle of Murfreesboro
December 31, 1862 - January 2, 1863

On January 2, General Bragg decided to force the enemy to withdraw with artillery fire from the east side of the river. He ordered General Breckinridge to take high ground on his front in order to position batteries. General Breckinridge objected to the order, but his anger could not prevail over General Bragg's seniority.

At 4:00 P.M., the Confederates formed their lines and struggled forward through sleet into heavy artillery fire. The lead brigade quickly closed with the Union regiments and broke their line. A second line crumbled and the Union soldiers splashed across Stones River; the Rebels occupied the hill Bragg coveted.

Forty-five artillery pieces blasted Breckinridge's Butternuts back to their departure point faster than they had advanced. The blueclads counterattacked and captured a battery, but were halted when the Confederates rallied on their own artillery. As he viewed survivors of the 2nd, 4th, 6th and 9th Kentucky Regiments, General Breckinridge cried: "My poor Orphans! My poor Orphans! My poor Orphan Brigade! They have cut it to pieces!"[7] Thus was born the Orphan Brigade and so ended the Battle of Murfreesboro.

General Bragg responded to the failure by shifting Hardee's Corps across the river to support Breckinridge. This left Generals Cheatham and Withers alone on the west side of Stones River. A little after midnight they visited General Polk with a message for their commanding general. Polk read the note and composed one of his own. One of Polk's aides awoke Bragg at 2:00 A.M. and the North Carolinian snorted: "Say to General Polk we shall hold our own at every hazard."[8]

Shortly thereafter, a senior officer in Cleburne's Division encountered Bragg. Brigadier General St. John R. Liddell (1815-1870; resigned after one year at West Point) sought shelter from a cold rain at army headquarters; he found Bragg in a pensive mood. General Bragg feared his army was too weak to risk another serious engagement. He also believed, incorrectly, that General Rosecrans had received heavy reinforcements. Liddell encouraged Bragg to remain on the battlefield and discounted the arrival of Union reinforcements. He left convinced that Bragg was wrong, which he was. That night, the Army of Tennessee withdrew from Murfreesboro and set up winter camp at Tullahoma.

General Bragg's empty success cost the Confederacy 10,266 casualties out of 35,000 men engaged. The Army of the Cumberland lost nearly 12,000 out of a strength of 45,000 men. Unlike the Confederate commander, the Union commander was praised by the press and politicians. Bragg's controversial and weak reputation eroded even more and the confidence of his soldiers ebbed. On December 31, General Bragg had all but guaranteed the southern public a great victory in his dispatches. His subsequent retreat produced disappointment, and anger. Another "victory" could only be measured in terms of retreat. Bragg was scourged by the southern press. In a series of editorials, the *Chattanooga Daily Rebel* claimed that Bragg had lost the confidence of his soldiers and generals, who had advised against retreat. Amid rumors that he would be replaced, General Bragg's staff informed him that the army had indeed lost confidence in him; he should resign.

Instead of offering his resignation to the government, Bragg retaliated against his tormenters. The following is a circular letter that he composed and sent to his senior generals.

> Headquarters Army of Tennessee
> Tullahoma, Tenn. January 11th 1863

General

Finding myself assailed in private and public by the Press, in private circles by officers and citizens for the movement from Murfreesboro, which was resisted by me for Sometime after advised by my Corps and Division commanders and only adopted after hearing of the enemy's reinforcements by large numbers from Kentucky: it becomes necessary for me to Save my fair name, if I cannot Stop the deluge of abuse which will destroy my usefulness and demoralize this army. It has come to my Knowledge that many of these accusations and insinuations are from Staff officers of my Generals who persistently assert that the movement was made against the opinion and advice of their chiefs and while the enemy was in full retreat. False or true the Soldiers have no means of judging me rightly or getting the facts and the effect on them will be the Same, a loss of confidence and a consequent demoralization of the whole army. It is only thro[ugh] my Generals that I can establish the facts as they exist. Unanimous as you were in Council in verbally advising a retrograde movement I cannot doubt that you will cheerfully attest the Same in writing. I deem that you will consult your Subordinate commanders and be candid with me as I have always endeavored to prove myself with you. If I have misunderstood your advice and acted against your opinions, let me Know it in justice to yourselves. If on the contrary I am the victim of unjust accusations Say So and unite with me in Staying the malignant Slanders being propagated by Men who have felt the Sting of discipline.

Gen'l [E. Kirby] Smith has been called to Richmond, it is Supposed with a View to Supersede me. I shall retire without a regret if I find I have lost the good opinion of my Generals upon whom I have ever relied as upon a foundation of rock.

Your early attention is most desirable and is urgently Solicited.

> Most Respectfully
> Your Ob't Sv't
> Braxton Bragg
> Gen'l C.S.A.

Head Quarters Army of Tennessee
Tullahoma Tenn— January 11th 1863

General

Finding myself assailed in private and public by the Press, in private circles by officers and citizens for the movement from Murfreesboro, which was resisted by me for sometime after advised by my Corps and Division commanders and only adopted after hearing of the enemy's reinforcements by large numbers from Kentucky; it becomes necessary for me to save my fair name, if I cannot stop the deluge of abuse which will destroy my usefulness and demoralize this army. It has come to my knowledge that many of these accusations and insinuations are from Staff officers of my Generals who persistently assert that the movement was made against the opinion and advice of their Chiefs and while the enemy was in full retreat. False or true the Soldiers have no means of judging me rightly or getting the facts and the effect on them will be the same, a loss of confidence and a consequent demoralization of the whole army. It is only thro my Generals that I can

Page one of the circular letter sent by General Bragg to General Polk

59

establish the facts as they exist, Unanimous as
You were in Council in virtually advising a
retrograde movement I cannot doubt that
you will cheerfully attest the Same in writing,
I ask that you will consult your Subordinate
commanders and be candid with me as I
have always endeavored to prove myself with
you, If I have misunderstood your advice
and acted against Your opinion, let me know
it in justice to Yourselves, If on the contrary I
am the victim of unjust accusations Say
to and unite with me in Staying the malignant Slanders being propagated by One
Who have felt the Sting of dicipline

Genl Smith has been called to
Richmond, it is Supposed with a View to
Supersede me, I Shall retire without a
regret if I find I have lost the good opin-
ion of my Generals upon whom I have ever
relied as upon a foundation of rock
Your early attention is most desirable
and is urgently Solicited,
Most Respectfully
Your Obt Servt
Braxton Bragg
Genl C. S. A.

Page two of General Bragg's letter to General Polk

I enclosed copies of a joint note received about 2 O'Clock A.M. from Majs Genls Cheatham and Withers on the night before we retreated from Murfreesboro: with Lt Genl Polks' endorsement and my own verbal reply to Lt Richmond Polks' Aid de Camp.

Lt Gen'l Polk
Commdg Polks' Corps
[*OR* XX Series I Pt.1 p.699]

End of General Bragg's letter to General Polk

"A"

12.15 A M   Head Quarters in the field
                                                      Murfreesboro Tenn
                                                      January 1863

Genl,

   We deem it our duty to say to you frankly that in our judgment this army Should be promptly put in retreat. You have but three Brigades that are at all reliable and even Some of these are more or less demoralized from having Some Brigade commanders who do not possess the confidence of their commands, Such is our opinion and we deem it a Solemn duty to express it to you. We do fear great disaster from the condition of things now existing and think it should be averted if possible.

                                        Very resply Genl Yours &C
                                        B F Cheatham
                                           Maj Genl C.S.A
                                        J M Withers
                                           Maj Genl &C
To
   Genl Bragg   A true copy
   Comdg &C   Kinloch Falconer A.A.G
                         A true copy
                         W D Gale   A.D.C

[*OR* XX Series I Pt.1 p.700]

"B"

"Copy"   1.30 A.M. January 3rd

My dear General

   I send you the enclosed paper as requested. And I am compelled to add, that after seeing the effect of the operations of to day, added to that produced upon the troops by the battle of the 31st, I very greatly fear the consequences of another engagement at this place on the ensuing day. We could now perhaps get off with some safety and with some credit, if the affair was well managed. Should we fail in the meditated attack, the consequences might be very disastrous.

   Hoping you may be guided aright, whatever detirmination [*sic*] you may reach

                                        I am very truly yours
                                        (S.G.) L. Polk.
                                        Lieut Genl.
   I certify the above is a true copy

                                        (Sg) Kinloch Falconer
                                             A.A.G
   To this Genl. Bragg replied through Lieut Richmond "Say to Genl. Polk we shall hold our own at every hazard."

   (A true copy)   T.B. Roy
                                        Chfofstaff

[*OR* XX Series I Pt.1 p.700]

"a"

12.15 A M

Head Quarters in the field
Murfreesboro Tenn.
January 3 1863

Genl

We deem it our duty to say to You
frankly that in our judgment this army
should be promptly put in retreat, You have
but three Brigades that are at all reliable
and even some of these are more or less demoralized from having some Brigade
commanders who do not possess the con
fidence of their commands, Such is
our opinion and we deem it a solemn
duty to express it to You, We do fear
great disaster from the condition of things
now existing and think it should be averted
if possible —

Very respy Genl Your &C
B F Cheatham
Maj Genl C. S. A.
J M Withers
Maj Genl &C

To
Genl Bragg
Commdg &C

A true copy
Kinloch Falconer a. a. g
A true copy
M L Fall a. d. c

Enclosure mentioned by General Bragg

"*B*"

"*Copy*"   1.30 A. M. January 3rd   (43)

My Dear General

I send you the enclosed paper
as requested. And I am compelled to add, that
after seeing the effect of the operations of to-day,
added to that produced upon the troops by the
battle of the 31st. I very greatly fear the conse-
=quences of another engagement at this place on
the ensuing day. We could now perhaps get off
with some safety and with some credit, if the
affair was well managed. Should we fail in
the meditated attack, the consequences might
be very disastrous.

Hoping you may be guided aright, whatever
determination you may reach

I am very truly yours
(Sg)   L. Polk,
Lieut Genl,

I certify the above is a true copy
(Sg) Kinloch Falconer
A. A. G

To this Genl. Bragg replied through Lieut Richmond
"Say to Genl. Polk we shall hold our own at every
hazard."

(A true Copy)
J. B. Roy.
Chf of staff

Enclosure mentioned by General Bragg

General Bragg's attempt to salvage a modicum of his reputation back fired. His generals offered him unsolicited advice. General Hardee replied that he had agreed with the decision to retreat, but had not advised it. Further, in consultation with Generals Cleburne and Breckinridge, Hardee concluded that Bragg should be replaced. Breckinridge admitted he had pushed for the retreat from Murfreesboro. The Kentuckian also informed Bragg that he and his brigade commanders were unanimous: Bragg should go. Cleburne's response provided no answer concerning the question of responsibility for the retreat. He too had consulted with his brigadiers who all expressed the opinion that the army lacked confidence in Bragg. General Withers made no answer while General Cheatham asserted he was among the first to propose retreat.

General Polk had been on leave when the circular appeared. Upon his return to duty, he asked Bragg to clarify the intent of the circular in light of the negative opinion Hardee's subordinates had expressed regarding his fitness to command the Army of Tennessee. The following is the exchange which took place between them.

Tullahoma 30th Jany 1863

General

I hasten to reply to your note of this morning, So as to place you beyond all doubt in regard to the construction of mine of the 11it [instant].

To my mind that circular contained but one point of enquiry and it certainly was intended to contain but one. And that was to ask of my Corps and Division commanders to commit to writing what had transpired between us in regard to the retreat from Murfreesboro. I believed it had been grossly and intentionally misrepresented_ not by any one of them __ for any injury. It was never intended by me that this should go further than the parties to whom it was addressed and its only object was to relieve my mind of all doubt, whilst I Secured in a form to be preserved the means of defense in the future when discipline might be proper.

The paragraph relating to my Supercedure was only an explanation of the feeling with which I Should receive your replies Should they prove I have been misled in my construction of your opinions and advice.

I am Genl very respelly &c
Braxton Bragg
Genl comdg

Lt Genl L Polk
&c. &c. &c.
[*OR* XX Series I Pt.1 p.701]

Tullahoma Jany 30 1863

General

 I am in receipt of yours of the 30th in reply to mine of the Same date. In it you Say you designed your circular Should contain but one point of enquiry and that was whether your Corps and Division commanders would give you for future reference a statement of what transpired between us in regard to the retreat from Murfreesboro.

 I have therefore now to say that the opinions and counsel which I gave you on that subject prior to the retreat are those that are embodied in the endorsement of the note of my Division commanders, Genls Cheatham and Withers of the 3d January which are in your possession, and I have to add that they were deliberately considered and are Such as I would give again under the Same circumstances.

Resply Genl yrs
L Polk Lt Genl Com'g

Genl Bragg
[*OR* XX Series I Pt.1 p.702]

General Bragg forwarded a letter to President Davis that offered reasons to justify the retreat; it included a feeble offer to resign. He warned the chief executive that political and military critics would press for his removal. President Davis responded to the awkward situation by sending General Johnston to investigate reports of discord in the Army of Tennessee. General Johnston met with Bragg, Hardee, and Polk, and the governor of Tennessee, Isham Harris. Polk learned that Hardee and the others felt that he had avoided the real issue, Bragg himself. After a conversation with Johnston, the bishop forwarded the previous documents to Davis; they were accompanied by an epistle, of which the following is the last page.

[Last page of February 4, 1863, letter from L. Polk to Jefferson Davis per Frances McClure.]

 ...to be permitted to do this urgently. The state of this army demands immediate attention, and its position before the enemy, as well as the mind of the troops and commanders could find relief in no way so readily as by the appointment of Genl. Johnston. I send this by mail and will send copies by my aid de Camp Lt. Richmond who I send to Richmond on business with the Department & by whom I also send my report of the battle of Shiloh. In it I have taken care that the presence or our valued friend on that field shall not be ignored.

I remain faithfully
your friend
L. Polk
Lt. Genl. &c

The president's representative learned that Bragg's troops were not dispirited. In fact, the Army of Tennessee was stronger numerically than it had been on December 31. Concerning his visit, Johnston wrote in his memoir: "I bestowed three weeks upon this investigation, and then advised against General Bragg's removal, because the field-officers of the army represented that their men were in high spirits, and as ready as ever for fight; such a condition seemed to me incompatible with the alleged want of confidence in their general's ability."[9]

General Johnston returned to Mobile to inspect the city's defenses; however, President Davis remained unconvinced that all was well with the Army of Tennessee. On March 9, the Secretary of War ordered General Bragg to Richmond while General Johnston was directed to Tullahoma. When Johnston arrived at Bragg's headquarters, he found that Mrs. Elsie Bragg was thought to be near death. General Johnston assumed command of the army as General Bragg cared for his wife. When Mrs. Bragg recovered, General Johnston's poor health rendered him unfit for duty. General Bragg "was automatically restored by default...."[10]

General Polk wrote yet another letter to President Davis at the end of March. He urged the president to move General Bragg up to the Inspector General's office where his organizational abilities could be used by the entire Confederacy. A year later Bragg served at Richmond, but for the present, in spite of his own declaration that he would resign without the confidence of his generals, he retained command.

> To the average commander, the very suggestion, the barest hint of such want of confidence would furnish compelling reason for resignation, but Bragg—sometimes so supersensitive—seemed suddenly to have developed a skin of elephantine toughness...the unhappy Army of Tennessee continued to function under the impossible condition of command by a man whose ability was openly and unreservedly distrusted by his subordinates. It is a monument to the mettle of the army's personnel that it was able to function at all in such distressing circumstances.[11]

The Civil War entered a decisive phase when General Grant's Army of the Tennessee besieged Vicksburg in May. The following month, Lee's Army of Northern Virginia marched into Pennsylvania. General Bragg's Army of Tennessee remained inactive in camp around Tullahoma. Relations between Bragg and Polk remained strained while the other generals tried to make the best of an awkward situation. In contrast to General Polk, General Hardee inspected his troops frequently. Occasionally he would challenge Polk's Corps to a drill contest. Hardee's reviews became an institution, and one event in April attracted 500 female observers.

Active campaigning for the Confederacy's second most important army resumed when General Rosecrans assumed the offensive in June. His campaign, which maneuvered Bragg out of Tullahoma, was a masterpiece. General Bragg relied too heavily on his frontal defenses and expected his opponent to march conveniently in that direction. Not until Rosecrans had outflanked him to the east did Bragg realize, belatedly, what had happened. "Though he had been in position for six months, he seems never to have thought of the possibility of flank attack, and in the early stages of the turning movement he showed a fumbling in decision and action that filled his corps commanders with dismay."[12]

On July 4, General Pemberton surrendered Vicksburg to General Grant. By mid-July the Army of Tennessee was encamped around Chattanooga; General Hardee left the army to labor in Mississippi. Hardee organized, trained and equipped paroled soldiers from the Vicksburg garrison. He also acted as General Johnston's second in command. When he returned to Tennessee at the end of October, General Hardee found an army in disarray: Bragg had won another tactical victory.

General Hardee was replaced as a corps commander by D.H. Hill, who had been appointed a lieutenant general in July. Porter Alexander wrote of him: "...there was never a harder fighter than General D.H. Hill."[13] Hill's reputation was more important to him than life and like his brother-in-law, "Stonewall Jackson," he adhered to Christian principles. General Hill had submitted his resignation early in 1863 for reasons that remain obscure, but he was persuaded to remain in the service. Until he reported to Bragg on July 19, Hill commanded the Department of North Carolina. His greatest fault was in his propensity to over-criticize the perceived failings of others.

The Army of Tennessee awaited the resumption of the campaign as the Army of the Cumberland built up supplies and secured its long line of communications. With the fall of Vicksburg, General Rosecrans expected to receive troops from General Grant's army, but they did not arrive until November. Some of Grant's excess strength was diverted to East Tennessee to threaten Knoxville. The corps commanded by Major General Simon B. Buckner (1823-1914; West Point 1844) retreated to join Bragg's army.

Late in August, the Army of the Cumberland resumed its advance toward Chattanooga. To drive the Confederate army away from the gateway to the deep south, General Rosecrans maneuvered against General Bragg's supply line from Georgia. The Union army crossed the Tennessee River into Alabama and spread across northwestern Georgia. General Crittenden's 21st Corps marched due east toward Chattanooga and occupied it on September 9. The 14th Corps under General Thomas advanced in the center as General McCook's 20th Corps, the southernmost segment, advanced on the right

General Daniel Harvey Hill

The Army of Tennessee had withdrawn to LaFayette, Georgia, to await an opportunity to attack the Army of the Cumberland as it pushed through the mountains. Two divisions from Mississippi reinforced Bragg, who organized his army into four corps commanded by Hill, Buckner, Polk, and Major General William H.T. Walker (1816-1864; West Point 1837).

Lookout Mountain, a chain of peaks nearly 100 miles long, stretches southwest from Chattanooga. A few miles east of Lookout Mountain, a spur known as Missionary Ridge rises. Between Missionary Ridge and Pigeon Mountain, another spur farther east, a stream called Chickamauga Creek flows toward Chattanooga. On September 9, General Negley marched his division, 14th Corps, toward Dug Gap into an area known as McLemore's Cove. Isolated from the main body, Negley's three brigades invited attack.

General Bragg recognized the opportunity to smash the vulnerable division. He detached a division from Polk under Major General Thomas C. Hindman (1828-1868; Mexican War) and planned to attack on the tenth. General Hill was ordered to cooperate with General Hindman. Throughout the day Hill and Hindman waited for each to go into action which allowed a division commanded by Brigadier General Absalom Baird (1824-1905; West Point 1849) to march to Negley's assistance. Despite the fact they were outnumbered more than two to one by the grayclads, the bluecoats were allowed to retreat through Lookout Mountain by way of Stevens Gap and escape destruction.

Though he was concerned by the threat the 20th Corps posed to his vunerable communications, Bragg learned on the twelfth that Crittenden's entire corps was exposed, just as part of Thomas' had been. General Polk received orders to attack but he declined to give battle. Bragg was not as well informed as Polk, who knew that the 21st Corps was concentrated and therefore not exposed to defeat in detail. If he encountered difficulty, General Crittenden could not be assisted by General Thomas or General McCook. It is possible that the Confederates could have crushed Crittenden if they had moved rapidly. The failure to attack the 21st Corps rests with Bragg, who did not oversee the operation.

Writing after the war, D.H. Hill explained the reason why Braxton Bragg's generals failed to attack isolated elements of the Army of the Cumberland.

> The trouble with him was: first, lack of knowledge of the situation; second, lack of personal supervision of the execution of his orders. No general ever won a permanent fame who was wanting in these grand elements of success: knowledge of his own and his enemy's condition, and personal superintendence of operations on the field...Bragg's want of definite and precise information had led him more than once to issue 'impossible' orders, and therefore those entrusted with their execution got in the way of disregarding them. Another more serious trouble with him was the disposition to find a scapegoat for every failure and disaster. This made his officers cautious about striking a blow when an opportunity presented itself, unless they were protected by a positive order.[14]

Braxton Bragg's reputation crippled his efforts. His senior generals did not trust or want to fight under him.

On September 12, General Rosecrans, who believed the enemy was in retreat, finally realized that General Bragg's army was prepared to offer battle. Intelligence sources also indicated that Bragg would be reinforced from Virginia. He directed General McCook to retrace his steps and join General Thomas near Stevens Gap. This movement was completed by September 17. Major General Gordon Granger (1822-1876; West Point 1845) with his Reserve Corps of three brigades was positioned at Rossville, Georgia, to cover Chattanooga.

General Bragg planned another attack for September 18 against General Crittenden, whose corps was in position near Lee and Gordon's Mill on Chickamauga Creek. While Polk demonstrated against Crittenden, other divisions would cross the stream at three points and force the Federals into McLemore Cove. The attempt to bag General Crittenden failed to develop because Federal cavalry and mounted infantry armed with repeaters disputed the crossings. The Confederates were unable to cross until late afternoon by which time the opportunity no longer existed. Three brigades from the Army of Northern Virginia, commanded by General Hood,[15] with two more on the way, united with the Army of Tennessee on the eighteenth.

Throughout the nineteenth, General Rosecrans reinforced his left to guard bridges across Chickamauga Creek and the LaFayette Road which led to Chattanooga. The 14th Corps drew this vital assignment. The 20th Corps held the right while General Crittenden's 21st Corps remained in the center of the Union line. General Bragg expected to be able to turn General Rosecrans' left flank which he still believed was fixed at Lee and Gordon's Mill.

Around 8:00 A.M., the battle opened when General Thomas struck first. Informed of an isolated enemy brigade, Thomas sent a division under Brigadier General Joseph M. Brannan (1819-1892; West Point 1841) with General Baird's Division in support, to destroy the Rebels. The intelligence proved erroneous as the Federals engaged cavalry. Walker's Reserve Corps counterattacked and knocked out Brannan and Baird. Johnson's Division of McCook's Corps repelled Walker, who was reinforced by Cheatham's Division, Polk's Corps.

General Cheatham formed four of his brigades and attacked around noon. His advance drove the Federals back until their defense stiffened on a line of breastworks which were thrown up the night before. The Tennesseans could

General John Bell Hood

71

not break the Yankee brigades; Cheatham threw in his reserve brigade. Federal reinforcements entered the contest and Cheatham's veteran division broke in mid-afternoon. Only the effective work of his artillery saved Cheatham's Division from disaster.

All through the morning, General Bragg persisted with his plan to turn General Rosecrans' left flank. Without an effective body of scouts, Bragg was unaware that a large gap existed in the Union line. By chance, this gap was exploited by the "Little Giant Division" of Buckner's Corps.

Instead of rushing to the support of General Cheatham as ordered, Brigadier General Alexander P. Stewart (1821-1908; West Point 1842) attacked. His three brigades forced the Federals to retreat beyond the LaFayette Road where two of General Van Cleve's Brigades formed a line. Stewart's men punched through the new line, captured numerous cannon and advanced to within sight of the Dry Valley Road. Massed artillery fire dropped Stewart's men in heaps. General Thomas sent Brannan's Division to the center while Negley's Brigades, which had seen no action, approached from the south. Their appearance suggested to Stewart that it was time to withdraw his spent units.

General Bragg's poor generalship precluded victory that day. Stewart's men fought unsupported because the Confederate divisions had been fed into the battle one at a time. The disjointed pattern of attacks continued when General Hood's Division and Brigadier General Bushrod R. Johnson's (1817-1880; West Point 1840) Provisional Division attacked the Union right in mid-afternoon. Four Union brigades representing three different divisions were pummelled by the Confederates. The timely arrival of divisions under Generals Sheridan and Wood, 20th and 21st Corps respectively, prevented the collapse of the Army of the Cumberland's right flank. Combat on the west side of Chickamauga Creek, however had not finished for the day.

While Stewart, Hood, and Johnson carried Bragg's attack south, General Cleburne had been marching his men toward the Rebel right. At twilight he set a line in motion that was a mile wide toward Baird and Johnson. In the forest darkness, sound and musket flashes guided the combatants as the lines closed. Though the center of the Federal line held, both flanks were gnawed away. Only darkness saved the Yankees from further punishment. The next day, General Thomas, a Virginian by birth, acquired glory as the "Rock of Chickamauga," when he did not allow a severe defeat to become a turning point in the war.

Most of the soldiers were unable to sleep that night. Both sides suffered from the first cold snap of the season. Though many Northerners kept warm as they fortified their positions, no adequate source of water was available to them. The Southerners, however, could obtain water from the creek. Union wounded crawled to a stagnant pool of water near the Widow Glenn House which became known as "Bloody Pond."

At 11:00 P.M., General Rosecrans met with his three corps commanders who believed General Bragg would renew the battle in the morning. General Thomas advised his commander to strengthen the left because it covered the roads back to Chattanooga. General Rosecrans was confident that with a shorter line, he could hold his position and claim victory.

General Longstreet arrived at General Bragg's gloomy headquarters at about the same time Rosecrans began to adjust his line. Two more fresh brigades from Virginia accompanied him. General Bragg decided then to reorganize his army into two wings. Longstreet took over the left and Polk the right; a simple plan was discussed. The Army of Tennessee would attack at daylight from right to left *en echelon*, Bragg's customary tactic.

General Hill, demoted by the new command structure, never received the order from General Polk to attack at an early hour. Meanwhile, General Bragg became impatient. He sent a staff officer in search of General Polk for an explanation. Major Pollock B. Lee found Polk at breakfast, instead of at the front, and when informed of the situation, an enraged Bragg set off to find his troublesome subordinate. General Polk in the meantime had located Hill, who protested that the delay was due to his men drawing rations. The explanation did not satisfy Polk, therefore he ordered an immediate attack, and galloped away. Shortly thereafter, Bragg arrived and demanded of Hill the reason why he had not already attacked. Hill claimed he had received no such order, whereupon Bragg told him to begin the attack when it was practicable.

By 10:00 A.M., the attack General Bragg desired was underway. General Polk's wing, led by Breckinridge and Cleburne, conducted a series of uncoordinated attacks. Two of General Breckinridge's Brigades turned the Union left and briefly held the LaFayette Road. If Polk had sustained the triumph with available reserves, "they might readily have rolled up Thomas' flank."[16]

Despite General Polk's inept handling of his assignment, General Thomas called on his commander for reinforcements. Shortly before 11:00 A.M., General Wood was ordered to the assistance of the Union left. His division's departure left a large gap in the center. General Longstreet found the flaw in General Rosecrans' line of battle.

Longstreet had waited all morning for the fight to carry to his sector. During the delay, he had deployed eight brigades into a column five lines deep. General Johnson's Provisional Division, the tip of Longstreet's lance, was backed by the veterans from Virginia. The divisions of General Hindman and Brigadier General William Preston (1816-1887; Mexican War) were fresh because they had seen limited action the day before. Just after 11:00 A.M., Bushrod Johnson advanced straight toward the spot recently vacated by Wood.

The Confederate attackers pierced the center of General Rosecrans' army with ease. A few Federal regiments tried to make a stand but they were swept away by the surging tide of exultant Butternuts. Hindman went into action on the left and with their escape route threatened, the divisions on the Army of the Cumberland's right flank broke and ran. Generals Rosecrans, Crittenden, and McCook joined fugitives in flight up the Dry Valley Road toward Chattanooga. Fighting on the Union left, directed by General Thomas, developed into some of the most desperate of the war.

General Thomas' two lines were perpendicular to each other. The eastern line confronted General Polk's right wing and covered the LaFayette Road. A makeshift line that faced south evolved on a series of hills known as Horseshoe Ridge. It protected the Dry Valley Road. When the action on Horseshoe Ridge intensified, the fighting on the eastern line died down. Many defenders on Horseshoe Ridge thought that the numerous Rebel brigades thrown against them constituted one continuous attack. The 21st Ohio, armed with five-shot Colt repeating rifles, was deployed on the right of the ridge. Their attackers thought they faced an entire division.

Between Thomas' two lines, a six hundred yard gap existed. If General Longstreet had located it, no Union army could have prevented the Army of Tennessee from taking a drink from the Ohio River. Longstreet and Bragg met around 3:00 P.M. General Bragg responded unenthusiastically to the Georgian's report of a stunning success. Despite the capture of dozens of enemy cannon, General Bragg believed that the battle had been lost: Rosecrans had not been driven into McLemore Cove. Bragg offered the commander of his left wing no additional troops to exploit the unprecedented achievement; he retired to his headquarters.

Reinforcements reached General Thomas, however, when General Granger marched from Rossville to the sound of the guns. General Johnson, who now led Hood's Division after that officer had been wounded, threatened General Thomas' right flank on Horseshoe Ridge. Granger's Brigades entered the hard-pressed line at the proper place at a crucial time to throw back the oncoming Southerners. The arrival of these fresh troops averted the crisis and allowed Thomas to defend Rosecrans' broken army.

Longstreet's last division, General Preston's well-rested men, hit the Federals at 3:30 P.M. In spite of their spirited effort and fierce fighting, the Confederates failed to carry the position. At Confederate Memorial Hall in New Orleans, the flag of the 2nd Alabama Battalion is on display. The eighty-odd bullet holes in it testify to the determination of the Southerners on September 20, 1863.

Shortly after General Polk's wing re-entered the fight at 5:00 P.M., General Thomas began to withdraw. A Federal counterattack against General Liddell's Division bought time and the colonel of the 30th Mississippi was captured.

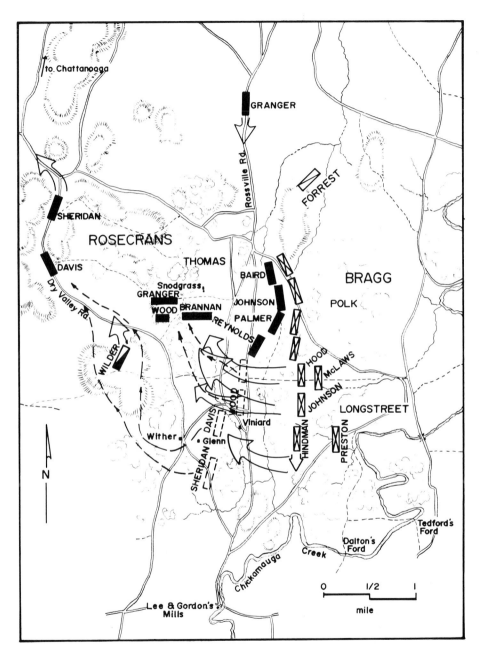

The second day at the Battle of Chickamauga
September 20, 1863

Amid the combat and confusion on Horseshoe Ridge, the 21st and 89th Ohio along with the 22nd Michigan were cut off. Only George Thomas' devotion, energy, and skill (with some luck) prevented even greater losses to the Army of the Cumberland.

During the course of the Civil War, the Battle of Chickamauga was the only major battle where the Southerners (68,000) enjoyed numerical superiority over the Northerners (57,840). Rosecrans lost 16,170 men while Bragg's losses approached 20,000.

The greatest Confederate victory in the west brought no joy to General Bragg. Even though his foe was very demoralized, he considered his own army to be too disorganized for a prompt advance the next day. Instead, the befuddled Bragg ordered his generals to gather discarded muskets and equipment from the battlefield. General Bragg thought that General Rosecrans would abandon Chattanooga without further fighting. His inaction brought about another conflict with his disgusted generals and an extraordinary confrontation.

Generals Polk, Longstreet, and Hill conferred to establish a course of action that would result in Bragg's removal. Longstreet communicated with the Secretary of War and Polk wrote to the president. General Bragg was also busy; he had resumed his customary practice of searching for scapegoats. He demanded that Polk give him an explanation for disobeying the order to attack at daylight on the second day. After some delay, General Polk responded by blaming General Hill unfairly. Polk's sloth and his previous displays of minimal military prowess suggest that he expected Hill to function as executive commander and direct the right wing in battle on September 20.

Tired of his insubordinate attitude, on September 29, General Bragg ordered General Polk to Atlanta to await further orders, even though he did not have the authority to do so. General Hindman, also on Bragg's short list of irritants, departed the army as well. Polk's pen stayed busy as more letters were dispatched to Richmond from Atlanta.

On October 4, General Buckner composed a document that petitioned President Davis to remove General Bragg from command. Signed by a dozen general officers, it included the endorsement of Buckner, Longstreet, Hill, and Cleburne. Unexpectedly, the president arrived at army headquarters on October 9, accompanied by the disgraced John Pemberton. The "Memorial" to Davis was never submitted, but Bragg was aware of its existence.

In a discussion with Davis, Bragg offered his resignation. The president resorted to an unprecedented procedure in an attempt to restore harmony in the troubled army. He summoned the corps commanders to a council where General Bragg was present. To Davis' surprise, first Longstreet, then Buckner, Hill, and Cheatham (in Polk's place) told him that Bragg should go. The subject of the interview, who seemed confused, remained silent during the discussion that questioned his fitness for command. Davis decided to retain Bragg, much to the dismay of the Confederacy. "The fact that Davis kept Bragg in command in the face of this formidable resistance represents one of his greatest errors in judgment."[17] Yet, even if Davis had lost confidence in Bragg, who would replace him? General Johnston was personally repugnant while General Hardee had no desire for the responsibility. General Longstreet, who claimed that he was offered the position, did not accept; General Lee would not leave Virginia. The problem of replacing General Bragg would soon resurface to bedevil President Davis.

After Davis departed, General Buckner took leave and eventually transferred to the Trans-Mississippi Department. Before Davis' departure, General Hill became another command casualty. Unflattering remarks he had made were reported to Bragg, who disliked his subordinate and had become exasperated with him. On October 11, Bragg requested permission from Davis to relieve Hill. His reasons were Hill's failure to follow orders in a timely manner and the negative impact he had on the morale of troops in his corps. As the following letter to General Breckinridge indicates, General Hill believed that he was a victim of a conspiracy.

Charlotte, N.C.
Oct. 26" 1863.

General,

    I reached home on the 24" & expect to remain until I hear from Richmond. I met Genl. Polk at Atlanta, who professed much friendship and kindness. I regret that I spoke unkindly of him in regard to the coalition Bragg proposed. I am satisfied that Polk is too much of a man to make a compromise. The plan was to make me responsible for Polk's supposed delinquency & give Pemberton the corps. Polk's manliness and P's sense of propriety defeated the scheme. Bragg's great object was to please the President & at the same time account to the country for his failure. It pained me inexplicably to part with the corps & to be absent from the stirring incidents of the campaign. But it is all right. I hope you remain permanently in charge of the corps. It is reported that Rosencrantz [*sic*] has been relieved and Grant placed in charge. If so, you will have heavy odds against you as Grant will unite his army to that of R. Surely, Johnston will be brought up to command at Chattanooga. It cant be possible that the destiny of the South will still be committed to Bragg.

    Will always be glad to hear from you, I write now, not merely out of friendship, but to ask that you will forget what I said about the coalition. Please mention the matter to Genl Cleburne & tell him that I am now convinced Genl Polk never became a party to it & that Pemberton also declined, when he found the Division commanders adverse to him.

May great success attend you,
Yours truly
Signed D.H. Hill

Due to his dismissal, D.H. Hill's name became associated with the carnage at Chickamauga, a charge he resented bitterly. His request for a Court of Inquiry from General Cooper was refused. Early in November a meeting with the president produced a heated exchange between the two when Hill protested his treatment in comparison to Polk. On November 16, Hill apologized in a letter to Davis and repeated his request of a Court of Inquiry to obtain justice. The following is the reply from President Davis.

> Richmond, Nov. 17th 1863
> Gen'l D.H. Hill:
> Richmond,

Sir:_____ Yours of yesterday has just come to hand, and I hasten to reply that the conversation, before it closed, removed every impression which was personally disagreeable and the whole matter was restored to its official character so far as I was concerned.

I am not sure whether you intend your letter to be an application for a Court of Inquiry or whether you had made at a previous time such [a] request. The latter is to be inferred from the language employed, but I am not informed as to the application, or the "refusal" if one was made, and cannot judge of the grounds taken in either.

You say you are relieved from the army of Tenn. "for expressing want of confidence in Gen'l Bragg." That reason was not given to me in the note through which Gen'l Bragg recommended your removal, and on which I authorized him to relieve you. The discrimination of which you complain is made to rest upon a reason which was not offered to me or acted on by me, and therefore the complaint is not warranted by the fact.

Need I repeat that no charge was preferred against you, and that no application for a Court of Inquiry by you was before me, and again call your attention to that difference between your case and that of Gen'l Polk.

If you have not forgotten my reply to you when you first referred to my note to Gen'l Polk, I am surprised that you should again adduce it in your list of grievances.

> Very respectfully,
> (signed) Jeffn. Davis

[*OR* LII Series I Pt.2 p.562]

For the rest of the war, General Hill was never employed in a position commensurate with his rank. His pride suffered another blow when Davis refused to nominate his name to the Senate for confirmation as lieutenant general. After the events of 1865, D.H. Hill became an editor and an educator. The following two letters written by Hill indicate the depth of feeling that remained with him after the war regarding his damaged military reputation.

Charlotte NC
Nov 30th 1867

Hon Jefferson Davis

Dear Sir

Permit me to offer my sincere congratulations upon your escape out of lawless &
bloody hands.

I am editing a Magazine here & wish to illustrate it with the daughters of the South.
Have you any objection to our having a steel plate engraving of your oldest daughter (Miss
Maggie I believe?) A simple refusal to answer will be construed into a negative.

Although I felt you had ruined my reputation, I defended you in the Magazine when
the papers of the South were afraid to say a word. I risked arrest and suppression of the
Magazine to do so. Your old enemy Pollard has made atrocious charges against me
arising out of my removal from the Western Army. I told you in Richmond that my
removal after a battle and reduction of rank, would be ruinous to my military character
and asked you to put in writing what you did not hesitate to say in writing that there was
no fault to be found with me as a soldier. Such a statement even now would repel the unjust
charges which have been made. I leeve [*sic*] it to your sense of right and justice. I can
hardly conceive that you can have any desire to crush one who tried to serve you faithfully
& honestly, as well as our poor unhappy country.

With sincere wishes
for your health & happiness
I am your obt servant
DHHill

Charlotte NC
Dec 11th 1867

Hon Jefferson Davis

Respected Sir

Hon Wm B. Reed was supplied with some of L. W. L ["Land We Love"] containing
the defence & he wrote to me that you were much gratified by it. From time to time, I sent
to Fortress Monroe copies of L. W. L containing poetic tributes from Mr. Danning and
others. Whether they reached you or not, I never learned. If I knew certainly your address,
I would send a bound copy of 1st Volume, as we have no single copy on hand.

My recollection of Beauregard's Report is that it was published simply as "Supple-
mental part of Beauregard's Report of Battle of Manassas", and without comment. If any
comment was made, it was done by myself. I never doubted the facts were as Genl B
represented them to be that the Confederate Government suppressed a portion of his
Report.

Genl. D. H. Hill
no ans.
Charlotte NC
Dec 11th 1869

Hon Jefferson Davis
Respected Sir

Hon Wm B. Reed was supplied with some copies of S. W. & containing the defence & he wrote to me that you were much gratified by it.. From time to time, I sent to Fortress Monroe copies of S. W. & containing poetic tributes from Mrs Downing & others. Whether they reached you or not, I never learned. If I knew certainly your address, I would send a bound copy of the volume, as we have not single copy on hand.

My recollection of Beauregard's "Report" is that it was published simply as "Suppressed part of Beauregard's Report of Battle of Manasses", and without comment.. If any comment

Letter from D.H. Hill to Jefferson Davis (4 pages)

was made, it was done by myself. I never doubted that the facts were as Genl ⟶ represented them to be that the Confederate Government suppressed a portion of his Report.

Pollard says that I was relieved from the Army of Tennessee for continuously refusing to attack in the Mo & More love. Genl Bragg told me that he had no fault to find with me as a Soldier. In truth, he relieved me for signing the Memorial to the President suggested by Genl Polk and written by Buckner. Polk told Bragg that I wrote the Memorial & hence Bragg's exasperation. I had nothing to do with it beyond approving & signing it.

A statement from you, that I was relieved on personal grounds and not because of military delinquency, would enable me to reply to Pollard. Whatever charge I am amenable to, a hesitation to fight seems the last I deserved.

Page 3d

#134

It has always seemed strange to me that you never could per-ceive the injury done me by relieving me after a battle and reducing my rank. Genl Polk's case is not parallel. He was relieved, it is true, but the President quashed the charges against him, wrote him a complimentary letter and gave him another & a more important command. The whole onus of failure to reap the fruits of victory at Chickamauga was thrown upon me, though I did my whole duty there and won the confidence of my officers & men. Breckinridge, Claiborne, young Polk, Stovall, Lewis, Brown & ... wrote me warm & enthusiastic letters commending me as a ... soldier, after I had been relieved & they had nothing to expect from me.

I have always supposed that

you degraded me because
I was so unfortunate as
to offend you in an interview
in Richmond.

I then told you that a
simple statement from you
that no imputations had ever
been made upon my military
character would be entirely
satisfactory. It was not given,
And in consequence I have
had to writhe for four years
under slanders named and
un named. Every body thinking
that there was something wrong,
but no one knowing what and
each one supplying from his
own imagination the supposed
offence.

In no battles of this war did I
my duty more fully than in Chickamauga and in none did my
personal exertions & personal
exposure contribute so largely to
the victory. But it has brought
me nothing but unutterable suffering & the opprobrium of
my countrymen

Very Respectfully
D. H. Hill

Pollard says that I was relieved from the Army of Tennessee for continuously refusing to attack in McLemore Cove. Genl Bragg told me that he had no fault to find with me as a soldier. In truth, he relieved me for signing the Memorial to the President suggested by Genl Polk and written by Buckner. Bate[18] told Bragg that I wrote the Memorial & hence Bragg's exasperation. I had nothing to do with it beyond approving & signing it.

A statement from you, that I was relieved on personal grounds and not because of military delinquency, would enable me to reply to Pollard. Whatever charges I am answerable to, a hesitation to fight seems the last I deserved.

It has always seemed strange to me that you never could perceive the injury done me by relieving me after a battle and reducing my rank. Genl Polk's case is not parallel. He was relieved, it is true, but the President quashed the charges against him, wrote a complimentary letter and gave him another & a more important command. The whole onus of failure to reap the fruits of victory at Chickamauga was thus thrown upon me, though I did my whole duty there and won the confidence of my officers & men. Breckinridge, Cleburne, Young Polk,[19] Stovall[20] [illegible] Brown[21] &c wrote me warm & enthusiastic letters commending me as a soldier, after I had been relieved & they had nothing to expect from me.

I have always supposed that you degraded me because I was so unfortunate as to offend you in an interview in Richmond. I then told you that a simple statement from you___ that no imputations had ever been made upon my military character would be entirely satisfactory. It was not given, but in consequence I have had to writhe for four years under slanders named and unnamed. Every body thinking that there was something wrong, but no one knowing what and each one supplying from his own imagination the supposed offense.

In no battles of the war did I [do] my duty more fully than in Chickamauga and in none did my personal exertions & personal exposure contribute so largely to the victory. But it has brought me nothing but unutterable suffering, & the opprobrium of my countrymen.

> Very Respectfully
> DHHill

Braxton Bragg copied the letter written October 26, 1863, by Hill to Breckinridge. Bragg sent it to Davis with a cover letter, which appears below.

> Mobile 27" June, 1872

My dear Sir:

I enclose for your information, a copy of a characteristic letter from that sore-headed Bear D.H. Hill, just published in a Yankee Magazine called historical, at Morisania [Morriasana], N.Y.

The paragraph marked [see above] will show you the accuracy of the whole thing. My recollections of the whole encounter are very clear, but I should like to be justified by your remembrance_ If I mistake not Pemberton's name was never mentioned between us until both Polk & Hill had been relieved, and then it first came from you. Indeed, I did not know he had been exchanged and was available.

#138

Mobile. 27th June. 1872

My dear Sir:

I enclose for your informa-
tion, a copy of a characteristic letter
from that sore-headed Bear, D.H. Hill.
just published in a yankee Magazine,
called Historical, at Morisania. N.Y.

The paragraph marked will show
you the animus of the whole thing. My
recollections of the whole matter are very
clear, but I should like to be justified
by your own remembrance. If I
mistake not Pemberton's name was
never mentioned between us until both
Polk & Hill had been relieved, and then
it first came from you. Indeed, I did

Letter from Braxton Bragg to Jefferson Davis (3 pages)

not know he had been exchanged and
my available,

The Army was so small, it was
my wish, afterwards executed, to consolidate
all but Longstreet's comd. into two corps,
under Hardee & Hood, the latter recommend
-ed to you for promotion with that view —

I only consented to use Pemberton, if I
found him available, after consulting
those he would command — and, I think,
expressed strong doubts of success — Not
that I doubted Pemberton — one of the
truest and most gallant men we had — but
I knew the prejudices exciting and excited
against him by such malignants as
Hill — and the danger of running counter thereto, even in justice to a good man
in a good cause —

The effort resulted as I feared, and
like a true man Pemberton accepted
his fate — Resigned his commission

as Lieut. General, and fought through the war as Lieut. Colonel. How with the other man who aspired too, He hides away under the look of a Lieut. General and devotes his abilities to the injury of his country by endeavoring to pull down the constituted authorities thereof, in order to build himself up —

I have now before me, Genl Polk's letter explaining his failure to attack the enemy as ordered — He puts the whole blame on D. H. Hill, who did not obey him — and I should have accepted the same as satisfactory, if the Genl had been in place on the battle field to enforce which he ordered —

The thanks I got for thus protecting Hill, you will find in this charge of conspiracy.

Mrs. B. joins in kind regards to Mrs. D & yourself.

Jeffn Davis

Very truly. Braxton Bragg.

The Army was so small, it was my wish, afterwards executed, to consolidate all but Longstreet's comd. into two corps, under Hardee & Hood, the latter recommended to you for promotion with that view _ I only consented to use Pemberton, if I found him available, after consulting those he would command _ and, I think, expressed strong doubts of success _ not that I doubted Pemberton _ one of the truest and most gallant men we had _ but I knew the prejudices existing and created against him by such malignants as Hill_ and the danger of running counter thrusts, even in justice to a good man in good cause _

The effort resulted as I feared, and like a true man Pemberton accepted his fate _ resigned his commission as Lieut. General, and fought through the war as Lieut. Colonel [around Richmond]. How with the other man who as feared him. He hides away under the coat of a Lieut Genl and devoted his abilities to the injury of his country by endeavoring to pull down the constituted authorities ["of his country" lined out] thereof in order to build himself up _

I have now before me, Genl. Polk's letter explaining his failure to attack the enemy as ordered _ He puts the whole blame on D.H. Hill, who did not obey him _ and I should have accepted the same as satisfactory, if the Genl had been in place on the battlefield to enforce what he ordered _ The thanks I got for thus protecting Hill you will find in this charge of conspiracy.

> Mrs. B. joins in kind regards to Mrs D & yourself.
> Very truly. Braxton Bragg.

Jeffn Davis

Memphis Tenn., 29th June 1872

Genl. B. Bragg.
My dear Sir,

Yours of the 27th just received. In regard to the main facts of the case to which you refer, my recollection is quite distinct. Genl. Pemberton left by the fall of Vicksburg without a command reported to Richmond for duty as soon as his exchange permitted him to do so. I then as now, held him in high estimation and regarded him as an officer most unjustly censured. Being about to visit the army under your command I invited Genl Pemberton to accompany me under the hope that some duty appropriate to his rank might be found and his desire for active service be gratified. After reaching your Hd. Qurs. and the fanciful fact had been realized as was manifest in the council held with the senior officers, that there was not the harmony and subordination essential to success, my thoughts were directed to the changes which the good of the service required. You had, previous to the meeting of that council requested to be relieved, and the answer to your request had been delayed. The conference satisfied me that no change for the better would be needed in the commander of the Army. That decision made it necessary to consider other changes, and I found there, as on other occasions, that your views and recommendations rested upon facts which had been developed and pointed only to the efficiency of the army as the object. Thus, when I inquired, whether Genl. Pemberton could be advantageously employed, you said you would have to make inquiry before expressing an opinion, not that you esteemed him less than I did, but that notwithstanding your confidence in his worth and your personal attachment to him you did not wish him assigned to a command in that army unless he would be acceptable to the troops. Subsequently you informed me that after consultation with officers you thought it would not be advisable to carry out my suggestion. Having recently assigned an officer to the command of a corps in that army who had not previously served with it or been applied for by you, and the result having proved unsatisfactory I had no disposition to insist on repeating the experiment. The subsequent conduct of Genl. Pemberton in resigning his commission as Lieut Genl. when he found there was no corps for him, and applying for duty in his [1861] army rank of Lt Col of artillery, maintains my opinion of his zeal and soldierly spirit.

Very respy &truly yours
(signed)   Jefferson Davis

The following letter from Jefferson Davis written to William Hardee underlines the president's error in not removing Braxton Bragg from command and points toward the future.

Atlanta Geo
October 30th 1893

My dear Hardee

I regret very much not having seen you before leaving. Delay in receiving information from General Bragg prevented me from communicating with you from Mobile, but hearing that you were on the road I had hoped to see you here.

The information from the army at Chattanooga painfully impresses me with the fact that there is a want there of that harmony among the highest officers which is essential to success. I rely greatly upon you for the restoration of a proper feeling, and know that you will realize the comparative insignificance of personal considerations when weighed against the duty of imparting to the army all the efficiency of which it is capable.

With my earnest prayers for your welfare, I am very truly

your friend
Jefferson Davis

To
Lieut Genl Hardee
Atlanta
Geo
[*OR* XXXI Series I Pt. 3 p. 609]

Three days after the Battle of Chickamauga, the Army of Tennessee appeared before Chattanooga. Instead of taking a risk by crossing the Tennessee River to force the evacuation of the town, General Bragg occupied

Missionary Ridge and Lookout Mountain to starve the Yankees out. This was another poor decision on Bragg's part, for time was not on his side. With greater resources in men and the sinews of war, the Federals would eventually be able to rescue the Army of the Cumberland. Reinforcements from Virginia and Mississippi were soon on the way to relieve the hungry men and animals trapped at Chattanooga.

General Grant assumed control of military operations south of the Ohio River and east of the Mississippi River as commander of the Military Division of the Mississippi, created on October 16. Three days later General Rosecrans was sacked and replaced by General Thomas. Grant established his head-quarters at Chattanooga on October 23. Five days later the siege was broken by the capture of Brown's Ferry below Lookout Mountain. By mid-November, four divisions from the Army of the Tennessee and three divisions from the Army of the Potomac had arrived.

While the Union army's strength grew, General Bragg made no less than eighteen organizational changes in his command. General Hardee traded places with General Polk. General Breckinridge remained in command of the corps once led by D.H. Hill. Bragg also broke up Cheatham's Division because he mistrusted the Tennesseans and regarded them as a source of trouble. His soldiers were fed poorly and their bivouacs around Chickamauga Creek became bogs when heavy rain fell. Sickness was rampant and dissatisfaction among the ranks increased as their morale decreased. General Bragg committed another error in judgment on November 5. He weakened his long lines by sending General Longstreet and three divisions on a questionable mission to recapture Knoxville from the Army of the Ohio. When General Grant's army attacked three weeks later, it outnumbered the Rebels about 70,000 to 50,000.

On November 23, the Federals took possession of Orchard Knob, a Confederate strong point below Missionary Ridge. The following day, General Hooker, who commanded the troops from the Eastern Army, pushed the Johnnies off Lookout Mountain. Survivors of four brigades rejoined the main force on Missionary Ridge. General Sherman's powerful force crossed the Tennessee River on November 24 to threaten the right flank of General Bragg's line, held by Cleburne's command.

Despite their presence on Missionary Ridge for two months, the Confeder-ate defenses were weak. A line of rifle pits ran below the high ground while another was located half way up the slope. The main position had been dug at the crest of the ridge instead of slightly below, which would have provided the artillery with a better field of fire. General Bragg considered his position to be impregnable, but without Longstreet's Brigades, sufficient reserves were unavailable to plug a breakthrough. General Grant devised a simple plan to defeat his imprudent adversary. While Sherman directed the main attack against the northern end of Missionary Ridge, Hooker would assail the other end. Four divisions from the Army of the Cumberland, drawn up on the plain below, could assist either flank.

Pat Cleburne was well-prepared at Tunnel Hill when the veterans of Vicksburg tried to storm his position on the morning of November 25. Even though elements of five divisions participated in the attack, they were repulsed by General Cleburne's stubborn brigades. On the opposite end of the Confederate line, General Hooker could not bring his men into action due to an inability to bridge Chattanooga Creek which flowed between Lookout Mountain and Missionary Ridge.

At 3:00 P.M., General Grant ordered an attack from the center. Four divisions advanced against the rifle pits and overwhelmed the defenders without difficulty. He merely wanted to take the pressure off Sherman and expected the excited regiments to halt in place. To his astonishment, after a brief pause, they continued up the two hundred foot high ridge. Turning to Generals Thomas and Granger, General Grant demanded angrily to know who ordered the men to keep moving. Neither subordinate could furnish the answer, since it was a spontaneous response to the tactical situation. Grant promised to exact a penalty on the person responsible and turned to watch one of the most dramatic episodes in military history.

As the first line of Johnnies scrambled up Missionary Ridge to safety, the Yankees were right behind them. Casualties were few among the attackers as they approached the summit. Defenders higher up were reluctant to fire on comrades and the poor placement of the main line left many areas free from fire. The Federals penetrated the Confederate line at several places which allowed them to enfilade strong points that continued to hold out.

The low morale of the Confederate soldiers, who believed Hooker had outflanked them and gained their rear, caused the collapse of the Bragg's center. The display of massed military forces below Missionary Ridge by an army they had beaten two months before had already sapped their will to resist. Panic gripped a brigade in Hindman's Division and the Alabamians ran to avoid death or capture. Others units began to break up before the surging mob of attackers. A trickle of fleeing defenders swelled into a flood as hundreds threw away their weapons to escape the trap they thought was closing on them. Generals Bragg and Breckinridge narrowly avoided capture as they tried to rally Hindman's broken division, now commanded by Brigadier General James Patton Anderson (1822-1872: Mexican War). General Cheatham managed to contain the breakthrough which enabled Hardee's Corps to withdraw in good order. Except for pickets, by 9:00 P.M., the last of Cleburne's Division had crossed Chickamauga Creek. Darkness ended effective pursuit by the victorious, redeemed, Army of the Cumberland.

In 1913, a proud veteran of Cleburne's Division, P.D. Stephenson of Company K, 13th Arkansas, uttered words that assigned the verdict of responsibility for the calamity. "The truth as to that shameful disaster is that General Bragg, and not his army, was to blame. It was a case of glaring outgeneralship as to our commander, not of cowardice as to our men. Bragg was a good officer in some respects, but had not 'military genius' nor capacity for handling great bodies of men. He was a brave and Christian gentlemen, but a 'routine man,' not equal to emergencies."[22]

As dispirited survivors of the disaster trudged toward Dalton, Georgia, General Cleburne's Division covered itself with more glory in a sharp rear guard action at Ringgold Gap on November 26. The Battles of Lookout Mountain and Missionary Ridge cost the Army of the Cumberland 5,824 men. General Bragg lost 6,667 men, including 4,146 prisoners and 37 cannon. It also, finally, ended Braxton Bragg's career as captain of the Army of Tennessee.

On November 28, General Bragg telegraphed a report to Richmond on the condition of the army and asked to be relieved of command. General Cooper notified General Bragg that his request had been granted. The most senior of the remaining generals, William Hardee, assumed Bragg's role.

This unexpected calamity was another severe blow to the South. Morale in the Army of Tennessee settled at a new low. As for General Bragg, he became President Davis' military advisor, which indirectly caused the army's destruction as a fighting force almost exactly a year later.

3

GETTYSBURG

On January 4, 1864, the Alabama legislature passed a resolution that called for the 26th Alabama Regiment to return home. Before the Gettysburg Campaign, Edward A. O'Neal (1818-1890; lawyer), former colonel of the 26th, had been recommended for promotion to the rank of brigadier by General Lee. O'Neal's commission, dated June 6, 1863, reached Lee's headquarters, but for a reason (or reasons) unknown, the president cancelled the promotion. Historians have pointed to the poor performance of Colonel O'Neal's brigade on July 1 outside of Gettysburg as the cause. The following letter written to an Alabama Congressman indicates army politics as the reason.

Richmond January 25, 1864

Hon. James Phelan,

Sir,

Having requested of me a short history of the humiliating treatment I have received at the hands of my Division commander, Gen. R.E. Rhodes [*sic*], I submit the following facts. I took charge of the Brigade _(Rhodes' Brigade)_ on the 25th of January 1863. I commanded it from that time till the 25th of July, after we had returned from Pennsylvania, when I obtained a short leave of absence and went home. After my return, I commanded 'til a few days since. I led it in the battle of Chancellorsville. On the march to Pennsylvania, I led it in the battles of Berryville, Martinsburg, and the bloody three days fight at Gettysburg, and the skirmish at Manassas Gap, and the skirmish at Mine river. In fact I commanded the Brigade for the last twelve months, except the time I was absent on leave. Gen. Rhodes was promoted on the field at Chancellorsville[1] and said he owed his

93

General Edward Asbury O'Neal

appointment, greatly to the charge, which his old Brigade made on Saturday, when it broke and routed the 11th army corps of the enemy. He was told by Col., now Gen., Battle,[2] who was present, and did not participate in that battle [Battle had fallen off a horse] that the same order which announced his promotion, should have announced mine. After the Pennsylvania campaign and when I had commanded the Brigade since January, all the field officers present voluntarily recommended me for promotion, including Gen. Battle, then Colonel. These officers were Col. Battle; Lt. Col. [Charles] Forsyth, Maj. [Robert M.] Sand[s], 3rd Ala. Col. [J.M.] Hall and Maj [Eugene] Blackford, 5th Ala. Col. [Samuel B.] Pickens, Lt. Col. [John C.] Goodgame and Maj. [Adolph] Proskaner, of the 12th Ala._ Lt. Col. [E. Lafayette] Hobson, 5th Ala. Lt. Col. [John S.] Garvin and Maj. [David F.] Bryan 26th Ala. were absent wounded, but they have told me that they would have signed the paper if they had been present. This paper is in the hands of the President and was drawn up voluntarily and sent [to] him after I had led the Brigade in the great battles of Chancellorsville and Gettysburg, and skirmishes of Berryville, Martinsburg and Manassas Gap and had commanded them in camp, on the march, and in battle for some six or seven months. which gave them opportunity to test my capacity.

On the 6th of June the President appointed me a Brigadier General, as the records of the War Department, will show, and the commission, from some cause, has been witheld. Three officers, all my juniors in rank, have been appointed over me. One of them, Col. John T. Morgan, when he reached Richmond, in July last, and learned, from another,_

94

(Gov. Watts)[3] and not from me, the circumstances of his appointment,[4] declined the place, because of the injustice to me, who had led the Brigade in all the fights. I am the only Colonel in the Brigade who ranked these gentlemen. Col. Morgan belonged to the army of Tennessee. Gen. Battle was my junior, and he says he owes his appointment to the opposition of the Division commander to me; and that, like Col. Morgan, he, too would have declined, if I could have been recommended. It is proper to add that all the field officers except, two, Col. [James N. Lightfoot] Lyghtfoot and Maj. [Isaac F.] Culver of the 6th Ala., as soon as they heard I had been superseded by the appointment of Col. Morgan, drew up and sent Gen. Rhodes a paper protesting against his treatment of me. This paper was handed him while we were at Greencastle, Pa., on the march to Gettysburg.

I have thus hurriedly, and without any feeling, given you a short history of Gen. Rhodes' conduct towards me. But it is proper to add, that he came to me, the other day, and after a long and candid conversation, acknowledged he had done me injustice and remarked that as an honorable man, he would do all he could to repair the wrong. He said he never had any thing to complain of me in action and referred to his official reports to show that he had borne testimony to my good Conduct and gallantry in battle, and he now says he attributes my discipline less rigid than his _ to the fact that I held a pro tem appointment as Commander of the Brigade. As an honorable man anxious for the ["good" lined out] success of our Arms & the triumph of our Cause _ though feeling deeply the wrongs inflicted on me _ I did not hesitate, for the good of the Service, to accept his proffered offer of reconciliation & agree to bury the past. And yet, as a true Soldier _ I can not cease to feel the humiliation of my condition & situation & wish to be relieved, and would be greatly relieved if the President could look into the facts of my case and give it a few moments consideration. I refer you to the various recommendations on file in the War Department in reference to me. _ Some from the Legislature of my state, and many from those with whom I have served in the field _ Genl Wilcox & others and especially from the Field officers whom I have commanded.

Three Regmts from Ala. & one Battalion in the Army of Miss _ towit _ the 27 - 35 Col [John W.] Portis (number forgotten) [42nd Ala.] & Col [George H.] Forney'[s] Bat. [1st Confederate Battalion of Infantry] have requested that I should be placed over them. I would like to be transferred to that Department _ as it would relieve me of my present position more or less humiliating. Why can not this be done in my case _ when it is done in so many others_? But if this cannot be done _ & Ala. Troops must be kept under a key commander _ who has not seen half the service I have _ then I wish to have the power authority & rank to increase my Regmt into a Brigade and will raise it in those Counties in North Ala. where it is impossible to enforce the Conscript Law. I would like to have this power now as this is the moment to effect it in North Ala. Will you see his Excellency this morning and let me know today _ as I wish to leave the city in the morning on a Short leave of absence to my family. I have fought in every battle from Williamsburg to Gettysburg _ except Sharpsburg & the first battle of Fredericksburg, where I was detained from wounds from the field.

> I am very respectly
> Edward A O'Neal
> Col 26th Ala. Regmt.

in all humiliating. Why cannot this be
done in my case - when it is done
in so many others? But if this cannot
be done - if Ala. Troops must be kept
under a [?] Commander - who has not
seen half the service I have - then I wish
to have the power authority & rank
to increase my Regiment into a Brigade
and I will raise in those Counties in North
Ala. where it is impossible to enforce
the Conscript Laws. I would like to
have this power now as this is the mom-
-ent to effect it in North Ala.
Will you see his Excellency this morning
and let me know to day - as I wish
to leave the city in the morning on
a short leave of absence to my family.
I have fought in every battle from Williamsburg
to Gettysburg - except Sharpsburg & the first
battle of Fredericksburg - where I was detained
by wound from the field.
I am very respectfully
Edward A. O'Neal
Col 26th Ala. Regmt.

Last page of Colonel O'Neal's January 25, 1864 letter to Congressman Phelan

General Lee responded to the Alabama legislature's request at month's end. "I do not see how the good of the service can be promoted by detaching this regiment, thus breaking up a veteran brigade which has just set the glorious example in this army of re-enlisting for the war...If Colonel O'Neal desires duty in some other army I will interpose no objection. I regret that he feels injustice has been done him here. I have a just appreciation of his gallantry[5] and worth. I recommended another officer to the command of the brigade because I believe him better qualified to perform the duties of the position."[6]

Despite the objections of General Lee, Colonel O'Neal and his fine regiment departed the Army of Northern Virginia. From February to June, the 26th Alabama guarded prisoners on their way to Andersonville Prison. During the Atlanta Campaign, the Alabamians served as members of the brigade commanded by Brigadier General James Cantey (1818-1874; Mexican War). Colonel O'Neal, who led the brigade at the Battle of Peachtree Creek, was assigned to round up deserters in northern Alabama. The 26th Alabama served in the Tennessee and Carolina Campaigns under Major Bryan.

General Lee arrived at the Second Corps headquarters near sunset on July 1, 1863. Though Longstreet's Divisions had not yet reached Gettysburg, Lee was determined to strike Meade's army early the next day. Ewell's Corps, closest to the enemy and in better condition than Hill's Corps, became the logical choice to conduct the attack. While Lee discussed the condition of the corps with Generals Ewell and Rodes, General Early returned from an inspection of his troops and assumed the role of spokesman for the other two. Early argued against Lee's proposal to attack Cemetery Hill in the morning. He pointed out that the Union army would concentrate against the Second Corps during the night and the ground before Cemetery Hill was unfavorable to an attacker. The ground south of Gettysburg, Early suggested, presented a more favorable opportunity; the capture of Big Round Top and Little Round Top would allow the Army of Northern Virginia to dominate the battlefield.

Generals Ewell and Rodes agreed with Early. General Lee responded to General Early's arguments by suggesting:

> Then perhaps I had better draw you around towards my right, as the line will be very long [five miles] and thin if you remain here, and the enemy may come down and break through it?
>
> Again it was Early who answered, not Ewell, and it was pride, not tactics, that shaped his reply. He felt that his men had won a victory and they would consider their success empty if they were ordered to give up the ground they had gained. Besides, he could not move his seriously wounded. Lee need not fear, he asserted, that the enemy would break through. The Second Corps could hold its own against any troops that might be sent down from the hills to attack it.[7]

Early's attitude, combined with the reticence of Ewell and Rodes, pressured Lee into making his main attack against the Union left flank with Longstreet's troops. Any advantage gained by Longstreet's Corps against the Union left would be supported by Ewell's Corps. Jubal Early upset the most favorable plan to deliver a massive blow against the enemy's left flank on July 2. Success on July 1, which was secured largely through Early's efforts, became a partial success on July 2 and a sanguinary disappointment on July 3. The greatest measure of blame for the Southern failure at Gettysburg can be assigned to Early. Colonel Alexander's non-partisan observations about Gettysburg corroborates this conclusion. He believed the placement of Ewell's Corps had involved "one of the vital points of the battle." General Ewell's infantry and artillery were "practically paralysed & useless by its position during the last two days of the battle."[8]

In a postwar letter to Early, Lee suggested that "all controversy, I think, will only serve to prolong angry and bitter feeling, and postpone the period when reason and charity may resume their sway. At present the public mind is not prepared to receive the truth."[9] After the death of his former chief in 1870, General Early emerged as the unofficial historian of the Army of Northern Virginia. He defended the image of Lee, the symbol of the "lost cause," throughout the 1870s. Early was very sensitive to criticism about Lee's obvious failure at Gettysburg. William Swinton, who had reported on the war for the *New York Times*, published *Campaigns of the Army of the Potomac* in 1866. His work contained offensive remarks attributed to Longstreet regarding Lee's conduct of the battle and the campaign. Lee partisans were particularly offended by the statement: "Having, however, gotten a taste of blood in the considerable success of the first day, the Confederate commander seems to have lost that equipoise in which his faculties commonly moved, and he determined to give battle."[10]

On the occasion of Lee's birthday, January 19, 1872, Jubal Early spoke out against James Longstreet which triggered a feud between them. Early suggested that the defeat at Gettysburg was due to Longstreet's failure to attack at dawn on July 2, as Lee had intended. Early may have also recognized his own shortcomings at Gettysburg. Both he and Ewell share blame for not moving against Cemetery Hill and Culp's Hill on July 1.

General Early's career after Gettysburg was also vulnerable to criticism. On November 7, 1863, one of his brigades held a bridgehead across the Rappahannock River. The Army of the Potomac's 5th and 6th Corps approached the *tete-de-pont* and Early rushed reinforcements to the threatened point. Lee surveyed the scene "and agreed with Early that the position could be held during the night without further reinforcement."[11] Brigadier General David A. Russell's (1820-1864; West Point 1845) Division of the 6th Corps attacked unexpectedly at dusk and overwhelmed the bridgehead. General Early, who lost 1,674 men, a battery, and eight flags, did not feel responsible for the disaster since the army commander "shared his estimate of the situation. Still, it might be wondered why so exposed a point should have been reinforced after the enemy advance began; still greater wonder that Early did not urge complete withdrawal of the defenders despite the strategic importance of the position."[12]

On May 29, 1864, Early replaced Ewell as commander of the Second Corps; two days later Early received promotion to lieutenant general. Two weeks later, the Second Corps returned to the Shenandoah Valley to save Lynchburg. The approach of the Second Corps on June 18 caused the army led by Major General David Hunter (1802-1886; West Point 1822) to withdraw into the mountains.

Lee's orders permitted Early to conduct a campaign north of the Potomac River in order to draw Union troops away from the Army of Northern Virginia. In the spirit of "Stonewall" Jackson, Early and his army of 14,000 men crossed the river at Sheperdstown, Maryland, on July 6. On the ninth the Confederates routed 6,000 Federals at Monacacy Junction south of Frederick. Two days later, in one of the most remarkable feats of the war, Early's four divisions were in position at Silver Spring, Maryland, ready to assault the United States' capital. The arrival of reinforcements from the 6th Corps and the 19th Corps convinced Early not to risk his small force in an attack. After severe skirmishing on July 12, which Abraham Lincoln witnessed, the Rebels withdrew during the night. General Early's army retired unmolested and recrossed the Potomac at White's Ferry on July 14.

Grant assigned Sheridan the task of defeating Early and eliminating the Valley as a source of supply for Lee's army. Sheridan assumed command of the 6th, 8th and 19th Corps on August 7. With a numerical superiority of about 3 to 1, Sheridan attacked Early at Winchester on September 13. Casualties were very heavy in proportion to the effectives engaged; General Rodes was among those killed. Superior numbers carried the day for Sheridan. Late in the afternoon the Confederates were forced to retreat after inflicting 5,000 casualties and suffering a loss of 3,900 men.

Three days later, Sheridan's army attacked the dispirited Rebels at Fisher's Hill, some twenty-five miles southwest of Winchester. Again, superior numbers allowed the Federals to outflank the enemy position. The Johnnies were put to flight with the loss of more than 1,000 prisoners. On September 29, the Yankees began burning the barns and crops of the Shenandoah Valley. "The red glow from those fires signaled the dawning of a new and terrible age—the era of total war. There had been foraging aplenty in the past three years of conflict, there had been individual acts of vengeance and rage, and there had been criminal behavior masquerading as military necessity. But never before in this war, if ever in history, had military force on such a scale been applied to the economic resources of civilians."[13]

As the enemy retreated north, General Early received reinforcements from Lee. On October 19, Early attacked the Federal encampment near Cedar Creek at first light. With the element of surprise on their side, the Confederates routed the 8th and 19th Corps. The 6th Corps stood its ground and Early hesitated to attack in the belief that the battle had been won. Delay in launching a decisive final blow to drive the 6th Corps allowed General Sheridan to snatch an amazing victory from "Stonewall" Jackson's successor in the Valley.

On October 16, General Sheridan had traveled to Washington for a conference at the War Department. When the unexpected battle erupted at dawn, Sheridan had been asleep at Winchester. Though the sound of heavy firing south of Winchester was audible, Sheridan did not believe a major battle was underway. Around 9:00 A.M., he left Winchester with his escort. As signs of defeat became evident, Sheridan became anxious. The sight of a disorganized wagon train halted on the Valley Pike convinced Sheridan that his army was in trouble. As he encountered survivors of broken units, Phil Sheridan rallied his men. A sergeant in the 110th Ohio heard his general shout: "Come on back, boys! Give 'em hell, God damn 'em! We'll make coffee out of Cedar Creek tonight!"[14]

Sheridan reorganized his troops and just before 4:00 P.M., the 6th and 19th Corps advanced toward the center of the Confederate line. Strong cavalry columns tore at Early's flanks. After fighting most of the day and looting the enemy camps, the Southerners were unable to resist the onslaught of Union soldiers who had been inspired by "Little Phil." The entire Rebel line splintered and the veterans of Chancellorsville and Gettysburg fled panic-stricken up the Valley.

Newmarket, October 20 '64

Col. W.H. Taylor, A.A.G.

The sixth and nineteenth corps have now left the Valley. I fought them both yesterday. I attacked Sheridan's camp on Cedar Creek before day yesterday morning and and [*sic*] surprised and routed the eighth and nineteenth corps and then drove the sixth corps beyond Middletown capturing eighteen pieces of Artillery and thirteen hundred prisoners. But the enemy subsequently made a stand on the pike and in turn attacked my line and my left gave way and the rest of the troops took a panic and could not be rallied, retreating in confusion. But for their bad conduct I should have defeated Sheridan's whole force. On the retreat back to Fisher's Hill the enemy captured about thirty pieces of Artillery and some wagons and ambulances. The prisoners were brought off. My loss in men was not heavy. Genl. Ramseur [15] was seriously wounded while acting with gallantry and was captured by the enemy.

J.A.Early
Lt Genl.

[*OR* XLIII Series I Pt.1 p. 901]

The disaster at Cedar Creek ended Confederate control of the Shenandoah Valley; it could no longer feed the Army of Northern Virginia. Out of 31,000 men present, Sheridan lost 5,600 men; Early's army of 18,500 suffered nearly 3,000 casualties. Most of the survivors returned to Lee's army while Early retained a very small force in the Valley. On March 2, 1865, a cavalry division led by Brigadier General George A. Custer (1839-1876; West Point 1861) annihilated the Confederacy's last force at Waynesboro, Virginia. Jubal Early escaped and Lee relieved him at the end of the month as commander of the District of Western Virginia. With no command in Virginia to occupy him, Early chose to cross the Mississippi River and fight on. By the time he reached Texas, the Trans-Mississippi Department had surrendered. Early entered Mexico, without giving his parole to Federal authorities, then traveled to Canada. While exiled north of the border, Early published *A Memoir of the Last Year of the War for Independence in the Confederate States of America* in 1866. Three years later, having never formally surrendered, Jubal Early returned to the United States and settled in New Orleans. Many ex-Confederate generals, including James Longstreet resided in the Crescent City after the war.

New Orleans May 30th 1877

Dear Sir:

I regret very much that I did not see you when you were in the city _ your card was not received by me until after 5.P.M. yesterday and that was the first intimation I had that you had been here, and you were then gone. _

Mr [J. William] Jones, the Secretary of the Southern Historical Society, informed me in a letter received therein four days ago, that you intended having my notice of the Count de Paris' book [*History of the Civil War in America*] translated into French, and published in some French journal _

As the article in the Southern Historical Society Papers contain some rather awkward typographical errors, I have corrected a copy and herewith send it to you, in order that the errors may not be continued in the translation _ I sent a copy in manuscript to the Count, along with a letter on the Campaign in Pennsylvania and the Battle of Gettysburg, in reply to some points suggested by him upon which he desired to have the views of several Confederate officers, including myself. _ From one or two letters he has written to Mr Jones, he appears to be well disposed, but he is very badly informed in regard to all questions [in] relation to our struggle _ I therefore made my comments on his book as mild as possible.

Last year I had a controversy with Longstreet in regard to the Battle of Gettysburg, and as I think it possible you may not have received the copies of my articles, which were sent to you at Memphis, I now send other copies _ _ ["Since" lined out] After the publication of my last article I received a letter from Genl A.L. Long, [16] who was on Genl Lee's staff at Gettysburg, stating that Longstreet arrived in person on the field at Gettysburg on the first day, after the close of the fighting that day _ when doubtless he received his orders in person. Long also says that Genl Lee was very impatient all the morning of the second, and went there several times to meet Longstreet & hurry his march _ I have also a copy of a letter from Governor John Lee Carroll of Maryland to Fitzlee, in which he says that shortly after the war, General Lee told him that if Longstreet had obeyed his orders and attacked early instead of late, we would have gained the victory _ at Gettysburg Of this I have never had a doubt myself.___ I regretted the necessity of the controversy with Longstreet, but his communications were of such a character that I could not avoid it_ When I was in New Orleans last winter, I was very much astonished at his calling at the St Charles, and leaving his card for me in my absence _ Though I was at first puzzled as to how I should meet this advance on his part,_ yet I became convinced that his sufferings from his tregioisation had been so great, that I could not but have compassion on him so when we met on the street I shook hands with him _

I am glad to hear that your health is good, and trust that I may have the pleasure of meeting you this summer _

I will return to Virginia the last of next week__

With the highest esteem, I am
Very Respectfully &Truly
Yours
JA Early

Hon. Jefferson Davis_

Despite his failure as an independent commander and unpopularity during the war, General Early remained a favorite with Confederate veterans. In his feud with Longstreet, Early gained allies such as Brigadier General William N. Pendleton (1809-1883; West Point 1830) and Major General Fitzhugh Lee (1835-1905; West Point 1856), nephew to both R.E. Lee and Samuel Cooper. James Longstreet, who had embraced the Republican Party and accepted Reconstruction, defended himself in the Northern press. Jubal Early, however, won the war of words: he was permanent president of the Southern Historical Society, "the most influential Civil War history association in the South...."[17]

The Southern Historical Society, founded in 1869 at New Orleans, began publishing its "Papers" in 1876. Many of the articles that appeared during the next few years were devoted to the war in the east and praise of General Lee. This Virginia bias upset Western veterans who published the *The Annals of the Army of Tennessee and Early Western History* in 1878. The Virginians criticized their former president because they believed the chief executive had dominated their hero. Davis grew to resent the exaltation of Lee and told a friend that "if Lee's eulogists could better comprehend his character they would not seek to build for it a fiction in disparagement of others."[18]

Longstreet endured the most unjust treatment from Lee partisans in the pages of the "Gettysburg Series" published in the "Papers." Beginning in August 1878, twenty articles appeared which cast Longstreet in the role of scapegoat for the failure of Southern arms at Gettysburg, and consequently, eventual defeat. Any article written by Longstreet received a reply from the

war, General Lee told him that if Longstreet had obeyed his orders and attacked early instead of late, we would have gained the victory of Gettysburg. Of this, I have never had a doubt myself. — I regretted the necessity of the controversy with Longstreet, but his communications were of such a character that I could not avoid it. When I was in New Orleans last winter, I was very much astonished at his calling at the St Charles, and leaving his card for me in my absence — Though I was at first puzzled as to how I should meet this advance on his part, — yet I became convinced that his sufferings from his trepidation had been so great, that I could not but have compassion on him — So when we met on the street I shook hands with him —

I am glad to hear that your health is good, and trust that I may have the pleasure of meeting you this summer. —

I will return to Virginia the last of next week —

With the highest esteem, I am
Very Respectfully & truly,
Yours &c
J A Early

Hon. Jefferson Davis —

Last page of Jubal Early's May 30, 1877 letter to Jefferson Davis

"Virginia crowd" until his death in 1904.[19] The following letter written by Jubal Early to Jefferson Davis, recounts his ignominious dispute with the officer Lee called "my old War Horse."

Lynchburg Va Jany 19th 1888

My Dear Sir:

Your letter of the 9th was received on my return here on the 13th, but, not having been able to get a copy of the Century [Magazine] for February 1887 until today, and not knowing whether Longstreet's article in it was one which I had seen, I have delayed answering you _ I now find that the article is the one I had before seen, and to which I refer in the enclosed communication which appeared in the Richmond State [newspaper] of the 11th of May 1887, and which was copied into two or three New Orleans papers, and also in a number of other papers in different parts of the country. I sent you a copy of the paper containing my communication, but supposed you overlooked it, as you get a number of papers _

As to General Longstreet's statement that at the close of the fight on the first day his command was "fifteen to twenty miles west of the field," that is intended to produce an erroneous impression _ [20] The first day's fight was at an end about 4 O'Clock P.M., and Longstreet's two divisions, Hood's and McLaws', camped that night within four miles of the battle field __ See General Lee's report in the July number of the Southern Historical Papers for July 1876 (Vol. 2nd) page 33 _ The statement being on page 41._ It was on the 2nd that Longstreet was remiss, in not attacking early in the morning, and General Hood, in a letter, an extract from which is given by Longstreet in the February number of the Southern Historical Papers for 1878, (Vol 5th) page 79, says he arrived in front of the heights of Gettysburg shortly after daybreak on the 2nd, and his division soon commenced filing into an open field near him _

If Longstreet was so far from Gettysburg at the close of the fight on the first, it was due to his own tardiness. The news of the movement of Mead[e]'s army north, was received by General Lee on the 28th of June at Chambersburg, where his head quarters were, and where Longstreet's Corps was _ He immediately issued orders for the concentration of his army East of the South Mountain, at or near Gettysburg _ These orders were sent to Ewell who was at Carli[s]le, fully thirty miles from Chambersburg, and Ewell sent them to me at York, fully thirty miles from Carlile, and thirty two miles from Gettysburg. These orders were received by me on the morning of June 29th. Ewell, with Rodes' division, moved down from Carlile, and I moved from York on the 30th, and we both arrived at Gettysburg in time to take part in the first day's battle, though we did not take the direct routes to Gettysburg _ Chambersburg is only twenty -five miles from Gettysburg, and how was it that Longstreet was fifteen or twenty miles from the field at the close of the fight? I have had two controversies with Longstreet in regard to the Battle of Gettysburg _ One was in the New Orleans papers, previous to 1877; and the other in the Southern Historical Papers._ You will find my articles in the Papers December number for 1877 (Vol 4th), pages 241 to 302, and the June number for 1878 (Vol 5th) pages 270-287.

Longstreet's articles to which mine are replies, are in Vol 5th pages 54 to 86 and pages 257 to 270. In printing my articles in the 4th volume, there are a number of typographical errors which are corrected on page 94, Vol 5th.

I think I fully demonstrated the falsehood of many of Longstreet's statements, and the absurdity of his pretensions and criticisms _ I trust you will have the time and patience to read the whole of my articles _ Having thus fully answered all of his absurd criticisms, I did not deem it necessary to go over the task again, when his article in the Century appeared, though I received several written applications to do so, but contented myself with the brief notice of his article contained in the communication to The State _

You will see that he criticizes the appointment of Ewell and A.P. Hill as Lieutenant Generals after the death of Jackson and imputes unworthy motives to General Lee in pursuing their promotions. He intimates that D.H. Hill [and] McLaws were the proper parties to have been promoted, yet D.H. Hill was not at that time on duty with the Army of Northern Virginia, having been relieved at his own request, as I have always understood, because he could not get along very well with General Jackson, though they were brothers in law _ Longstreet, himself, relieved McLaws [21] from the command of a division in his corps after his campaign in East Tennessee, and imputed to him a failure of duty when he besieged Knoxville in the spring of 1864 [November, 1863]._ This shows you how little insight is to be attached to his criticisms.

He seems to have lost all sense of decency and propriety, and I think in his misstatements in regard to the Gettysburg Campaign, as well as the Seven Days' battles around Richmond,[22] and the campaign into Maryland in September 1862, [23] about both of which he has published articles, he has demonstrated his want of sense as well as his utter disregard for the truth, as he had before shown his utter want of principle by his political course.

In what I say in my communication to The State in regard to the opinion expressed by [Lord] Wolsel[e]y [24] in respect to General Lee, I wish you to understand that I by no means endorse his criticism of you_ When I wrote that communication, I had only seen his opinion of General Lee as copied into many of our papers, and did not see the full article until some time afterwards._

Trusting that you and all your household are enjoying good health, I am,

Very Truly & Sincerely Yours

Hon. Jefferson Davis   JA Early

Early's criticism of Longstreet's conduct on July 2, 1863, rests upon the fact that the 1st Corps did not engage the Army of the Potomac's left flank until 4:00 P.M. His contention that Longstreet disobeyed orders to attack at sunrise "has fallen apart, both from time and from lack of substance. During the re-examination of the evidence, the prosecution's case collapsed." [25]

The fact that Lee intended Longstreet to attack earlier in the day is not disputed. Captain Samuel R. Johnston scouted the Union left at daylight but he did not return to headquarters until 9:00 A.M. He reported that the Round Tops were clear of enemy troops and this intelligence supported Lee's intention to outflank the Federals, crush their left flank, then drive the survivors toward Cemetery Hill. Lee ordered Ewell to pressure the enemy force on his front when he heard the sound of Longstreet's guns. General Hill received a similar order.

A division under Major General Richard H. Anderson (1821-1879; West Point 1842) was designated to protect Longstreet's left and advance "if the success should warrant it." [26] At 11:00 A.M., Lee ordered Longstreet to move his men toward assembly areas in preparation for the assault.

Lee was already aware that his most experienced corps commander disagreed with his desire go on the offensive. The previous day Longstreet had "urged quite vehemently that the Confederates avoid any attack on the Union position at Gettysburg. Instead he suggested that Lee make a sweeping movement southward along the Confederate right and then veer toward the east so as to get around the left of Meade's army and between it and Washington. In this way, he said, Lee could force Meade to attack him in a place of his own choosing."[27] Longstreet wanted to fight the decisive battle of the campaign with the same tactical advantage they had enjoyed at Fredericksburg. Lee, however, was determined to attack because he believed the Army of the Potomac had not yet fully concentrated at Gettysburg. Longstreet's uncooperative attitude provided his postwar critics with another plausible explanation to pin the cause of the defeat on him. They believed Longstreet's failure to attack promptly at daylight allowed Union reinforcements to reach the field and determine the outcome of the battle. This is a myth since the 2nd, 3rd, and 5th Corps were available to Meade before Lee's plan had matured.

General Richard Heron Anderson

Longstreet delayed his attack because only two of his three divisions were up. Major General George E. Pickett's (1825-1875; West Point 1846) Division was on the march from Chambersburg; it did not arrive at Herr Ridge, behind McPherson's Ridge, until 4:00 P.M. Longstreet remarked to Hood: "I never like to go into battle with one boot off."[28] One of General Hood's own brigades, commanded by Brigadier General Evander M. Law (1836-1920; The Citadel 1856), did not join the division until noon, whereupon the 1st Corps began its march to assemble behind Seminary Ridge, opposite Cemetery Ridge.

Around 1:00 P.M., forward elements of Major General Lafayette McLaws' (1821-1897; West Point 1842) Division reached high ground in the vicinity of Black Horse Tavern. General Lee had hoped that the movement of Longstreet's troops would be unobserved by the enemy to retain the element of surprise. General McLaws thought that his column was visible to Federal observers on Little Round Top. When he became aware of McLaws' opinion, Longstreet ordered his corps to countermarch along another route that followed Willoughby Run, which flowed in the rear of Seminary Ridge. These delays, combined with evidence already presented, make it clear that Longstreet's delay in attacking on July 2 was justified.[29] It did not serve Jubal Early's self-interest to evaluate the evidence against James Longstreet fairly.

When General Hood's four brigades advanced at 4:00 P.M., Major General Daniel E. Sickles' (1819-1914; lawyer) 3rd Corps defended, but did not occupy the Round Tops. Brigadier General Andrew A. Humphrey's (1810-1883; West Point 1831) Division was positioned parallel to the Emmitsburg Road south of town; it connected the 3rd Corps with the 2nd Corps to the north. One brigade of Major General David B. Birney's (1825-1864; lawyer-businessman) Division occupied the Peach Orchard on Humphrey's left while the other two brigades held Houck's Ridge which angled southeast away from the Emmitsburg Road. Devil's Den is located at the eastern end of Houck's Ridge below Little Round Top.

Major General Gouverneur K. Warren (1830-1882; West Point 1850), the Army of the Potomac's chief engineer, stood on Little Round Top as General Hood's Division approached the weak Union left. Warren noticed that the Rebel line outflanked Birney's Division and sent a subordinate to secure troops for the defense of the high ground. If the Rebel army had exploited the soft spot, the Army of the Potomac could have been assailed in its rear.

Lee wanted Longstreet to attack directly north up the Emmitsburg Road toward Cemetery Hill, but most of General Hood's Division struck Houck's Ridge. Though his division fought magnificently, its efforts were uncoordinated because Hood was wounded early in the action. General Sickles' men clung desperately to Houck's Ridge. Longstreet did not commit McLaw's four brigades until 5:30 P.M. when Hood's Division, now commanded by General Law, was fully

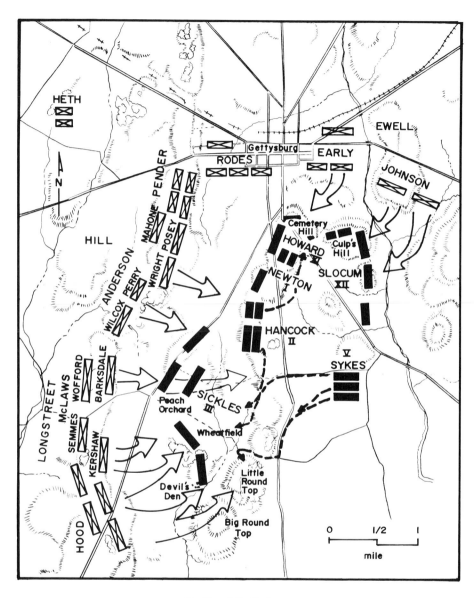

Battle of Gettysburg
July 2, 1863

engaged. Around this time, the Rebels captured Devil's Den but the timely arrival of two Union brigades from the 5th Corps prevented the fall of Little Round Top.

Two of McLaws brigades blew across the Emmitsburg Road and maintained pressure on the Union brigades trying to retain control of the Wheatfield, northwest of Little Round Top. Brigadier General William Barksdale's (1821-1863; politician) Brigade of Mississippians broke General Birney's line near the Peach Orchard, captured Brigadier General Charles K. Graham (1824-1889; engineer), and continued an irresistible advance. Barksdale wheeled three of his regiments north in the direction of Cemetery Hill while the 21st Mississippi charged straight ahead. A brigade of Georgians, under Brigadier General William T. Wofford (1824-1884; Mexican War), cleared the Peach Orchard.

Barksdale's maneuver conformed with Lee's design for victory and his brigade gained the most glory of the day. The 13th, 17th, and 18th Mississippi Regiments ripped apart General Humphrey's left flank while four regiments under the command of Brigadier General Cadmus M. Wilcox (1824-1890; West Point 1846) of Anderson's Division hit the Federals in the front. Perry's Brigade of Floridians, led by Colonel David Lang of Anderson's Division, [30] advanced on Wilcox' left. The small brigade outflanked the Federals and forced them to retreat to Cemetery Ridge.

South of General Humphrey's hard-pressed division, General Birney's survivors along with elements of the 2nd and 5th Corps, were finally expelled from the Wheatfield. Lieutenant Colonel Freeman McGilvery established a line of batteries at Plum Run which bought time for the Federals to bring up fresh brigades to counterattack. The 21st Mississippi overran two batteries but fell back when the Pennsylvania Reserves, 5th Corps, charged across the northern slope of Little Round Top. The Rebels who swarmed below were driven back across the Wheatfield around 8:00 P.M.

Major General Winfield S. Hancock (1824-1886; West Point 1844), leader of the 2nd Corps, served as Meade's tactical commander during the fight for Cemetery Ridge. He responded to the crisis created when the 3rd Corps line ruptured by sending 2nd Corps units to support the crumbling left flank. A brigade of New Yorkers charged the exhausted Mississippians, who fled back across the Emmitsburg Road when Barksdale received a mortal wound. Humphrey's Division was reforming on the flank of the 2nd Corps when Wilcox and his Alabamians appeared. Hancock sent his only available reserves, the 1st Minnesota, to tackle the threat. A survivor of the charge remembered: "It seemed as if every step was over some fallen comrade. Yet no man wavers; every gap is closed up—and bringing down their bayonets, the boys pressed shoulder to shoulder and disdaining the ficticious courage proceeding from noise and excitement, without a word or cheer, but with silent, desperate determination, step firmly forward in unbroken line...forward...." [31]

The blow staggered the 1,600 Butternuts. Out of 262 men who participated in the gallant charge, less than 50 survived to rally on their colors. When General Wilcox observed that his unsupported brigade was exposed to additional counterattacks, he withdrew his weary men. Colonel Lang followed Wilcox and both brigades retired to Seminary Ridge. This caused a third brigade from General Anderson's Division to retire. The Georgians under the leadership of Brigadier General Ambrose R. Wright (1826-1872; lawyer) had charged across the Emmitsburg Road with light losses. They had driven off the opposing infantry on their front and captured a battery. General Wright sent a courier to General Anderson asking for support on his left flank from the division's two remaining brigades commanded by Brigadier General Carnot Posey (1818-1863; lawyer) and Brigadier General William Mahone (1826-1895; Virginia Military Institue 1847). Without the firepower of the additional brigades, and observing the withdrawal of the Floridians, General Wright ordered his band to fall back. A senior staff officer wrote in his autobiography that General Anderson "was a very brave man, but of a rather inert, indolent manner for commanding troops in the field, and by no means pushing or aggressive."[32]

Anderson's inability to coordinate the action of his five brigades character-ized the overall Confederate effort on July 2. Ewell, whose corps did not act until 6:30 P.M., "turned in a performance that was less than mediocre."[33] Part of Major General Edward "Allegheny" Johnson's (1816-1873; West Point 1838) Division gained a foothold on Culp's Hill but most of his men were repulsed. The Louisiana Tigers and a brigade of North Carolinians of Early's Division captured the crest of Cemetery Hill along with cannon and prisoners. This was the key to the entire Union line, but like the Georgians an hour before, the Tigers and the Tar Heels "had to retreat for lack of help at the decisive moment."[34] If Carnot and Posey had advanced against Cemetery Ridge, the brigade commanded by Brigadier General Samuel S. Carroll (1832-1893; West Point 1856), 2nd Corps, would have been pinned on the ridge near Ziegeler's Grove. It is unlikely that General Carroll's counterattack against Cemetery Hill would have developed since he received no orders to do so and acted on his own initiative.[35]

Unlike Hancock and Warren, Hill and Ewell were relatively inactive during the day and did not oversee their subordinates properly. The Army of Northern Virginia's divisions acted independently; brigades fought isolated actions. The loss of General Hood early in the battle along with the high rate of casualties among brigade and regimental commanders in McLaws' Division increased the odds against the Southerners. Though the Army of the Potomac had been staggered, the Confederate combinations never connected for the knockout blow. "After Longstreet drove the troops in his front and wrested about a mile of ground in depth from the Federals, there was ample time to win a victory had he received the full and prompt cooperation of Hill and Ewell."[36] Lee bears the overall responsibility for the disappointment on July 2, but he cannot be blamed for the inefficiency of his experienced generals.

Colonel Alexander believed that "None of Longstreet's three divisions were any better than any other divisions of the other corps...But now there came into play one of the well recognized forces in all military affairs—the difficulty in securing concentration of effort over long lines. To read military history is calculated to make one think that it should be stated not as a difficulty but an impossibility, & that certainly seemed to be the case at Gettysburg. Our line was like a big fishhook outside the enemy's small one...Our only hope was to make our attacks simultaneous."[37]

Lee's original plan had been to lead with his left, Ewell's Corps, and then follow with his right, Longstreet's Corps. General Early's misguided opposition caused his army commander to reconsider his operations for July 2. At this point, Lee could have decided to keep Early's Division in a defensive posture before Cemetery Hill and Culp's Hill while General Rodes occupied Gettysburg with minimal risk. Broken terrain made the Union right the strongest part of their line, and though Lee did not know it, Meade was committed to a defensive battle. By detaching Johnson's Division to participate in the main assault directed by Longstreet, problems of coordination would have been reduced. Hood's Division could have remained at Herr Ridge in strategic reserve to protect the army's line of retreat. In this scenario, Lee could have committed seven fresh brigades, in "Hood's Charge" on July 3. Would the Texas Brigade, perhaps the finest shock troops in either army and eager to fight, been defeated by the 2nd Vermont Brigade?

The Confederates suffered defeat at Gettysburg and the French were smashed at Waterloo for a related reason: the deficiency of an experienced senior officer. On June 18, 1815, Marshal Michael Ney committed the bulk of Napoleon's cavalry prematurely. The "bravest of the brave" compounded his mistake by not coordinating his continuous charges against the sturdy British squares with infantry and artillery. The square, a tactic developed to repel cavalry, was vulnerable to massed musketry and cannonballs since it was a compact target. Forty-eight years later, Jubal Early robbed the Army of Northern Virginia of its best opportunity to overwhelm the Army of the Potomac, in a decisive battle, by downplaying the aggressive spirit of his corps. Early's unwillingness to cooperate with Lee, approved by Ewell and Rodes, diminished the fearsome offensive potential of the finest body of American soldiers to ever take the field. Confederate confusion, manifested as poor coordination between divisions, Anderson in particular, became the deciding factor in the battle's outcome, notwithstanding the superb tactical decisions made by Union officers such as Hancock, Dawes, and Carroll.

General Robert Emmett Rodes

Following the war, Lee wrote to William M. McDonald of Berryville, Virginia concerning Gettysburg. "Its loss was occasioned by a combination of circumstances. It was commenced in the absence of correct intelligence. It was continued in the effort to overcome the difficulties by which we were surrounded, and it would have been gained could one determined and united blow have been delivered by our whole line."[38]

Lee's desire to shorten his line, frustrated by Early, would have increased the synchronization of the divisions involved in the attack on July 2. Early's advice to Lee was more critical than any criticism that can be levelled at Longstreet. Major John W. Daniel, a member of Early's own staff, strengthens the case against Longstreet's chief detractor. Daniel declared to fellow veterans in 1875:

> General Lee's plan was for Ewell to attack Cemetery Hill "by way of diversion at dawn," to be converted into a real attack, if opportunity offered, while Longstreet was to make the main attack...The secret of that fatal delay, which, to my mind, was the great mistake or misfortune of the campaign, may perhaps be forever buried in our commander's bosom. I apprehend that the tardiness of General Longstreet's movements, and the prolonged absence of Pickett's division was the cause; but lest injustice be done to General Longstreet I forbear expressing an opinion. [39]

112

On the third day of the battle, nine Confederate brigades participated in the attack on Cemetery Ridge known as "Pickett's Charge." Lee has been criticized for sending his soldiers over nearly a mile of open ground. His last attempt to secure victory did not fail due to distance. Both flanks were improperly covered and supports (again Anderson) failed to follow and exploit success when the Virginians, Tennesseans, and North Carolinians reached the Union line. The number of unwounded prisoners (approximately 1,500) taken from Pickett's three brigades indicates that the Virginians lost heart when they saw no friends coming up behind them. Lee accepted responsibility for the disaster but his true error was choosing the wrong point to attack.

By using their exterior lines, the Confederates could have smothered Cemetery Hill with converging artillery fire. If Pickett's Charge had been directed there, the assaulting column would have avoided the artillery fire from Little Round Top and had a greater chance for success. Porter Alexander, who commanded Longstreet's artillery reserve at Gettysburg, thought

> there was no reason why Ewell's whole corps could not have been drawn to the right, enough to spare fully two divisions, say 9 brigades more & three fourths of his artillery. And then, had the assault been delivered upon the head of the fishhook [Cemetery Hill], & all the artillery, of all three corps, handled as one mass, the heavier guns everywhere put to enfilading fire, & the lighter saved up to be used on the flanks as I proposed to use [Major Charles] Richardson's 9 [howitzers], [40] we should have practically forged our storming column into a sort of armor piercing projectile, & could surely have driven its head a long way into Meade's body, & stood a fair chance of precipitating a panic. What we did, under all our disadvantages, with only 9 brigades in the storming column, surely justifies sanguine anticipations of what might have been done by 22 [including four of Anderson's brigades] at a more favorable locality, & with more artillery. [41]

The Army of Northern Virginia numbered 75,000 and the Army of the Potomac had a strength of 95,000 men during the Gettysburg Campaign. Lee lost 28,000 soldiers while Meade's army suffered more than 23,000 casualties. Although Lee must bear the main responsibility for the defeat at Gettysburg, no single individual can be assigned sole blame. The late Douglas Freeman pointed out that there is no single "secret" as to why the Army of Northern Virginia was defeated. General Early contributed more to the crucial factor of command chaos than anyone else because he exacerbated the obvious tactical disadvantages the Confederates confronted when he persuaded Lee to leave Ewell's Corps on the left. Robert E. Lee, more so than any other American general, believed in the god of history, who determines the outcome of battles. Therefore, a fair conclusion concerning the Confederate effort at Gettysburg may be found in the concept that they were destined to lose. [42]

4

WEST OF THE MISSISSIPPI

The Trans-Mississippi Department, created on May 26, 1862, encompassed the Confederate states of Arkansas, Texas, and western Louisiana, and the Indian Territory (present day Oklahoma), and nominally neutral Missouri. Major General Thomas C. Hindman took command of the department on May 31. He had no organized army, only poorly armed militia companies to defend his territory. Two months earlier, the Army of the West, under Major General Earl Van Dorn (1820-1863; West Point 1842), had crossed the Mississippi River to reinforce the Army of the Mississippi.

The selection of Hindman proved to be wise since he was energetic and capable of meeting the challenges of creating an army. Through stern measures under martial law, General Hindman raised a force that numbered 20,000 men with ample artillery, as well as adequate supplies. President Davis, however, considered the pre-war civilian from Helena too young and inexperienced to handle the responsibility. Although he was warned that a change of commanders would be a mistake, Davis wanted a West Point graduate to replace Hindman. Major General Theophilus H. Holmes (1804-1880; West Point 1829), who had proven to be a failure during the Seven Days, established his headquarters at Little Rock in August. Davis' appointment of

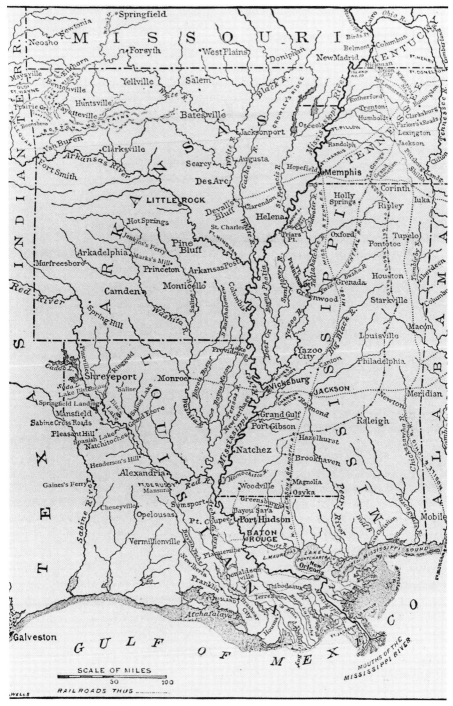

An 1864 map of Arkansas, Louisiana and Mississippi

Holmes "would be the most completely incomprehensible assignment he made as president, explicable only as an example of Davis's frequent poor judgment of men, his reliance on even unexperienced or demonstrably weak West Point graduates, his unswerving loyalty to friends from his own army days...."[1] Davis' decision to replace Hindman was most unfortunate because it carried unforeseen consequences. General Hindman, who had served Arkansas in Congress before the war, felt disposed to assist the war effort east of the Mississippi. General Holmes, a stiff soldier past his prime with restricted strategic vision, focused on the defense of his department. He did not recognize that defense of the Mississippi Valley, rather than Little Rock, shaped the strategic imperative.

Following the fall of Memphis in June 1862, Vicksburg remained the only major point in Confederate hands on the Mississippi River. Control of Vicksburg became essential to maintaining communications as well as the flow of men, arms, and supplies between the two sections of the Confederacy. Cooperation between Generals Pemberton and Holmes was crucial since the loss of Vicksburg would allow the Federals to concentrate overwhelming numbers of troops against the Trans-Mississippi Department. In October, President Davis and Secretary of War Randolph communicated to Holmes the importance of transferring troops to Pemberton.

Secretary Randolph irritated the president when he authorized General Holmes to cross the river with a prudent number of troops and assume command of the combined forces. Randolph believed that he expressed Davis' policy, but he resented his cabinet officer's impudence. Davis allowed pride to overwhelm his military sense and he rebuked Randolph by stating that there had been no specific plan for Holmes to cross the river. The president ordered his subordinate to withdraw the instructions for Holmes to join Pemeberton; the Secretary of War resigned on November 15. "Davis was now bound by his pride not to allow the trans-Mississippi forces to cross the river and join in a unified campaign. To do so would be to admit that Randolph had been right. The uncoupling of the Confederate defenses on either side of the Mississippi was now complete."[2]

Instead of issuing a direct order to General Holmes, President Davis detached a division from the Army of Tennessee to assist Pemberton. Davis attempted to "persuade" the North Carolinian into believing that he could send some of his troops across the Mississippi River without endangering the department, but "Holmes continued to insist that he could spare no forces, and there the matter rested. That Davis allowed Holmes to persist in this folly was another manifestation of the president's favoritism for his pre-war friends."[3] This failure of President Davis to exercise his authority over Holmes resulted in the waste of scarce Confederate manpower in a secondary theater.

On December 7, at the Battle of Prairie Grove, General Hindman suffered a loss of 1,300 men out of 10,000 men engaged. Hundreds of soldiers deserted during the retreat, unable to withstand winter hardship and endure defeat. A month later, almost 5,000 Confederates were captured 117 miles below Little Rock at Arkansas Post when Brigadier General Thomas J. Churchill (1824-1905; Mexican War) surrendered Fort Hindman. General McClernand's land force was five times the size of the Rebel garrison. In less than five months, the military strength of General Holmes' department had been reduced by a third. If a division from Holmes' department had served in Mississippi instead of Arkansas, the Army of Tennessee might have routed the Army of the Cumberland at Murfreesboro with Carter Stevenson's Division. Combined with the defeat at Fredericksburg and a deteriorating domestic situation, the North might have accepted a political solution to the advantage of the South.

Union strategy to gain control of the Mississippi Valley in 1863 focused on the capture of Vicksburg, which fell on July 4, 1863. General Grant's success in the Vicksburg Campaign was due in part to his ability to concentrate masses against General Pemberton's fractions at Port Gibson (May 1) and Raymond (May 12). On May 16, at the decisive Battle of Champion Hill, General Stevenson's Division crumbled. The momentum of a Confederate counterattack by Brigadier General John S. Bowen's (1830-1863 West Point 1853) Division which threatened to split General Grant's army could not be sustained. Two additional brigades could have given General Pemberton a victory. A strategic reserve composed of Arkansans and Texans based in central Mississippi would have provided John Pemberton with that additional manpower.

Jefferson Davis eliminated these possibilities (and others) when Theophilus Holmes assumed command of the Trans-Mississippi. Among the many errors in judgment that Davis made regarding his choice of senior generals, the appointment of Holmes was perhaps the worst because it occurred in 1862 rather than 1863 or 1864. The following two letters were written by President Davis to General Holmes.[4]

Richmond, Feb. 26th 1863.

Lt. Gen'l T.H. Holmes,
Trans Miss. Dept.

General:

Your letter borne by Mr. Holmes was duly received, and the sad condition of things in Arkansas is the more painful because of our little ability to correct it. When I possessed the power to suspend the writ of habeas corpus I sent you the requisite authority, and, with the camp regulations which you had the power to establish, hoped it would avail somewhat to repress the violent disturbance, the increase of which you describe. From your letter I infer that authority did not reach you, and now the power conferred on me by

Congress has expired by its own limitation. If another act should be passed, again investing me with power to suspend the writ, I will again act under it. In the meantime the arrangement which you have made will, I hope, effect much to suppress the disorders which, in the absence of civil tribunals for the punishment of crime, certainly leaves the good people in a condition greatly to be deplored.

In conjunction with the arrangements for military defence you will not fail to appreciate the importance of using all practicable means to promote the cultivation of the land and the production of the supplies necessary as well to support the people of the State as to maintain the army serving in it. The withdrawal of the enemy from the Post of Arkansas enables you to revive previously adopted plans for the defence of that line of approach, whether by works upon the banks of the Arkansas River and obstructions and torpedoes in the stream or otherwise, as may be most ["possible" lined out] feasible. If we lose the valley of the Arkansas I feel we shall not be able to obtain the supplies hereafter necessary to occupy the northern part of the State and carry operations into or across Missouri. It is, therefore, of vital importance that the enemy should not be permitted to ascend the Arkansas and White Rivers, and that such security should be given as will induce the planters of the valley to reoccupy and cultivate their fields.

Since my last letter to you, Gen'l Kirby Smith was ordered to proceed to the command of the Dept. to be composed of Louisiana and Texas. Subsequently hearing of the fall of the Post Arkansas, the enemy's ascent of White River, and the retreat of our forces from the N.W. portion of the State, it was deemed advisable to reestablish the unity of the Trans Mississippi Dept., at least for the present, and General Smith, as the ranking officer, will, during the continuance of this latter organization, command the Department. I need hardly say that this has been done for no want of confidence in you, but I may say that it was not in compliance with your wish to have some commander substituted for yourself, and that I hope, in the progress of events, that we shall be able to carry out the other purpose of two Departments west of the Miss., and that you will yet be able, reoccupying the whole of Arkansas and placing it in safety, to advance to the redemption of Missouri. You have later information than I can give you of events on the lower Mississippi. I am aware that the present stage of the river is unfavorable to the operation of field batteries against transports, and am quite sure that you will not neglect any opportunity which may offer to embarrass the enemy by operations against his river transportation. It is reported here that the enemy are attempting to open lateral channels from the Miss. so as to pass around the Tensas [River] and Bayou Macon. I do not think either of these practicable, but, to guard against possibilities, it might be well to have obstructions, such as rafts made of felled timber, thrown into those streams below the points where the artificial channels would enter them. Your knowledge of the country will enable you to suggest to Gen'l Smith whatever may be desirable in this connection.

I hope you will soon be supplied with the requisite funds for which estimates have been received, and that with the close of the winter the sickness in your army will disappear, and that you may yet be able to carry out the plans heretofore devised so that all past disappointments will be swallowed up in future success.

As ever, very truly your friend,
(Signed) Jeffn. Davis.

[*OR* LIII Series I p.849-850]

Richmond, Nov. 19th 1863.

Lt. Gen'l Holmes

Comdg. &c.

General:_____ I heard with great regret of your serious illness, and congratulate you on your reported restoration to health Your military views are so well known to me that I can appreciate your disappointment at having to fall back from the valley of the Arkansas. Concurring fully with you as to the importance, I might say the necessity, for the reoccupation of that region, I hope that we shall be able to regain possession of it.

I have not attempted to draw any conclusions from the reports as to the strength of the enemy or his withdrawal from Little Rock, having long since learned how little reliance is to be placed upon such statements as are made by those who come from among the enemy or by those who so often startle the East with very late and important intelligence from the West.

Reduced therefore to speculation upon probabilities, I have assumed that you would only regain the valley of the Arkansas by active operations either against the enemy's forces or his lines of communication and means of supply. The arms which are now en route to the trans Mississippi Dept. will, I hope, be followed by an increase of your military force and an improvement in the confidence of the people.

Col. Northrop[5] communicated to me the remark in your letter to him which related to myself. Events have been to both of us the source of disappointment and sorrow, but I have been as little disposed to blame you as you have been to censure me for those results which we both strove but failed to avert. I heard with much gratification that the persons who had previously been busy in detracting from you were equally prompt, after the attack upon Helena,[6] to render to you the tribute which was due; and I have an abiding faith that, under the blessing of Providence you will yet convince all fair-minded men as well of your zeal and ability as of your integrity and patriotism. I know your devotion to the cause in which you are engaged too well to suppose that my personal consideration can influence your conduct, and feel that I only do you justice when I say that I am sure you would sacrifice yourself at any time if you could thereby best promote the success of your country in the struggle in which She is engaged.

With high regard and cordial good wishes, I am

Your friend

(Signed) Jeffn. Davis

[*OR* LIII Series I p.915-916]

General E. Kirby Smith, who had been promoted to lieutenant general in October 1862, replaced General Holmes as head of the Trans-Mississippi Department on February 9, 1863. He had commanded the Department of East Tennessee and participated in the Perryville Campaign with an independent column; Smith became one of Bragg's chief critics.

Dick Taylor, a resourceful and touchy general, commanded the District of West Louisiana. The Federal commander of the Department of the Gulf, General Banks, had been ordered to cooperate with General Grant. In April, Banks invaded Taylor's district with 16,000 men. The 19th Corps advanced

General Edmund Kirby Smith

from Brashear City, seventy-five miles west of New Orleans, and despite spirited resistance at Fort Bisland and Irish Bend (April 12-14) Taylor was compelled to withdraw his 3,000 men toward Opelousas. The Yankees continued their advance up Bayou Teche into south central Louisiana, burning and pillaging along the way; they reached Opelousas on April 20. Taylor dispersed his small command and retreated to Natchitoches with a thousand infantry and his artillery and supply wagons, deep in the interior of the Red River Valley north of Alexandria.

Union gunboats that appeared on the Red River, the highway into central Louisiana, arrived at Alexandria just before the Union army did. General Banks occupied Alexandria on May 8 and began to confiscate cotton along with public property. Five days later the Federals departed the town. The invaders marched east to the Mississippi River for a campaign against Banks' new objective, Port Hudson, Louisiana, which was situated 125 miles below Vicksburg by land.

General Grant had already invested Vicksburg. The Richmond government as well as the Southern people demanded action from Kirby Smith. The department commander responded by sending General Taylor a division from northern Louisiana led by a veteran of Lee's army, Brigadier General John G. Walker (1822-1893; direct commission Mexican War). Taylor saw an oppor-

General Richard Taylor

tunity to operate against Banks' communications with New Orleans because he "recognized it as Banks's Achilles Heel. In much the same way that Jackson had used the Shenandoah Valley as a corridor to threaten Washington, Taylor could threaten New Orleans and thereby force Banks to retire from Port Hudson."[7]

Smith did not give Taylor approval to pursue this sound strategy. Instead, he ordered Taylor to threaten Grant's supply line in Louisiana opposite Vicksburg. This decision revealed Smith's limitations as a strategist. Grant's communications were no longer vulnerable. In May, when Grant's campaign had depended on the flow of men and supplies through eastern Louisiana across the river into Mississippi, Smith had allowed Walker to remain idle. Now, in June, Grant's supply line was protected by gunboats. Smith insisted on action. He believed that Grant's outposts were weakly defended by convalescents and colored troops. On June 7, Walker's Texans attacked Miliken's Bend but they were repulsed by a small brigade of former slaves and the 23rd Iowa. Two gunboats forced the Rebels to retire. Taylor wrote in his autobiography: "As foreseen, our movement resulted, and could result, in nothing."[8]

Despite the disappointment, Smith refused to release the Texas division to Taylor for an advance against New Orleans. Taylor, disgusted and determined to do something for Vicksburg, decided to proceed with the forces available to him. On June 23, the Union garrison at Brashear City fell to less than 3,000 Confederates. Most of the 1,700 Federals captured were convalescents. Their captors acquired a dozen heavy cannon, thousands of rifles and a large amount of stores. Taylor's accomplishment almost achieved the affect he desired. Rebel scouts were reported in Kenner, a New Orleans suburb, which created great excitement in the city. Early in July, Brigadier General William H. Emory (1811-1887; West Point 1831), in charge of the Crescent City, informed Banks that he had to decide between taking Port Hudson or holding New Orleans. Port Hudson surrendered on July 9.

Later in the year, Yankees again appeared in the Bayou Teche region. Vermillionville and Opelousas were occupied in October. The Federal troops advanced slowly, tormented by sudden cavalry strikes against their long columns. On November 3, the blueclads were roughly handled at Bayou Bourbeau near Opelousas by a veteran of the War for Texas Independence, Brigadier General Thomas Green (1814-1864). His combined force of infantry, cavalry, and artillery fought the more numerous Federals to a draw and captured 500 prisoners. After this display of fortitude, the Federals retreated south to New Iberia. Five months later they were back and Dick Taylor enjoyed his finest hour while Kirby Smith avoided another little known opportunity that could have impacted the outcome of the war.

President Lincoln's desire to impose political control of Texas and Louisiana, combined with French imperialism in Mexico, provided justification for an invasion of the Red River Valley. General Banks thought his presidential aspirations could be enhanced by the capture of Mobile, Alabama. He also realized that voters in his native Massachusetts would welcome bales of cotton for their idle mills. While Banks and 30,000 men marched northwest, another column 15,000 strong under Major General Frederick Steele (1819-1868; West Point 1843) would move southwest from Little Rock to divert Smith's attention. If the plan succeeded, the two columns would rendezvous at Shreveport (General Smith's headquarters). Steele never joined Banks; his men did not leave camp until March 23. By then, Alexandria had fallen, but General Taylor was preparing to strike back at the marauders.

Taylor concentrated his small army of 7,000 men thirty miles north of Alexandria around a supply depot. He pleaded with his superior for additional troops to repel the Yankees who were despoiling his state, but General Smith was more concerned with the threat to the capital of "Kirbydom" posed by General Steele. At the end of March, Banks resumed his advance. Taylor fell back before overwhelming numbers until he reached Mansfield, a point forty miles south of Shreveport. Three roads led to Shreveport from Mansfield; Taylor could not defend each of them adequately with his weak force. Early in April, General Green arrived with a cavalry brigade that had wintered in Texas. Even though he now commanded less than 9,000 men, Taylor decided he could wait no longer. Banks had moved inland away from the support of the powerful floating batteries on the Red River and his column stretched for miles. Taylor recognized the opportunity and seized it, without asking Smith for permission.

Smith had dispatched a division under General Churchill to Keatchie, halfway between Shreveport and Mansfield, but refused to reinforce Taylor with them. Smith, who saw glory for himself, planned to ride out from Shreveport, pick up Churchill's men on the way, and lead his little army to victory. Without Churchill's men, the Confederates were outnumbered more than two to one. Taylor, however, knew his available force was greater than the advance guard of General Banks' column, which stretched for twenty miles. The tactical advantage belonged to Taylor, and he deployed his army across the Mansfield Road on April 8 and waited for trouble.

The unavoidable clash occurred at Sabine Crossroads, three miles south of town. During the morning hours, the antagonists skirmished as Banks brought up reinforcements. He planned to attack on the ninth, but Taylor grew impatient. Just after 4:00 P.M., Brigadier General Jean Jacques A.A. Mouton (1829-1864; West Point 1850) received the order to attack with his Louisianians. Though Mouton was killed in the charge, the battle ended in a splendid victory. Two divisions of the 13th Corps were routed with the loss of 2,500 men. Twenty cannon were captured along with one thousand noncombatants and an entire wagon train. The Confederates lost about 1,000 soldiers and gained a moral victory over their numerically superior foe.

During the night Banks regrouped at Pleasant Hill. He believed that the campaign could be retrieved but Taylor intended to retain the initiative and complete the destruction of the enemy army before it could gain the security of its gunboats. Before Taylor began the fight on the eighth, he had ordered General Churchill to bring up his division, in disobedience of General Smith. Late in the afternoon Churchill's Missourians and Arkansans went forward, followed by Walker's Texans. The Rebels were successful at first, but a premature cavalry attack ordered by General Green was smashed. Taylor threw in Mouton's Division, now led by Brigadier General Camille Armand J. M. de Polignac (1832-1913; Crimean War) to maintain the pressure on his opponent but a Federal counterattack outflanked Churchill and broke his division. The Texans stopped the veterans of the 16th Corps and the battle became even bloodier. Taylor continued to assault the enemy line but his tired soldiers could not drive the Yankees.

Taylor admitted in his memoir that he had blundered at Pleasant Hill. He confessed that he should have employed the Louisianians during the initial attack instead of Churchill, and led them in person. Amid the confusion on the battlefield, Taylor's subordinates failed to exploit a gap between the Union left and center.[9] Poor reconnaissance had resulted in Churchill leading his men into a trap. Taylor's biographer concluded that "...Taylor failed to direct his troops effectively primarily because he underestimated the Federals' ability to repulse him. Believing that Banks's defenses at Pleasant Hill were merely designed to cover a withdrawal to the Red River, Taylor rushed into battle."[10] Taylor lost 1,600 men out of 12,500 engaged; Banks suffered 1,200 casualties from a force of 12,200.

Late that night Smith arrived at Taylor's headquarters and found a demoralized army. He expected the Federals to renew combat the next day. Like "Stonewall" Jackson's tactical defeat at Kernstown in 1862, however, the Battle of Pleasant Hill became a strategic victory. Taylor's aggressive posture combined with a lack of support from his generals convinced Banks to call off any further movement toward Shreveport. His army retreated to Grand Ecore, a few miles north of Natchitoches.

When Smith learned that the Federals were in retreat, he ordered Taylor to retire to Mansfield. Worried about the advance of General Steele's column toward Shreveport, he decided to concentrate against what he considered to be the most immediate threat. On April 14, Walker's and Churchill's infantry marched away. Smith promised to return the divisions to Taylor if Steele turned back. The Floridian also had dreams of recovering Arkansas and marching into Missouri; the people of Louisiana were less important. Taylor retained the Louisianians and several cavalry brigades (about 5,000 men). In an attempt to appease Taylor's disappointment, Smith issued an unofficial order on the sixteenth that promoted him to lieutenant general.

Banks retreated to Grand Ecore on the Red River but Taylor's ability to harass the Federal army was limited. General Green tried valiantly to block the descent of the fleet to Grand Ecore at Blair's Landing on April 12, but was killed. When the gunboats, ironclads, tugs, and transports under the command of Admiral David D. Porter reached Alexandria, they were trapped by low water. Upon learning this, Taylor's desire to finish off General Banks and capture his naval support intensified. He had returned to Shreveport only to discover on the fifteenth that Smith had broken his promise to him concerning the employment of Churchill's and Walker's Divisions. Steele had indeed begun to retreat, but Smith considered the threat of the column in Arkansas to be more important than the capture of a fleet or the destruction of an army.

Lieutenant Colonel Joseph Bailey, a pre-war lumberman from Wisconsin, saved Admiral Porter's boats which were stranded at Alexandria. Bailey constructed a series of dams that temporarily raised the level of the river and allowed the fleet to escape on May 13; the land retreat commenced the same day. Even though he was outnumbered greatly, Taylor tried to stop the retreating Yankees at Mansura on the 16th and Yellow Bayou on the 18th. Both attempts failed and the Federals crossed the Atchafalaya River to safety on May 19. The Red River Campaign was over, but a war of words between Smith and Taylor began. As his memoir shows, Dick Taylor became embittered by Kirby Smith's decision to deprive him of two divisions at a crucial juncture in the campaign.

> In all the ages since the establishment of the Assyrian monarchy no commander has possessed equal power to destroy a cause. Far away from the great centers of conflict in Virginia and Georgia, on a remote theater, the opportunity of striking a blow decisive of the war was afforded. An army that included the strength of every garrison from Memphis to the Gulf had been routed, and, by the incompetency of its commander was utterly demoralized and ripe for destruction...Instead of Sherman, Johnston would have been reinforced from west of the Mississippi, and thousands of absent men, with fresh hope, would have rejoined Lee.[11]

Taylor overstated the condition of Banks' army. The Union soldiers did not believe they had been whipped: their general would not let them fight. It is true, however, that without infantry support, Porter's fleet might have been captured, though not intact. The two 16th Corps divisions had been loaned to Banks by Sherman and were earmarked for the Atlanta Campaign. If Banks had been pressed by Taylor, the army might have abandoned the navy to its fate. No dams could have been built. Admiral Porter believed that if he had been compelled to sink his fleet, enough recoverable material would have remained for the construction of six ironclads. That would have taken months to complete, but with heavy cannon and iron plate, the Confederates could have established two strong batteries along a section of the Mississippi River. Such a strongpoint may have permitted troops to cross the river into Mississippi since the power of the inland navy to prevent such a movement would have been reduced severely. Whether or not reinforcements from the Trans-Mississippi would have affected the outcome of the Atlanta Campaign is debatable.

Major General Sterling Price (1809-1867), a popular but generally ineffective political general from Missouri, commanded a cavalry corps composed of three divisions led by Brigadier Generals John S. Marmaduke (1833-1887; West Point 1857), James F. Fagan (1828-1893; Mexican War), and Samuel B. Maxey (1825-1895; West Point 1846). As General Steele advanced into southwest Arkansas from Little Rock, the Confederates skirmished continuously with the Union column. On April 18, while at Camden, Steele learned of Banks' retreat to Grand Ecore. Five days later Steele received a dispatch from Banks that urged him to transport his command to the Red River Valley. In his reply, Steele did not commit to a retrograde or forward course of action. On April 25 a foraging expedition guarded by the 43rd Indiana, 36th Iowa, and 77th Ohio Regiments were annihilated at the Battle of Mark's Mill. The Rebels captured around 1,000 prisoners and an entire wagon train. This setback forced Steele to order a retreat back to the Arkansas River.

General Stirling Price

On April 30, sixty miles northeast of Camden, General Steele's column was crossing the Saline River at Jenkins' Ferry. Smith came up and attacked the rear guard with Churchill's and Walker's Divisions. Though he accomplished nothing and suffered 1,000 casualties in the process, Kirby Smith claimed a victory. Steele regained Little Rock on May 3. The following letter, from Taylor to Smith, speaks for itself.

> Head Quarters Dist Western La
> Near Alexandria June 5th 1864
> Genl. E. Kirby Smith
> Comdg Trans -Miss Dept

General

 I have the honor to acknowledge the receipt of your communication of May 26th.

 You are mistaken in supposing that my communications were intended as complaints. I have no complaints to make. My communications were statements of facts, necessary in my judgment, to the proper understanding of the campaign. I have not read the story of Gil Blas and the archbishop to so little purpose as not to know that truth is often considered "objectionable" by superiors, but I have not drawn the moral that it is therefore "improper" in subordinates to state it. The "regrets" I expressed at Mansfield on the 10th of May were drawn forth by your expressions of friendship for me, and assurances that you had given me all the support and assistance in your power. From no man living have I ever "begged" an indulgence for my acts whether personal or official.

So far from expressing my approbation of the movement of Walker, Parson[s][12] and Churchill against Steele, I stated to you on the 13th of May [April] at Mansfield, where you had come, because I had written to request permission to follow up my victories, that Steele must inevitably retreat. That every step he advanced insured his destruction. That the success of Maxey at Poison Spring [April 18] made assurance doubly sure, that the auxiliary columns must [torn] main one having been routed. You replied that Steele was [torn] "...to rashness," and that he would not hear of Bank's [sic] defeat, and insisted that the movement be made, proposing to select the troops from my command. It was then that I desired to accompany the troops, naming the Divisions above mentioned, and expressing my entire willingness to serve under Genl. Price, and give him all the assistance in my power. At the same time, I expressed my conviction that Steele would retreat, and understood from you, most distinctly, that in this event my movement northward would stop at once. My offer to serve under General Price drew from you many compliments, yet at that very time, as I subsequently learned, an order had been issued from your Head Quarters directing my chief q.m. [quartermaster] to send some captured wagons, as you intended to take the field. You permitted me to move forty miles to Shreveport, leave my command, and make all my arrangements for a campaign, which you had determined I was not to make. From the 13th to the night of the 15th I remained under this delusion, which you by a word could have dispelled. Arrived at Shreveport, I found myself deprived of my command, and that you had known for some time of Steele's retreat. I repeated the arguments against the movement, but was over ruled. In justification of your policy, you observed that it was an affair of a few days, and in answer to my inquiry, stated positively that Walker's Division was not to be removed from my command. You state that "the fruits of the victory of Mansfield were secured by the march of the column against Steele and that the complete success of the campaign was determined by his [torn] Jenkins Ferry."[13] After a series of engagements, Banks was driven into his works at Alexandria on the 28th of April _ two days before the fight at Jenkins Ferry, and on the day of that fight the river was completely blockaded below Alexandria against both transports and gunboats.[14] I am at a loss to conceive what connection the fruits of Mansfield have with the fight at Jenkins' Ferry. Sometime before this fight you directed Walker to report to me, but changed your mind and ordered him to Camden. Immediately after the fight, you ordered Walker and Churchill and Parsons to join me, which shows that even in your opinion the Red River was the theater of events.

At Jenkins' Ferry you attacked with your infantry alone. Nearly eight thousand men were not used at all _ either in the fight, or after it. This surplus of troops might well have enabled you to leave Walker with me. At Jenkin's Ferry you lost more heavily in killed and wounded than the enemy. This appears from the Official report of Steele __ confirmed by our officers who were present. You lost two pieces of artillery which the enemy did not carry off, because he had previously been deprived of means of transportation by Maxey and Fagan. He burned his ponton [pontoon bridge] for the same reason, and because after crossing the Saline he had no further use for it. He marched to Little

Rock after the fight entirely unmolested. He would unquestionably have gone there had the fight never occurred. We do not to day hold one more foot of Arkansas than if Jenkin's Ferry had never been, and we have a jaded army and one thousand less soldiers. How then was the complete success of the campaign determined by Steele's overthrow at Jenkin's Ferry? In truth the campaign as [torn] a hideous failure. The fruits of Mansfield have [torn] turned to dust and ashes. Louisiana from Natchitoches to the Gulf is a howling wilderness and her people are starving. Arkansas is probably as great a sufferer. In both States Abolition conventions are sitting to overthrow their system of labor. The remains of Bank's army have already gone to join Grant or Sherman, and may turn the scale against our over matched brethren in Virginia and Georgia. On the 24th May [April] the affair of Monettes [Monett's] Ferry took place.[15] The Federals admit that a few hours more delay would have led to the destruction of their army. Admiral Porter in his official report states this army to be thirty five thousand strong: The destruction of the army would have led of necessity to the destruction of the fleet. These advantages were all thrown away to the utter destruction of the best interests of the country, and in their place we have Jenkin's Ferry. Our material of war is exhausted, our men are broken down with long marches from Red River to Arkansas and from Arkansas back to the Red River. About a thousand of the best officers and men were sacrificed and no result attained. The roads to St. Louis and New Orleans should now be open to us. Your strategy has rivetted the fetters on both. At Jenkin's Ferry the tactical skill which carried Churchills, Parson's and Walker's Divisions, successively into the fight, after its predecessor had been driven back, and which failed to use at all, either in the fight, or in a pursuit, a force of over seven thousand cavalry, succeeded the strategy which declined the capture of Bank's army and Porter's fleet to march after the comparatively insignificant force of Steele. The same regard for duty which led me to throw myself between you and popular indignation, and quietly take the blame of your errors, impels me to tell you the truth, however "objectionable" to you. The grave errors you have committed in the recent campaign may be repeated if the unhappy consequences are not kept before you.

After the desire to serve my country, I have none more ardent than to be relieved from longer serving under your command.

Your obedient Servt
(signed) R. Taylor
Lt. Genl.

Hd. Qrs. T.M.D.
Shreveport June 10/64

official
John G. Meem jr.
A.A.D.G.

[*OR* XXXIV Series I Pt.1 p.546-548]

Smith complied with Taylor's request to be relieved from duty. Severe criticism and the course of subsequent events that summer prompted General Smith to compose for President Davis an extensive review of operations since he had assumed command of the department.

Shreveport La Aug 21st 1864

To the
President of the Confederate States
Richmond, Va.

Sir,

I have the honor to report that the General Commanding the Department has been sick for the last ten days with an attack of Acute Dysentery. Being very weak, he directs me to write you as follows:

I was very much surprised at receiving your telegram informing me that no order was on file directing the infantry of my command to cross the Mississippi river. Your telegram implies that I should have followed the enemy's troops lately operating in this Department; and that I was expected to so employ my force as to prevent him from reinforcing the armies of Grant & Sherman.

I beg leave to submit the following resume of events which have transpired since my arrival in this Department, as also my plans for the last campaign and the reasons why I was unable to detain longer the armies opposed to me.

Soon after I reached this Department, and before I could become fully acquainted with the character and position of the troops, the operations against Vicksburg & Port Hudson absorbed all attention. Banks' first raid__ in which he overpowered Gen. Taylor, at Camp Bisland __ swept through the most productive portion of Louisiana and caused the loss of our works controlling the navigation of the Red river and the Atchafalaya. This was subordinate to the investment of Port Hudson.

I made the best dispositions I could of my troops to aid in the relief of Vicksburg & Port Hudson.

Genl. Taylor with Walker's Division drawn from Arkansas, moved secretly up the Tensas in transports and landing a few miles from where Grant crossed the Mississippi river attempted a "coup de main" upon his communications. The enterprise succeeded but did not produce the important results anticipated. Grant having previously acquired a base of supply upon the Yazoo river.

Genl. Taylor now moved into the LaFourche country where he operated successfully in interrupting the navigation of the Mississippi river between Port Hudson & New Orleans. His position became perilous after the fall of Port Hudson and he recrossed Berwick's Bay.

Genl. Holmes reported that it was practicable for him to take Helena, and permission was given him to attempt it. The position was unsuccessfully assailed on the 4th of July. The enemy subsequently advanced, Genl. Price abandoned Little Rock and our forces fell back to Camden.

In the fall of 1862 [1863] the enemy made two attempts upon Texas. In the first, he landed at the mouth of the Sabine [River] where by the gallantry of a single company occupying a small fort he was beaten, two of his gunboats captured, and his design frustrated. He then concentrated a column at Berwick's Bay in the season of low water, intending to proceed along the coast drawing his supplies from its numerous inlets. I met this by placing Magruder's[16] small force at the Sabine holding Taylor on his flank. The

129

latter by avoiding a general engagement while he harassed and menaced his communications caused him to retire, when by a brilliant rear guard action, Genl. Green punished him severely. Banks then commenced his series of grand manaeuvres [*sic*] upon the whole length of the coast of Texas. Genl. Green's Division [of cavalry] was transferred to Galveston and the mouth of the Brazos [River] to meet a powerful force landed on Matagorda Peninsula. Throughout the winter Genl. Magruder was occupied in foiling the design of the enemy who numerically was greatly his superior.

This brings me to the point of time when the Spring campaign opened, and I beg you to remark the position of the opposing forces:___ My lines extended from the Indian Territory through Arkansas to the Mississippi, and down to the mouth of Red river; thence by the Atchafalaya to Berwick's Bay, and from thence by the coast to the Colorado. A small body of troops was engaged in observing the enemy at Brownsville. My forces were massed in three principal bodies, to wit; under Magruder opposite Banks on Matagorda peninsula, under Price confronting Steele, under Taylor holding the lower Red river.

The immense transportation of the enemy admitted of his taking the initiative with his entire force, at any moment, against any portion of my extended lines, while my limited transportation and the wide distances which separated my commands made it impossible to effect rapid concentrations or assume the offensive. My only alternative was to wait the developments of the enemy's plans, to retire before him until I effected my concentration, and to endeavour to manaeuvre to throw the principal mass if not my whole force against one of his columns.

As I wrote you in the fall of '63, I was satisfied that the lines of Red river would be the line of his principal attack because, _ as I then said _ when the water rose so as to admit his gun boats he could employ his powerful naval armament in conjunction with the advance of his infantry column. In accordance with this view, I had established last fall, subsistence and forage depots along the roads through the barren country between Texas and Red river, and between Camden and Natchitoches.

I omitted to state that I had been obliged to keep a force in the Indian Territory to hold in check several thousand men under Thayer,[17] at Fort Smith, and to cover Northern Texas, filled with disloyal people.

The water in the beginning of February being in a state to admit gun boats into Red river, Genl. Banks suddenly transferred his force to New Orleans & Berwicks' Bay, leaving but six or eight thousand men on Matagorda peninsula who subsequently joined him at Alexandria, after the retreat from Mansfield. Between the 21st & 26th Feby. I directed Genl Magruder to hold Green's Division in constant marching order. On the sixth of March the Division was ordered to move with dispatch to join Genl. Taylor who was embarrassed for want of cavalry. On the 12th March, a body of eight or ten thousand men composed of portions of the 16th & 17th Army Corps under Genl. A.J. Smith,[18] moved down from Vicksburg to Simmsport [Simmesport], and subsequently advanced with such celerity on Fort De Russy _[19] taking it in reverse _ that Genl. Taylor was not allowed time to concentrate and cover this most important work _ our only means of arresting the progress of the gunboats. The fall of the work, and the immediate movement of the enemy, by means of his transports to Alexandria, placed Genl. Taylor in a very embarrassing situation. He extricated himself with his characteristic tact by a march of seventy miles through the pine woods.

Banks now pressed forward from Berwicks' Bay by the line of the Teche, and by the aid of Steamers, both on the Mississippi & Red rivers, concentrated at Alexandria a force of thirty thousand men, supported by the most powerful naval armament ever employed on a river.

As soon as I had received intelligence of the debarkation of the enemy at Simmsport, I ordered Genl. Price to dispatch his entire infantry to Shreveport, and Genl. Maxey to move towards Price, and, when Steele advanced to join Price with his whole command, Indians included.

The cavalry East of the Washita [River] was directed to fall back towards Natchitoches and subsequently to oppose, as far as possible, the advance of the enemy's fleet. It was under command of Genl. Liddell. All disposable infantry detachments in Texas were directed on Marshall; and although the enemy still had a force of several thousand on the coast, I reduced the number of men holding the defences [*sic*] to an absolute minimum. Genl. Magruder's field report shows that but 2,300 men were left in the entire District of Texas. Except these, every effective soldier in the Department was put in front of Steele or in support of Taylor. When this was accomplished, the disparity of numbers was frightful. Taylor had at Mansfield, after the junction of Green, eleven thousand effectives, with five thousand infantry from Price's army, in one day's march of him, at Kea[t]chie. Price, with six or eight thousand cavalry, was engaged in impeding the advance of Steele whose column did not number less than fifteen thousand of all arms. Banks pushed on to Natchitoches. It was expected he would be detained there several days in accumulating supplies. Steele on the Little Missouri, and Banks at Natchitoches were either but about one hundred miles from Shreveport or Marshall. The character of the country did not admit of their forming a junction above Natchitoches, and if they advanced equally I hope by refusing one to fight the other with my whole force. It seemed probable at this time that Steele would come up first. When he reached Prairie Dan [d'Ann] two routes were open to him _ the one to Marshall, the river crossing at Fulton; the other direct to Shreveport. I consequently held Price's infantry a few days at Shreveport when Steele's hesitation and the reports of the advance of Banks' cavalry caused me to move it to Keachi, a point twenty miles in rear of Mansfield, on the road where it divides to go to Marshall and Shreveport. It was directed to report to Genl. Taylor. I now visited and conferred with Genl. Taylor. Neither believed that Banks could yet advance his infantry across the barren country stretching between Natchitoches and Mansfield. I returned to Shreveport and wrote to Genl. Taylor, instructing him to choose a position in which to fight, and move forward a reconnoisance [*sic*] in force and compel the enemy to display his infantry, to notify me as soon as he had done so, and I would join him in the front. I hoped to derive an element of "morale" from the arrival of Churchill's command and my own presence at the moment of action.

The reconnoissance was converted into a decisive engagement with the advance Corps of the enemy (a portion of the 13th & his Cavalry) and by the rare intrepidity of Mouton's Division resulted in a complete victory over the forces engaged. Genl. Taylor pushed forward his troops in pursuit, met, engaged, and repulsed the 19th Corps which was hastening to the support of the 13th Corps. Price's infantry came up from Keachi that night. The next morning our whole army advanced & found the enemy in position at Pleasant Hill. Our troops attacked with vigor and at first with success, but by superiority of numbers were finally repulsed and thrown into confusion. The Missouri & Arkansas troops with a Brigade of Walker's division were broken & scattered. The enemy recovered cannon which we had captured, and two of our pieces were left in his hands. To my great relief, I found in the morning that the enemy had fallen back during the night. He continued his retreat to Grand Ecore where he intrenched [*sic*] himself, and remained until the return of his fleet and its passage over the bars, made especially difficult this season by the unusual fall of the river.

The question may be asked why the enemy was not pursued at once? I answer, because our troops were completely paraliysed [*sic*] by the repulse at Pleasant Hill, and the Cavalry, worn by the long march from Texas, had been constantly engaged for three days almost without food or forage.

Before we could reorganize at Mansfield, and get into condition to advance over the fifty five miles of wilderness which separated the armies, the enemy was reinforced and intrenched at Grand Ecore. If we could not whip him at Pleasant Hill in a fair fight, it would have been madness to attack him at Grand Ecore in his intrenchments supported by a formidable fleet of gunboats. No sustained operations for dislodging him could be undertaken because it was impossible to transport supplies for the entire army from Shreveport, distant one hundred miles. The enemy held possession of the river until they evacuated Grand Ecore. A large steamboat which had been sunk in the narrowest part of the channel for the purpose of obstructing the passage upwards of his fleet had to be removed before the river could again be used.   Here occurred the most perplexing moment of the campaign for me. Should I with the bulk of my forces, pursue Banks until he left the Red river valley; or should I march against Steele who threatened my Depots & Work Shops __ the loss of which would well nigh have closed operations in this Department? I determined upon the latter, and for the following reasons:_

I have stated that my original plan was, if possible, to mass my whole force against a single column of the enemy. This had been done successfully against Banks. Steele was still slowly advancing from the Little Missouri to the Prairie Dan. I deemed it imprudent to follow Banks below Grand Ecore, and leave Steele so near Shreveport. Were I able to throw Banks across the Atchafalaya, the high water of that stream would arrest my further progress. If Red river continued to fall, it seemed probable that Banks would be compelled to withdraw to Alexandria. It was hoped that the Falls would detain him there until we could finish Steele, when the entire force of the Department would be free to operate against him.

I confidently hoped that if I could reach Steele with my infantry to beat him at a distance from his Depot ["and" lined out] in a poor country ["where" lined out] and with my large cavalry force destroy his army. The prize would have been the Arkansas valley and the fortifications of Little Rock _ now too strong to be taken by either siege or assault with any force at my command. By the time my infantry reached Shreveport, Steele had moved by his left flank to Camden. He held the fortifications we had constructed there. They were strong. I could not think of allowing Steele time to establish himself finally in Camden. I moved upon the place. The enemy abandoned it. I pursued, overtook and beat him at the Saline. I failed to accomplish what I had reasonably hoped for, but succeeded in driving Steele from the valley of the Wachita [Washita]. with signal loss of men and material, and left myself free to move my entire force to the support of Taylor.

After the enemy left Grand Ecore, Genl. Taylor attacked his rear at Cloutierville, while a part of his force held his front in check at Monette's Ferry. Genl. Taylor's force was too weak to warrant the hope that he could successfully impede the march of Banks' column. After the latter reached Alexandria, Taylor transferred a part of his command to the river below Alexandria, and with unparralled [*sic*] audacity and great ability so operated on the enemy's gun boats and transports as to compel him, with a force quadruple his own, to abandon that important position. A temporary rise in Red river enabled Admiral Porter to get his fleet over the Falls. Had he delayed but one week longer our whole infantry would have been with Taylor.

Some idea may be formed of the character of our operations here when it is stated that, Walker's Division, from the opening of the campaign at Simmsport to the time of its arrival at Alexandria _ a period of about two months _ marched seven hundred miles and fought three pitched battles.

Information having been received that A.J. Smith's command was proceeding up the Mississippi river, I threw Marmaduke across from Camden to dispute its progress. He attacked the fleet, disabled or destroyed three of its boats, compelled it to halt and land its infantry which he engaged for several hours. Here ends the campaign in which, with a force of twenty five thousand men all told, _ in the entire department,[20] I drove back ["from" lined out] whence they came armies sixty thousand strong, supported by an enormous fleet, inflicting immense loss in both men and material. It is not difficult to understand, that at its close, my forces required rest and reorganization. Banks' or rather Canby's[21] army remained for sometime at Morganza [Louisiana], a strongly fortified position, & occupied at this time by a large force. The Atchafalaya still affording sufficient water for the use of gunboats, no operations could be undertaken across that stream.

You say that I should have followed the movements of the enemy. This was simply impossible. The 19th Army Corps was sent to New York, or Washington. The portion of the 16th & 17th Corps' under A.J. Smith, were withdrawn to Memphis _ delayed, as I have said, for a few days by Marmaduke _ while the 13th Corps was dissolved[22] by Mr. Lincoln: thus leaving in Louisiana, as far as we could ascertain the reenlisted men of the 13th Corps, and the only Corps D'Afrique [colored troops].

I should have mentioned that by a captured dispatch it was ascertained that the command of A. J. Smith, received on the 5th April, orders to immediately join Sherman, at Vicksburg. The operations of Taylor on Red River, and Marmaduke on the Mississippi, prevented Smith from executing this movement until the middle of June, or for a period of more than sixty days. I had not sufficient reason to believe that there remained a large force disposable for an attack on Mobile. How could I employ my command so as to attract a large force from either Sherman or Grant, or prevent a movement on Mobile? First, no serious demonstration could be made on New Orleans because of the Mississippi river. Any operations in the LaFourche country would necessarily be hazardous with the enemy at Morganza _ would have been barren of military results _ would have ravaged a country from which we should have been obliged to withdraw whenever the waters rose.

In the second place, if I had seized a point on the Mississippi river with the view of causing the enemy to send a large force to dislodge me, the attempt would have failed unless I had guns sufficiently heavy to contend with Iron clads. Had I had these, my entire army would have been committed to their defence, and the ultimate result would probably have been a repetition of the Vicksburg & Port Hudson affairs.

There remained a third plan, viz: _ To push a large Cavalry force into Missouri, and to support the movement by occupying my infantry in operations against Steele. Should he weaken himself to defend St. Louis, I might possibly take his works at Little Rock, Pine Bluff and Devall's Bluff, and recover the state of Arkansas. If he proved too strong for me, I would be at hand to help Price extricate himself in case of failure or disaster. This plan I was putting in execution, and had it not been for the telegrams of Genls. Bragg & [S.D.] Lee, herewith enclosed, my infantry would have been now in the Arkansas valley and Price would have been entering Missouri.

I have written thus at length in advance of my report _ delayed by being unable to get the reports of my subordinate commanders _ because I learn that my policy and plans have been much discussed at Richmond, and that it has been charged that, but for my errors much more important results would have been achieved. In this connection, I have only to remark that I have honestly done what appeared to me to be right and proper. I claim that my combinations have resulted in great success, and beg to doubt whether more would have been accomplished under a different system of operations.

Certain it is, that my heart overflowed with thankfulness when I realized the fact that the valor and good conduct of the officers and men of my command had enabled me to oppose and overcome the vast armies moving against me.

I care not for the censure of those who allege that I have exhibited a want of capacity. You, Mr. President, have honored me with your confidence of which I am proud. I beg if at any time I lose this, that you will relieve me of the weighty responsibilities with which I am now entrusted. I will always gladly serve in any other field or position to which you may fit to assign me.

> I am very respectfully,
> Your obt. svt.
> S, A, Smith
> Med Director Genl Hosps
> Dep of Trans Miss

[*OR* XLIX Series I Pt. 1 p.113-117]

General Smith's seventeen page apology mentions a contemplated move into Missouri with St. Louis as the ultimate objective. General Price carried out this operation with his cavalry corps in the Fall. It accomplished little and ended in disaster.

> Army Head Quarters Camp 60
> Boons b'ro Washn County Ark's
> 3d Nov. 1864

Col. S.S. Anderson
Asst. Adjt. Genl.

I have the honor to report my arrival at this point, being unable from the number of forces brought against me to maintain my Column in Missouri, encumbered as it was by unarmed men and undisciplined recruits.

Entering the State of Missouri [on September 19] from the South east in Ripley County, I marched northward, in three Columns, reuniting at Fredericktown; then moved on, and Carried Irontown & Pilot Knob, making a full reconai[ss]ance as far as St. Louis County, destroying the Iron mountain R.R. and S.W. Branch of the Pacific R_ then turned north west striking the Pacific R.R. at Franklin; from that the R.R. was destroyed at various points westward and the Crossings of the merrinral [Meramee] and Morran [Moreau] rivers; forced until the Enemy were driven into their works at Jefferson City: From positive information received of the forces there, my troops were drawn off and moved on Boonville where a Small force surrendered, thence west towards Lexington and Sedalia and Capturing both; at Lexington I met Genl. Blaunt's[23] force of Mo. Kansas & Calarado [Colorado] troops and drove them back towards Independence, they Contesting the Crossing of the [Big] Blue [River]; here, from intercepted dispatches and other Sources _ I learned that a heavy force under Generals A.J. Smith, McNeil,[24] Sannders [Colonel John P. Sanderson] and others were establishing their Lines about thirty miles South, and parallel to our line of march and the Missouri river, while Genl. Rasecrans[25] with a heavy Column of Infantry in all about thirty thousand Strong were following as fast as the impaired Condition of the roads would admit, and I was obliged after forcing the Enemy into Westport, to fall back Southward and, they were then enabled to mass their forces on my Column, and, when south of the Osage [River], by the rapidity of their marches, were enabled to come Suddenly upon my rear and Strike a Severe blow, Capturing Several pieces of artillery and between three and four hundred prisoners including Generals Marmaduke and Cabell,[26] and Cols. [W.F.] Slemons & [Lee] Crandall. The Enemy followed as far as Newtonia, where they were Signally repulsed and driven back, Since which time they have not been heard from as advancing.

The details of this expedition with Casualties will be given in a future report in full; an [on] account of the broken down Condition of the Stock, and Scarcity of forage I will divided the Command, Crossing the River at different points.

> Very Respectfullly
> Your Obt. Servt.
> Sterling Price
> Maj Genl. Comdg.

[*OR* XLI Series I Pt.1 p.623,624]

The Confederate defeat at the Battle of Westport on October 23, in terms of the numbers engaged, was the largest battle fought west of the Mississippi River. Sterling Price's report on the raid neglected to mention that the campaign had cost him half his men and all his cannon. General Price, "having never been on a cavalry raid, lacked that ability to judge the potential of his men and horses...he had concentrated on problems of supply and had been reluctant to live off the country. Finally, using tactics that were natural for an infantry commander, he had undertaken at Westport a full scale battle with a superior Union army...As the commanding general of the Department who chose Price to lead the operation, Edmund Kirby Smith must shoulder final responsibilty for the blunders that brought defeat and shattered dreams."[27]

Westport ended significant military action in the Trans-Mississippi Department. At the beginning of his report, General Smith referred to a telegram he had received from President Davis.

South Western Telegraph Company

Clinton Miss.   August 9 1864

By Telegraph from Richmond Va. August 8 1864
To S.A. Chipley
For Genl. E.K. Smith

Your telegram of 30th July 1864 is received and after inquiry can find no record of a telegraph ordering you to send Genl. Taylor and Infantry from Trans -Miss. Department across the Mississippi river. No such order was given by me, though propositions, to follow enemy's movements from your Department were referred to your discretion in terms which implied the expectation you would do all which was consistent with the desires of you position. You had not communicated the purpose to commence offensive operations in Arkansas and Missouri, and no indications of it had reached me.

I do not perceive how the success of a movement, the arrangement for which you say had been perfected, could depend on Infantry which was below the lower Red river. Be that as it may, you must expect frequent diversity of views, unless fuller information is given.

I directed Genl. S. D. Lee to keep you informed, so as having co intelligence, there might be the more effective co operation :_ if our fources [sic] succeed on the east side they will make easy the plan for the west side of the Mississippi :_ if our forces on the west side of the river should allow the enemy to leave that section and, by concentrating, defeat those on the east side, your projected campaign could not fail to end in disaster.

This was so obvious that I expected you to act, without waiting for orders, so as to counteract the movements he was reported to be making with troops that you had lately defeated.

Your recommendation [for promotion to lieutenant general] in regard to Genl Buckner, has been referred to [the] War Department.

(Signed) Jefferson Davis _

Hd Qr Trans Miss. Dept
Shreveport La.   Official
                                   H.P.Pratt
                                   A.A.Genl.

[*OR* XLI Series I Pt.1 p.102]

South Western Telegraph Company
Clinton Miss. August 9th 1864
By Telegraph from Richmond Va. August 8th 1864
To S. A. Shipley
For Genl. E. K. Smith

Your telegram of 30th July 18..
is received and after inquiry can find no record
of a telegraph ordering you to send Genl. Taylor an
Infantry from Trans-Miss. Department across the
Mississippi river. No such order was ever given
by me, though propositions, to follow enemy's move
-ments from your Department were referred to your
discretion in terms which implied the expectation
you would do all which was consistent with the
desires of your position. You had not communicated
the purpose to commence offensive operations in Ar-
-kansas and Missouri, and no indications of it
had reached me.

I do not now perceive how the success of a movement, the arrangement
for which you say had been perfected, could depend upon difference
which was below the lower Red river. Be that as it may,
you must expect frequent diversity of views, unless fuller
information is given.

I directed Genl. S. D. Lee to keep you informed, so as
having Co-intelligence, there might be the more effective
Co-operation:— if our forces succeed on the east side,
they will make easy the plan for the west side of the
Mississippi:— if our forces on the west side of the river
should allow the enemy to leave that section and, by
concentrating, defeat those on the east side, your projected

Telegram from President Davis to General Kirby Smith (2 pages)

137

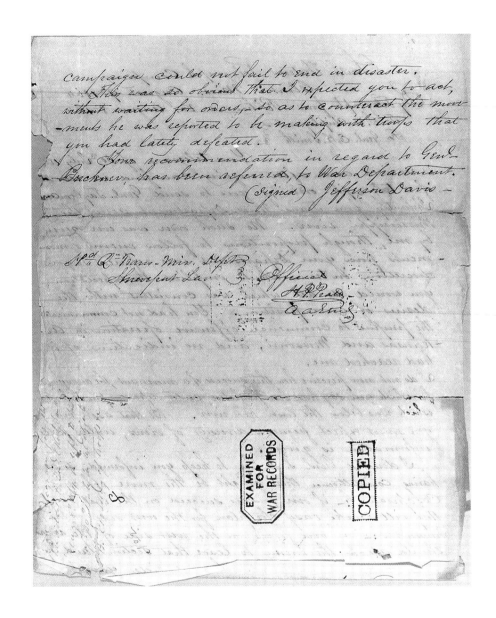

campaign could not fail to end in disaster.

This was so obvious that I expected you to act, without waiting for orders, so as to counteract the movements he was reported to be making with troops that you had lately defeated.

Your recommendation in regard to Genl. Buckner, has been referred to War Department.

(Signed) Jefferson Davis —

President Davis, in his customary style, had issued indirect orders to General Smith for direct action on July 16.[28] He feared that Union forces withdrawn from Louisiana would move on Mobile. A week later, the President's military advisor, General Bragg, directed Taylor to cross the Mississippi with his infantry corps, then replace Lieutenant General Stephen D. Lee (1833-1908; West Point 1854) as commander of the Department of East Louisiana, Mississippi, and Alabama. Bragg was unaware that Taylor had been relieved. Taylor, at Natchitoches with his family, received orders from Smith on July 28 to resume command of the District of West Louisiana, and take charge of the crossing operation. The attempt to again cross infantry from the Trans-Mississippi Department into the state of Mississippi produced a bureaucratic quarrel along with a blizzard of communications between Taylor and Smith. Included in their correspondence were the following two letters.

Alexandria, August 8th. 1864.

General,

Your communication of the 7th inst. were [*sic*] received last night. The importance of expedition in crossing the Infantry has fully impressed itself upon me, but the means of effecting it and the necessary co operation of other forces within this [district] are beyond my control.

On the 10th. of June, I was relieved from the command of Western Louisiana and ordered by you to Natchitoches "to await the pleasure of the Confederate States," on the 18th. [28th] of July, six weeks after I was relieved by you, the order for me to cross the river and assume command of the Department of Miss. & E. La. was issued from the War Dept. evidently under the belief that I was in command of the District of Western La. or commanding a Corps_ Your order directing me take command of the two Infantry Divisions reached me at Natchitoches on the 28th of July_ From the date of my being relieved until the receipt of these orders, I had no means of ascertaining the disposition of our own or the enemy's forces, on or near the Miss. river, the points at which the enemy's gun-boats were lying and such other necessary facts as would enable me at once to fix upon suitable places for crossing. Although the order from the War Dept. contemplated that I was in command, I can perceive nothing therein which instructs that the troops should "cross under my order" or that I "should conduct the operation of crossing in person" so long as the command is in this Department & it is subject to your orders, and without dispositions made by you as commanding General, I am powerless to effect anything.__ Simply to cross the men is but a portion of the movement; to submit [subsist] and transport them to localities where their presence and services are needed, involve the most important features. There is but one railroad in the State of Mississippi in use by our authorities and that lies east of Pearl river, its western terminus being quite a hundred miles from the Mississippi. While Lt. Genl. Lee states that he will establish depots of supplies, such depots can only be available if they are convenient to the points of crossing, and places previously selected would be liable to interference by the enemy at the very moment when the movement to a particular point was about to be undertaken, and this render an immediate change necessary; co-operation between the two sides of the river is therefore of the highest importance and a full understanding with Gen'l Lee can alone ensure the establishment of supplies at convenient and accessible localities. I had the honor to submit to you several days ago, with an endorsement of my entire approval thereof, the plan of Lt. Col. [Henry T.] Douglas, which I consider the most practicable one which can be adopted_ I have not heard from you on that subject. In accordance with your instructions, I furnished you, on the 28th of July, with the names of the Staff Officers, whom I desired to report to me_ only last night I received your answer, stating that a portion of these named and needed by me, should be assigned. I have been without Staff Officers, necessary to enable me to make even the requisite preliminary arrangements, and but for the kindness of Maj. Gen'l. Walker, who has allowed me to use a portion of his staff, I should have been entirely without any such assistance. Major [Alexander H.] Mason, my former chief Commissary, whose services are almost indispensable, and upon which I relied, you refused to allow me, no other Commissary is assigned me, and none could be so useful as this officer. Col. [J.L.] Brent also, who has been on my Staff for two years, and for whom I made application is withheld. Both these officers share my earnest desire to have them ordered to report to me. If the troops are to be used in the crisis to which you allude in your letter of yesterday, and if Atlanta is the "scene of action" to which you refer, the distance to be accomplished, even after they cross the river, would render it necessary for adequate arrangements to be made on the other side of the Mississippi as well as on this, to ensure rapidity of movement and preserve the efficiency of the men, so that they could arrive in time and in condition for the performance of the services required of them. With this view, therefore I applied, in a former communication, for permission to cross at once to the other side, where I could assume command of the Department as directed by the War Department, and hasten all the necessary arrangements. This permission having been refused by you, I am without knowledge of the location and number of our forces on the other side and as to the assistance they can give to a column of Infantry.___ For the reasons stated: the troops whose co-operation is necessary to ensure the success of the movement, being beyond my control, the plan of crossing being devised by yourself, the necessary provisions for subsistance [*sic*] and transportation, when the troops do cross, not being made and being myself powerless under your instructions, to remedy these vital deficiencies, I deem it proper to state to you, that while I shall to the best of my ability, carry out the instructions, contained in your communication of yesterday, I do not deem myself responsible for the failure or success of the undertaking you direct___

	Very Respectfully
	Your ob't Servt.
Gen'l E. Kirby Smith	(Signed) R. Taylor
Com'd'g Dept. of Trans-Miss.	Lieu't Gen'l.
Head Qrs. Trans Miss. Dept.	Official
Shreveport La. 1st Sept. 1864	H.P.Pratt
	A.A.Gen'l.

[*OR* XLI Series I Pt.1 p.100-102]

The following is Smith's reply to General Taylor.

Head Quarters Trans Miss Dept.
Shreveport La. Aug. 11th. 1864.

General,

I have the honor to acknowledge the receipt of your communication of the 8th inst. My letter written to you in Alexandria expresses clearly my views and the necessity for crossing immediately, the Miss, with the troops under your command The enclosed copies of dispatches from Genl's Maury[29] and Liddell are additional evidences of this necessity. The plan submitted and approved by your letter of August 8th for bridging the Miss. is simply impracticable and visionary. It necessitates the concentration of Engineer troops from Arkansas and Texas, virtually the establishment of a navy-yard at Shreveport, and building of boats. It makes requisition of material on the city of Houston, Texas which in all probability will have to be imported. Under the most favorable circumstances, it requires preparations, the collection of material, and construction, that would necessitate the delay of at least two months, and might fairly convey the impression that we were endeavoring to evade the order directing the crossing of the troops. You, certainly could not have carefully examined the plan proposed or you would not have approved and recommended a course which detains indefinitely the troops here, whilst the campaign East of the Miss. in which they were to participate has already reached a crisis In my letter of July 31st. the whole disposable force of the district was placed under your control, through Gen'l Walker its commander, the points and mode of crossing were left to you own judgment. It was only suggested that instead of sending the Cavalry on a distant expedition towards New Orleans, they with Artillery, should be used to cover the crossing by holding points above and below the point selected. In my letter of the 31st. I authorized you to send members of your staff east of the Miss. for the purpose of obtaining information and making provisions for your troops. Your experience on the Mississippi, your knowledge of the country and your personal interest in the success of the movement, make you the proper officer to command. Even had the dispatches from the War Dept. not so directed. The list of staff officers furnished by you, whom you desired might accompany you east of the river, was carefully considered by me in the intention of being liberal and with the desire of complying with your wishes. But two on the list were objected to: Maj. Mason and Col. Brent, their services are too indispensably necessary, without inflicting serious injury upon the interest of the District of West Louisiana. As an evidence of my liberality, I made no objection to either of the five Adjutants General whose names were on that list, viz: Col. [William M.] Levy, Maj. [Eustace] Surget, Captain [Charles Le D.] Elgin [Elgee], Captain [A.H.] May, and Captain [Andrew J.] Watts [Watt]. Gen'l S D. Lee has, I believe, gone to Atlanta The enclosed copies of dispatches would indicate that Gen'l Maury commands the Dept. and is besieged at Mobile. Gen'l Liddell, immediately commanding the District opposite to you, is at Clinton. You can communicate with him and obtain his co operation_ I again urge upon you the necessity of promptly crossing the force under your command_ at least the attempt should be made_ If there is any unnecessary delay, the authorities at Richmond can judge where the fault lies and upon whom the responsibility rests

I am General
Very Respectfully &c
(Signed) E. Kirby Smith

Lt. Gen'l R. Taylor
Comd'g. &c

Official
H.P.Pratt
A.A.Gen'l.

[*OR* XLI Series I Pt.1 p.103,104]

Taylor crossed the Mississippi with his body servant Tom Strother at the end of August. Lee[30] took command of a corps in the Army of Tennessee in July. For a brief period in early 1865, Taylor commanded the shattered Army of Tennessee. As late as January 31, 1865, less than ten weeks before Lee's surrender at Appomattox Court House, President Davis expressed to Smith the hope that troops could cross the river to assist the embattled Confederacy in the east. Mobile fell to General Canby on April 12, 1865, and by the end of the month, Taylor realized further resistance was hopeless. He surrendered his department to Canby on May 8 at Citronelle, Alabama. Smith surrendered the Trans-Mississippi Department to Canby on May 26, which ended the war. Thus, one may add E. Kirby Smith to the list of generals who were primarily responsible for the Confederacy's demise; the list also includes Braxton Bragg, Joe Johnston, John Pemberton, and Leonidas Polk.

5

ATLANTA TO NASHVILLE

General Hardee assumed temporary command of the Army of Tennessee on December 2, 1863. While he strengthened the army's defensive position about Dalton, Georgia, and reorganized its artillery, President Davis settled the problem of finding a permanent replacement for the disgraced Bragg. General Beauregard, in command of the coastal defenses of Georgia and South Carolina, received brief consideration. Davis soon discarded his name and decided to appoint General Johnston.

The choice of Johnston, personally painful for Davis to make, was the correct decision politically. Generals Lee and Polk, as well as the Secretary of War supported him. The anti-Davis faction of the government welcomed the idea as a way to embarrass the president, who truly abhorred Johnston.

Relations between Davis and Johnston had deteriorated during the Vicksburg Campaign. Just before General Pemberton's army had become besieged on May 18, 1863, General Johnston had arrived at Jackson to coordinate action in Mississippi. Johnston had quickly abandoned the state capital and retreated away from Vicksburg. He offered no help, only advice to Pemberton. Reinforcements that reached Johnston were assembled into the "Army of Relief." By the beginning of June, the combined strength of Pemberton's and Johnston's armies amounted to 58,000 men in comparison to Grant's 51,000. Instead of advancing to threaten Grant's lines around Vicksburg, "Johnston procrasti-

143

nated. He saw nothing but difficulties wherever he turned. To save Mississippi was to lose Tennessee, and to save Port Hudson was to lose Mississippi. While he meditated on his dilemma, thousands of reinforcements poured down the Mississippi to join Grant, redressing the balance of power in favor of the Union."[1]

In response to Johnston's telegrams that implied inaction, President Davis and Secretary of War James A. Seddon urged Johnston to do something. Davis even contemplated going to Mississippi to take charge himself but poor health prevented the journey. Evidence indicates that Grant would have turned on Johnston if the Army of Relief had assumed an offensive posture, which would have allowed Pemberton's army to escape from the trap. Even if Vicksburg had fallen, 25,000 Confederate soldiers would have remained in the field.

Johnston's army did not advance toward Vicksburg until July 1. Three days later, Vicksburg surrendered and the Army of Relief retired to Jackson. President Davis blamed Johnston more than Pemberton for the loss of Vicksburg which increased the hard feelings between them. In the following document, President Davis attempted to establish a sympathetic working relationship with his trying subordinate.

General John Clifford Pemberton

Richmond, Dec. 23d 1863.

Gen'l J.E. Johnston,
Comdg. &c., Dalton, Ga.

General:_____ This addressed under the supposition that you have arrived at Dalton and have assumed command of the forces at that place. The intelligence recently received respecting the condition of that army is encouraging, and induces me to hope that you will soon be able to commence active operations against the enemy.

The reports concerning the battle at Missionary Ridge show that our loss in killed and wounded was not great [2,521], and that the reverse sustained is not attributable to any general demoralization or reluctance to encounter the opposing army. The brilliant stand [November 26] made by the rear guard at Ringgold [Gap] sustains this belief.

In a letter written to me soon after the battle, General Bragg expressed his unshaken confidence in the courage and morale of the troops. He says: "We can redeem the past. Let us concentrate all our available men, unite them with this gallant little army, still full of zeal and burning to redeem its lost character and prestige, hurl the whole upon the enemy and crush him in his power and his glory. I believe it practicable, and trust I may be allowed to participate in the struggle which may restore to us the character, the prestige, and the country we have just lost. This will give us confidence and restore hope to the country and the army whilst it will do what is more important, give us subsistence without which I do not see how we are to remain united."

The official reports made to my Aide de Camp, Colonel [Joseph C.] Ives, who has just returned from Dalton, presented a not unfavorable view of the material of the command. The Chief of Ordnance reported that, notwithstanding the abandonment of a considerable number of guns during the battle, there were still on hand, owing to the previous large captures by our troops, as many batteries as were proportionate to the strength of the army, well supplied with horses and equipments [and] that a large reserve of small arms was in store at readily accessible points, and that the supply of ammunition was abundant.

Comparatively few wagons and ambulances had been lost and sufficient remained for transportation purposes if an equal distribution were made through the different corps. The teams appeared to be generally in fair condition. The troops were tolerably provided with clothing, and a heavy invoice of blankets and shoes daily expected.

The returns from the Commissary Department showed that there were thirty days provisions on hand.

Stragglers and convalescents were rapidly coming in, and the morning reports exhibited an effective total that, added to the two brigades last sent from Mississippi and the cavalry sent back by Longstreet, would furnish a force perhaps exceeding in number that actually engaged in any battle on the Confederate side during the present war. Gen'l Hardee telegraphed to me on the 11th inst.: "The army is in good spirits, the artillery reorganised [*sic*] and equip[p]ed, and we are ready to fight."

The effective condition of your new command, as thus reported to me, is a matter of much congratulation, and I assure you that nothing shall be wanting on the part of the Government to aid you in your efforts to regain possession of the territory from which we have been driven. You will not need to have it suggested that the imperative demand for

145

prompt and vigorous action arises not only from the importance of restoring the prestige of the army and averting the dispiriting and injurious results that must attend a season of inactivity, but from the necessity of reoccupying the country upon the supplies of which the proper subsistence of our armies materially depends.

Of the immediate measures to be adopted in attaining this end, the full of importance of which I am sure you appreciate, you must be the best judge ["of the after due" lined out] after due inquiry and consideration on the spot shall have matured an opinion. It is my desire that you should communicate fully and freely with me concerning your proposed plan of action, that all the assistance and cooperation may be most advantageously afforded to you that it is in the power of the Government to render.

Trusting that your health may be preserved, and that the arduous and responsible duties you have undertaken may be successfully accomplished, I remain

Very respectfully & truly yours
(Signed) Jeffn. Davis

[*OR* XXXI Series I Pt.3 p.856]

When General Johnston joined his command on December 27, the Army of Tennessee numbered 36,017 men. Davis' statement concerning the army's strength is absurd and reflects ignorance of its true condition. General Johnston, offended and puzzled by the optimistic opinion from Richmond, replied to Davis on January 2. "Having been here but six days, during four of which it rained heavily, I have not been able to observe the condition of the army. I judge, however, from the language of the general officers, that it has not entirely recovered its confidence, and that its discipline is not so thorough as it was last spring....I can see no other mode of taking the offensive here, than to beat the enemy when he advances, and then move forward."[2]

Soldiers in the Army of Tennessee were enthusiastic about General Johnston. He gave amnesty to deserters and instituted a policy of granting furloughs that increased the morale of his men, who began to receive adequate provisions and clothing. As part of a general reorganization, Johnston restored Cheatham's old division in February. The grateful Tennessean's paraded to Johnston's headquarters with a band to display their appreciation for him. Johnston emerged from the building with Cheatham, who patted his diminutive commander on his balding head and said: "Boys, this is Old Joe."[3] Along with Pat Cleburne's crack division, which had defended Ringgold Gap, Frank Cheatham's Division constituted the Army of Tennessee's heart and soul.

At the end of February, John Bell Hood, a presidential favorite, took over the corps (Beckinridge's) temporarily commanded by General Hindman. Hood had been elevated to the rank of lieutenant general on February 1. As recorded in the following letter from presidential aide Colonel William M. Browne, Hindman resented the change.

Feb. 14. 1864

My dear Mr. President

By this day's mail send you a detailed report of my observations & inquiry during my visit to the A. of Tenn.

I saw Genl. Johnston very often. He was exceedingly courteous, and evidently desired to be cordial & communicative. On the main point _ a plan for the future _ he was silent although I gave him many opportunities to speak freely. I infer from all he said that he believes that to attack the enemy at or near Chattanooga as impossible & that the only thing to do is to enter E. Tenn. & operate from there. He evidently thinks his present force insufficient, & I think you may look for a demand for reinforcements any day to be drawn from the coast. The defence of the latter to be left to militia or State Guards to be received by requisition on the Governors of States.

The general seems very proud of his army, and the army well contented with him; but he does not seem to be sufficiently impressed with the importance of getting ready to strike before the enemy is prepared to assume the offensive; nor does he seem to have any well matured plan of operations. Beyond the hint of advancing on E. Tenn. I could gather nothing, and Genls. Hardee & Hindman are equally in the dark.

Genl. J works hard, has cordial relations with his officers, and to them appears more hopeful, & more cheerful than they have ever seen him. He is very anxious that his army should be divided into 3 corps, "that it may be organized as it is to fight.", & he also lays stress on the appt. of E.P. Alexander[4] as Brig. Genl. & his appointment to the command of the Artillery of his army.

Genl. Hindman is very sore at the reported appointment of Genl. Hood to the command of the corps now under him He threatens to resign, Hood being his junior. Genl. Hardee thinks very highly of Hindman and will as[s]ert every means to keep him quiet.

On the whole, Mr. President I am much encouraged by my visit to the army. It is in magnificent order & spirits, cheered loudly for you wherever I went as if to ask me to report to you how devoted they are to your self personally. I am suffering very much from bronchitis caused by exposure on the cars; I hope to be better & able to go about in a day or two.

> With much respect & esteem
> I am, MrPresident
> yr friend &obt. Sert
> Wm M Browne

General Hood, who had lost the use of his left hand from shell fragments at Gettysburg, had spent the winter recovering from the amputation of his right leg at Chickamauga. Regarded by Richmond society as a hero, he frequently accompanied the president. By promoting Hood and assigning him to the Army of Tennessee, "Davis evidently sought to establish a major conduit of information, as well as an indirect measure of control over Johnston's operations...Much as a covert but highly placed watchdog, Hood might warn the administration of Johnston's failure to act, and relate the true circumstances of the army's condition and capabilities. It was an important assignment in a most crucial area. It was also highly unethical and improper."[5]

In an interview with Johnston, Hood proposed a plan for offensive operations. By drawing reinforcements from Mississippi and then uniting with Longstreet, whose corps was wintering at Greenville, Tennessee, Hood reasoned that the Confederates could force the Federals to retreat from Knoxville or defeat them if they chose to give battle. "But he found no responsive chord in Johnston. That commander, who seemed allergic to any offensive program, was quick to point out, along with other real or supposed difficulties, his own unfamiliarity with the country where the campaign would be waged."[6]

By the beginning of May, the Army of Tennessee numbered 53,859 men. Opposed to it was an army group of 110,123 men under the overall command of General Sherman. General Thomas commanded the Army of the Cumberland (4th, 14th, 20th Corps),[7] the largest component of the organization. Major General John M. Schofield (1831-1906; West Point 1853) led the Army of the Ohio (23rd Corps), the smallest of the armies. The Army of the Tennessee (15th and two divisions of the 16th Corps) was commanded by Major General James B. McPherson (1828-1864; West Point 1853). Sherman put his armies into motion on May 4 for the purpose of breaking up Johnston's army and inflicting all damage possible to Rebeldom. His strategy was to use Thomas in the center to pin the Confederates, then, using his numerical superiority, outflank the Army of Tennessee with Schofield and McPherson. Each time Sherman threatened his opponent's line of communications along the Western & Atlantic Railroad, Johnston retreated. Johnston played for time and waited for a favorable opportunity to attack. As the Northerners advanced deeper into Georgia and farther from their base at Chattanooga, their supply line lengthened. Detachments employed to guard tunnels and bridges would weaken Sherman's army. Johnston was also aware that the term of enlistment for many Union soldiers would expire in June.

After heavy skirmishing at Rocky Face Ridge, Johnston pulled back from Dalton when McPherson surfaced on his southwest flank at Resaca. From May 13-15 the Confederates confronted the Federals at Resaca, where reinforcements from Mississippi led by Polk began to arrive. Again threatened by McPherson from the west, Johnston abandoned his position and withdrew across the Oostanaula River. Ground around Calhoun was unsuitable for defense which caused the Rebel army to take up a position around Adairsville. Johnston, deceived by his maps, learned to his disappointment that the valleys in the area were too wide to be defended. General Hardee recommended that

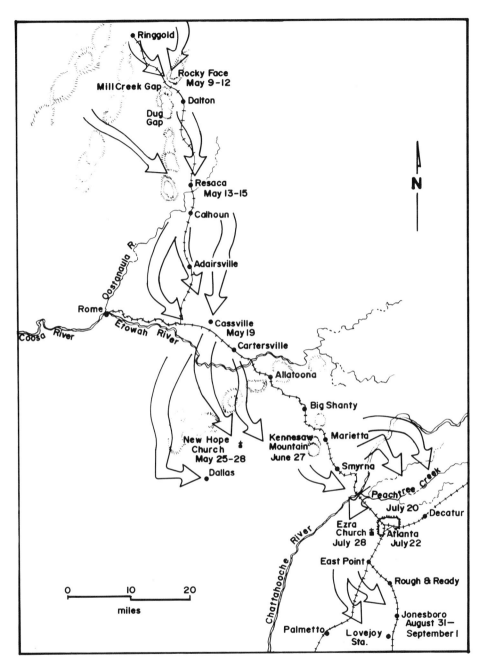

The Atlanta Campaign

his chief make a stand but Johnston saw a chance to attack one of Sherman's armies farther south.

Two roads led to Cassville from Adairsville. Johnston expected Sherman to divide his force along the roads and hoped to pounce upon the easternmost column before it could be supported. On the morning of May 19, Johnston issued a dramatic document that was read to each regiment. "Soldiers of the Army of Tennessee...By your courage and skill you have repulsed every assault of the enemy...Your communications are secure. You will now turn and march to meet his advancing columns. Fully confiding in the conduct of the officers, the courage of the soldiers, I lead you to battle...."[8]

Johnston designated Hood's Corps to deliver the blow. A stray body of Federal cavalry appeared unexpectedly in Hood's rear, which caused the Texan to cancel the attack. Johnston then deployed his army on a ridge southeast of Cassville that overlooked a broad valley. The armies of Thomas and Schofield occupied the opposite ridge. Both sides expected a battle the next day.

That night, Johnston and Hood conferred with Polk at his headquarters. Hood told Johnston that Union artillery would be able to enfilade his and Polk's lines, rendering them unsuitable for defense. He suggested to Johnston that it would be advisable to find a better defensive position if it was not his intent to attack. By the time Hardee arrived at 10:00 P.M., Johnston had decided to retreat. He ordered the army to cross the Etowah River, despite the protest of Hardee.

"Old Joe" exploited the episode to blame the attitude of Polk and Hood for his failure to fight under favorable circumstances at Cassville. Johnston's well-established reluctance to give battle and put his reputation at risk is better evidence to the contrary. If Johnston had fought a battle at Cassville, "It seems likely that the best he could have hoped for would have been a battle in which he inflicted slightly higher losses on the enemy before he was again forced to retreat to protect his railroad line of supplies."[9]

Sherman rested his men while the Army of Tennessee established itself eleven miles south of the Etowah around a gap through the mountains called Allatoona Pass. When the Union advance resumed on May 23, Sherman maneuvered to concentrate his entire force around Dallas, a town some fifteen miles southwest Allatoona's fortifications. Johnston anticipated the move and shifted his army toward Sherman's objective. Three small but hard fought battles occurred at New Hope Church (May 25), Pickett's Mill (27), and Dallas (May 28).

McPherson's army remained at New Hope Church while the Army of the Ohio and the Army of the Cumberland moved east toward Acworth, a few miles south of Allatoona. Sherman's strategy now changed. Instead of wide flanking maneuver's, the Ohioan intended to push south along the Western and Atlantic Railroad. His armies massed around Big Shanty and waited for the engineers to rebuild the railroad bridge across the Etowah River. On June 8, two divisions of the 17th Corps under Major General Francis P. Blair (1821-1875; politician) rejoined the Army of the Tennessee.

The Army of Tennessee had withdrawn from New Hope Church on the night of June 4. Despite public anxiety, Johnston's defensive strategy did not change. His army occupied prepared positions below Acworth that extended ten miles from Lost Mountain on the west to Brush Mountain, east of the railroad. In the center, Pine Mountain overlooked the two roads that led to Marietta. It projected a mile from the main line and a division from Hardee's Corps commanded by Major General William B. Bate (1826-1905; politician) held his sector.

On June 10, the Union army moved forward. The Army of the Cumberland encountered enemy skirmishers and entrenched before Pine Mountain. Schofield made little progress but the 15th Corps pushed past Big Shanty, less than thirty miles from the center of Atlanta. Sherman probed for a weak spot in the Confederate line while Johnston prepared for another retreat. He expected Sherman to outflank him with McPherson's army east of Brush Mountain. Hardee, concerned about Bate's vulnerable flanks, requested Johnston to investigate the matter and determine whether the position should be retained or abandoned. Johnston, Hardee, and Polk rode to the summit of Pine Mountain on the morning of June 14.

Below the high ground, Sherman noticed the cluster of generals and their staffs observing his own line. He issued an order and the 5th Indiana Battery opened fire. The third shell tore through General Polk's chest, killing him instantly, and then exploded against a tree. Bishop Polk's death did not deprive the Confederacy of a competent general officer, but his soldiers and peers respected him. When he rejoined the Army of Tennessee in May, the cleric had baptized Johnston and Hood. The following two documents were exchanged between Major Douglas West, Assistant Adjutant General, Polk's Corps, and General Hood.

My dear Genl

Enclosed herewith I send you a small tract, (one of four copies sent by its pious author Revd [Charles T.] Quintard) to Lt Gl Polk for distribution, and rec'd by him a few days before his death _. These little volumes are respectively addressed by his own hand to Genls Johnston, Hardee & yourself. Upon the fourth he wrote his own name, and placed them in the side pocket of his coat where they were found after his death __

I feel deeply honored my dear General in being the means of forwarding to you this posthumous testimonial of his affection for you, & I feel assured that you will not the less appreciate this priceless bequest that it is stained with the hallowed blood, which he shed in the holiest of causes. with my best wishes for the preservation of your valuable life

Lt Genl Hood}
I remain &c [unsigned]

Hd Qrts [torn]
June 16. 1864

My dear Sir

I have just received the Last you have been so kind to Send me. Tis useless for me to Say, that I most thoroughly appreciate it. I had grown to love Genl Polk with my whole heart. He was So noble, So generous, And Such an able Soldier. I Soon found myself very much attached to him.

Resply
J.B. Hood
To   Lt Genl
Major Douglas West
&c   &c

The Rebels gave up Pine Mountain on June 15. Continuous enemy pressure forced Johnston to retreat on the night of June 18 to a newly fortified line anchored by Kennesaw Mountain. Polk's Corps, now commanded temporarily by General W. W. Loring, held Kennesaw while Hardee's Corps was positioned south of the stronghold. Hood's Corps protected the area west of Hardee's command. When the 20th Corps and 23rd Corps threatened to outflank him to the west, Johnston pulled Hood out of line to contain the thrust. Without orders, Hood struck the 20th Corps on June 22 and lost 1,500 men for no gain. Johnston criticized the Texan for the costly action and Brigadier General Arthur M. Manigault (1824-1886; Mexican War), a brigade commander in Hindman's Division, wrote of Hood in his memoirs: "I formed my estimate of him on this occasion for the first time and subsequent events only confirmed me in the opinion that he was totally unfit for the command of a corps."[10]

General Sherman repeated his error at Chickasaw Bayou when he chose to assault Kennesaw Mountain on June 27. Soldiers of the 4th, 14th, and 15th Corps displayed great valor as they advanced over broken ground to close with the Confederates, who drove them back with severe losses. Sherman's attempt to break through the enemy line cost him around 3,000 casualties. The pattern of Federal flanking maneuvers and corresponding retreat continued until Johnston placed his army in strong fortifications before the Chattahoochee River. There the antagonists skirmished until the Army of the Ohio bridged the Chattahoochee near Roswell on July 8, upstream from the Confederate main works. Johnston, who expected the Northerners to try and cross downstream, though unprepared for that development, was ready to retreat. That night, the Army of Tennessee withdrew from the last important natural obstacle before Atlanta. Johnston deployed his divisions behind Peachtree Creek, nine miles from the city.

Hd Qrs
June 16. 1864

My dear Sir

I have just received the tract you have been so kind to send me. 'tis useless for me to say, that I most throughly appreciate it. I had grown to love Genl. Polk with my whole heart.—He was so noble so generous, and such an able soldier. I soon found myself very much attached to him.—

Reaspfy
JBHood
Lt Genl

To
Major Douglas West
&c &c

An example of a Confederate general's innermost thoughts

153

The presence of Yankees below the Chattahoochee alarmed the citizens of Atlanta as well as the government at Richmond. President Davis, under increasing pressure from Georgia politicians and worried that Johnston would give up the city without a fight, sent a representative to investigate the situation. On July 13, Johnston received a surprise visit from Braxton Bragg, who claimed to be just passing through. Bragg assured Johnston that his visit was unofficial. The intelligence that President Davis gained from General Bragg concerning the affairs in Georgia appears below.

Copy   Atlanta 15 July 1864

His Excellency Jefferson Davis,
President of Conf. States
Richmond,

Sir,

Unable to convey to you by telegraph all that you ought to learn from this quarter, & knowing the irregularity of the mail, I have determined to send you a special messenger.

I arrived here early on the 13th & immediately waited on Genl. Johnston, who received me kindly and courteously. Most of the day was spent with him in ascertaining the position of his army, its condition & strength, & in obtaining from him such information as he could give in regard to the enemy. The recent operations were explained to me more in detail, but in substance there was little, but what you have learned by telegraph. Our forces occupy the South East, and the enemy the North West bank of the Chattahoochie [Chattahoochee], on both sides of the rail road. The river is not fordable until you get twenty five miles above here. Within the past few days, three corps of Infantry have crossed to this side and are entrenched from nine to fifteen miles north east of this & near the River. The number is about twenty five thousand. A Brigade of cavalry in addition accompanies them. On the 13th this Brigade of the enemy's cavalry crossed the river at a point opposite Noonan and made a demonstration on the West Point Rail Road, but were met and driven back, & the bridge was burned by us. As far as I can learn we do not propose any offensive operations   but shall await the enemy's approach & be governed as heretofore by the developments in our front. All valuable stores & machinery have been removed and most of the citizens able to go, have left with their effects.   Much disappointment and dissatisfaction prevails, but there is no open or imprudent expression.

You will readily see the advantage the enemy has gained, & that it may not be his policy to strike us on this side of the river unless he sees his success ensured. Alabama & Mississippi will be devastated and our army will melt away. Our Railroad communication with Montgomery is now at the mercy of the enemy, & a mere raid may destroy Montgomery, and we would not even know it had moved. This is no fancy sketch Mr. President, & however painful, it is my duty to expose it to your view.

There is but one remedy—offensive action. This would now be assumed under many disadvantages. Position, numbers, and morale are now with the enemy, but not to an extent to make me despair of success. We should drive the enemy from this side [of] the river, follow him down by an atta[c]k in flank, & force him to battle, at the same time throwing our cavalry on his communications. Genls Hood, & Wheeler agree in this opinion, & look for success. But the emergency is so pressing, & the danger so great, I think troops should at once be drawn from the Trans Mississippi to hold the Trans Chattahoochie Department. On these points I inclose [*sic*] you a copy of a note from Genl. Hood. The suggestion to Genl Smith I fear will not answer & it is impossible for him to appreciate the vital position here, & delay for explanations may be fatal. I shall proceed to night or to morrow to confer with Genl. S.D Lee, aid him if possible in any arrangements to defend his department. At the same time I will endeavor to open communication with Genl. E.K Smith. The partial returns I have received so far, indicate a loss by us from Dalton, of more than 20000 of our effective force. The present effective[s] of all arms and kinds may reach 52000. The morale, though damaged of course, is still good & the army would hail with delight an order of battle. The enemy's morale has, no doubt improved as ours has declined, but his losses have been heavy and operates with great caution. His force has always been overestimated. It's now about 60,000 Infantry 5000 Artillery & 10,000 Cavalry, __ the latter defeated by us in every conflict during the campaign. During the whole campaign from & including our position in front of Dalton, Genl Hood has been in favor of giving battle & mentions to me numerous instances of opportunities lost. He assures me that Lt. Genl Polk after leaving Dalton, invariably sustained the same views. On the contrary Lieut Genl Hardee generally favored the retiring policy, though he was frequently noncommittal. Lieut Genl Stewart[11] since his promotion, firmly and uniformly sustained the aggressive policy. The Commanding General, from the best information I can gain, has ever been opposed to seeking battle, though willing to receive it on his own terms in his chosen position. You will see at once that the removal of the Commander, should such a measure be considered, would produce no change of policy, and it would be attended with some serious evils. A general denunciation by the disorganizers civil & military would follow. I do not believe the second in rank has the confidence of the army to the extent of the Chief. If any change is made, Lt Genl Hood would give unlimited satisfaction, and my estimate of him, always high, has been raised by his conduct in this campaign. Do not understand me as proposing him as a man of genius or a great General, but as far better in the present emergency than any one we have available. I enclose you a copy of Gov Brown's proclamation with Genl Johnston's note appended. Brown Toombs Stephens Wigfall, G.W. Smith &c &c[12] compose the cabal, & it has been most unfortunate for Genl Johnston that his name has been associated with the weak but treasonable document. His influence in the army is injured by it & the whole thing has recoiled on the head of the authors. But this will not prevent it from having its effect upon the enemy, where its sophistry will not be exposed or its assertions contradicted. It affords me great pleasure to report to you the entire & perfect satisfaction which has been given by your recent appointments in the army. I have not heard of a complaint & in Genl

Stewart's case the feeling is most gratifying. I would like to refer some other matters but must close to get my messenger [torn] by the train.

> I am Sir,
> most respectfully
> your obt. Servt.
> Braxton Bragg

Genl J. has not sought my advice, nor [torn] afforded me a fair opportunity of giving [torn] my opinion. I have obtruded neither upon him. Such will continue to be my course.

> B. B.

[*OR* XXXIX Series I Pt.2 p.712-714]

In 1864, during the course of the Atlanta Campaign, as in 1862 before Richmond and in 1863 during the siege of Vicksburg, General Johnston remained evasive about his plans. In practice, his plan in July to defeat Sherman had not changed from the program he had outlined to Davis in January.[13] Past performance and Johnston's failure to adopt an offensive posture eroded the president's confidence in him. Davis feared that the loss of Atlanta would result in devastation for much of the South. He could not allow Atlanta to fall without a struggle, and he feared that Johnston would retreat rather than make the fight. Before Bragg's letter arrived, President Davis asked R.E. Lee his opinion of John Bell Hood. Lee's reply foretold the future. "It is a bad time to relieve the commander of an army situated as that of Tennessee. We may lose Atlanta and the army too. Hood is a bold fighter. I am doubtful as to other qualities necessary."[14]

Lee preferred Hardee over Hood, but Davis promoted the crippled man to outrank the senior corps commander. By appointing Hood to command the Army of Tennessee, Davis expected offensive action and a miraculous victory. On July 17, Johnston received a telegram informing him of his removal from General Cooper that stated in part: "...as you have failed to arrest the advance of the enemy to the vicinity of Atlanta, far in the interior of Georgia, and express no confidence that you can defeat or repel him, you are hereby relieved from the command of the Army and Department of Tennessee, which you will immediately turn over to General Hood."[15]

Hood, uncomfortable with the unexpected promotion, took command on July 18 and spent most of the day at Johnston's headquarters. The deposed general explained to his successor that he planned to attack the enemy as they crossed Peachtree Creek. Hardee and Hood, along with General Stewart, who now led Polk's Corps, asked Johnston to ignore the order from Richmond. Johnston declined and set out for Macon that night.

The decision to remove Johnston endures as Davis' classic mistake in misjudging men. With his reputation and the fate of the Confederacy at stake, Johnston might have taken the offensive. Most of the soldiers who were affected by the change in commanders did not object. The popularity of "Old Joe" had peaked in June and though the majority did not disapprove of Hood, many were becoming apprehensive. Sherman and his generals were familiar with John Bell Hood's aggressive personality. General McPherson, Hood's roommate at West Point for two years remarked to members of his staff "...that we must now look out for different tactics; that Hood, though he might lack in judgment, would certainly fight his army at every opportunity that offered, and with desperation; and that we must take unusual precautions to guard against surprise."[16]

To the east of Atlanta, on July 19, the Army of the Ohio destroyed the Georgia Railroad's tracks at Decatur. The Army of the Cumberland began crossing Peachtree Creek and moved on Atlanta from the north while the Army of the Tennessee advanced between Thomas and Schofield. From his intelligence reports, Hood perceived that the 15th, 16th, 17th and 23rd Corps were not within supporting distance of the Army of the Cumberland. Hood believed the blunder would give him the opportunity to strike Thomas on July 20.

According to his design, Cheatham's Corps, formerly Hood's, would remain on the defensive east of Atlanta when the battle commenced at 1:00 P.M. Hardee's Corps was assigned to begin the action against Thomas' left. A delay developed when Hood directed Cheatham to support the cavalry which opposed the Army of the Tennessee approaching from the direction of Decatur. Instead of repositioning his corps one mile as ordered, Cheatham side-stepped two-miles. At the time designated for the attack, to Stewart's dismay, Hardee began a shift to the right in order to connect with Cheatham. Stewart knew the movement would compromise the attack and reported the matter to Hood, who allowed Hardee to continue his redeployment. Stewart's Corps dutifully closed up on Hardee's left with the result that seven divisions were a mile out of position. Hardee's line extended past the left of the 4th Corps while Stewart's Corps was overlapped on its left by the 14th Corps.

Around 2:30 P.M., Hardee sent a message to Stewart and informed him that he was prepared to attack. Stewart, who assumed the battle had begun, ordered an advance. Terrain features disoriented the attackers and favored the defenders, who had dug in deeper during the Confederate delay. The divisions of Brigadier General Edward C. Walthall (1831-1898; lawyer; Col. O'Neal's brigade) and General Loring suffered heavily but were unable to rout the Yankees. If circumstances had not forced Stewart to change his position, his corps could have conceivably rolled up the 20th Corps' right and scored a significant victory.

General Bate's Division, Hardee's Corps, stepped off around 4:00 P.M. and disappeared into the sector between Thomas and Schofield. Only one of Bate's Brigades became lightly engaged late in the day. General Walker's Brigades maneuvered with more precision and purpose. Two Georgia regiments gained ground and carried part of the 4th Corps' line before heavy fire forced them out. Though the Rebels rallied several times, they were unable to repeat their brief success. Brigadier George E. Maney (1826-1901; Mexican War), commanding Cheatham's Tennesseans, supported Walker but achieved little as only two of his brigades became fully engaged. General Cleburne's Division remained in reserve.

At 6:00 P.M. the attacks ceased; Hood's first sortie inflicted 1,900 casualties. The Army of Tennessee lost about 2,500 men and failed to drive the Yankees into the creek. Though Hood had devised a promising plan, his poor execution of it brought no positive tactical or strategic results. The true author of failure at Peachtree Creek, from a strategic perspective, was Jefferson Davis. Even though Hood had adopted his predecessor's plan and followed it closely, Johnston would have attacked a day sooner while Thomas' army was divided and more defenseless. According to Johnston: "If successful, the great divergence of the Federal line of retreat from the direct route available to us would enable us to secure decisive results; if unsuccessful, we had a safe place of refuge in our intrenched lines closed at hand."[17]

Generals Thomas and McPherson pressed closer to Atlanta on July 21; Hood conceived another attack. He chose Hardee's Corps to assault the rear left flank of the 17th Corps while Cheatham's Corps contained the 15th Corps. The Georgia Militia and Stewart's Corps would remain in the works around Atlanta.

During the night Union pickets noticed that Hardee's men had left their works. This intelligence resulted in the movement of two divisions from the 16th Corps, Major General Grenville M. Dodge (1831-1916; Iowa militia), to the left rear of the 17th Corps the following day. The divisions faced south to guard the army's flank and supply wagons. "In actuality Dodge had formed a new Federal line, refusing the left of the army and protecting the rear of McPherson. This was one of the most fortunate moves made by the Union armies in the war."[18] Hood was an unfortunate army commander.

Hood expected the attack to begin at dawn, but after marching all night, Hardee's four divisions reached their assembly points around noon. Swamps, thick undergrowth and dense forest had impeded their advance toward the enemy. General Walker had been killed by a picket as he observed the Union positions, which temporarily disrupted the division. Brigadier General Hugh W. Mercer (1808-1877; West Point 1828) assumed command of the division. "As it had done two days ago at Peachtree Creek, Hardee's Corps is making its attack in a disorganized, pell-mell, virtually blind fashion and for the same reason: already hours behind schedule, Hardee feels that he cannot take the time to conduct a reconnaissance for the purpose of ascertaining the location and strength of the enemy lines and the best way of approaching them."[19] From right to left, the divisions of Bate, Walker (Mercer), Cleburne, and Maney were deployed in line. When Bate and Mercer opened the ball shortly past noon, the Confederates were astonished to discover that the enemy's flank did not lead to their rear. Instead the Butternuts found a Yankee line of battle before them. Throughout the day persistent attacks by Bate and Mercer failed to crack the Union line. Had they succeeded, Rebel banners would have swept across the rear of the 15th and 17th Corps in an irresistible avalanche.

General McPherson had eaten lunch and was enjoying a cigar when the sound of combat became audible. He hurried to the front, concerned about a gap three quarters of a mile wide between Blair and Dodge. After studying the ground, General McPherson gave an order to a staff officer, then galloped off. A company of the 5th Confederate Infantry of Cleburne's Division waited one hundred yards away. McPherson and his escort ignored the summons to surrender and a volley followed their flight. Pierced in the lungs, the Ohio general fell from his horse and died twenty minutes later. McPherson, one of Grant's favorites, was the highest ranking Union soldier to die in the war.

General Cleburne, supported by General Maney, exploited the gap between the 16th and 17th Corps. An Iowa brigade in the division of Brigadier General Giles A. Smith (1829-1876; businessman), 17th Corps, withstood successive assaults but became outflanked. The hard-fighting Johnnies captured two cannon and most of the 16th Iowa before being stopped by the division commanded by Brigadier General Mortimer D. Leggett (1821-1896; school superintendent and lawyer) and Smith's remaining regiments. Leggett's Division occupied high ground denuded of timber. Despite repeated charges and hand to hand combat, the Confederates could not push General Leggett's men from the hill that today bears his name.

In mid-afternoon Hood learned that Hardee's attack had not achieved the important results he expected. Around 4:00 P.M., however, he received a report that Hardee was driving the enemy. Maney's men had carried the entrenchments held by Smith's Division; Leggett's Hill was attacked in the rear. Hood responded to the good news by ordering Cheatham's Corps to join the assault. Carter Stevenson's Division added its weight to the Confederate battle line on Frank Cheatham's right, but it could not take the works occupied by Leggett's battered brigades and Smith's survivors. Though the Georgia Militia also advanced, it contributed nothing.

General Manigault's Brigade of Hindman's Division, now led by Brigadier General John C. Brown (1827-1889; lawyer), spear-headed the attack in Cheatham's center. The Alabamians and South Carolinians who advanced over open ground near the Georgia Railroad endured enemy artillery fire yet maintained their formation. Supported by a brigade from Mississippi, Manigault's men routed a brigade of Ohioans of the 15th Corps. Two Illinois batteries were also captured as Brown's Division seized a chunk of ground a half mile wide from the Army of the Tennessee. From his headquarters, less than a mile away, Sherman recognized the makings of a disaster. He ordered Schofield to bring up all his artillery and five batteries went into action under the personal supervision of the army group commander. Manigault received insufficient support to exploit his success. A fresh Union division, along with a few reorganized brigades, counterattacked and the Rebels pulled back to their works.

At sunset, Hardee threw Mercer and Maney at Smith's line, now perpendicular and to the rear of Leggett's Hill in an all out attack. Smith's Midwesterners cut down Georgians and Tennesseans in bunches; the attempt to take the bald hill from the rear faltered. Bayonets flashed and fists flew along Leggett's Hill as Arkansans from Cleburne's Division grappled with Ohioans of Leggett's Division but the victory belonged to the Northerners. The battle ended at nightfall with a terrific bombardment of Leggett's Hill. Atlanta and the Army of Tennessee were doomed.

The Battle of Atlanta, Hood's second sortie, resulted in the loss of 5,500 men to the Confederacy; the United States lost 3,772 patriots. Hood conceived sound strategy for his effort of July 22 as he attempted to duplicate the Army of Northern Virginia's success at Chancellorsville, but he was no Lee, nor was Hardee a Jackson. General Blair stated that: "The movement of General Hood was a very bold and a very brilliant one, and was very near being successful.... The position taken up accidentally by the Sixteenth Corps prevented the full force of the blow from falling where it was intended to fall. If my command had been driven from its position at the time that the Fifteenth Corps was forced back from its entrenchments, there must have been a general rout of all the troops of the army commanded by General McPherson."[20]

General Howard, designated the new commander of the Army of the Tennessee, marched his divisions west of Atlanta on July 27. General Sherman intended to cut the Macon and Western Railroad as well as the Atlanta and West Point Railroad to force the evacuation of Atlanta. Hood was determined to keep the critical communication links under his control. He ordered General S.D. Lee, who had replaced Cheatham, to position two divisions at Ezra Church near a key crossroads, some three miles west of Atlanta. Stewart would follow with Walthall's and Loring's Divisions. After Lee's men entrenched on July 28, Stewart would maneuver against the enemy's rear and attack.

The 15th and the 16th Corps arrived at Ezra Church first, brought up artillery, and dug in. As Rebel patrols approached Ezra Church on the morning of July 28, Lee learned that the Federals occupied the crossroads. Lee decided to

General Stephen Dill Lee

attack immediately and sent Brown's Division into the forest. Before they realized it, the Southerners were engaged with the awaiting Northerners. One of General Brown's Brigades captured a hill and held it briefly before being routed by a counterattack. The other three brigades of the division were repulsed, regrouped, and again driven back.

Ten minutes after Brown's forward movement began, the division commanded by Major General Henry D. Clayton (1827-1889; lawyer) advanced. One of Lee's staff officers ordered Brigadier General Randall L. Gibson's (1832-1884; lawyer) Brigade of Louisiana troops to attack alone. Gibson's regiments were cut up in an hour long fire fight, and a brigade of Alabamians, which came to their support, fell back in confusion. Clayton suspended further assaults and assumed a defensive posture.

At 2:00 P.M., Walthall's Division attacked over the same ground Brown's Brigades had crossed. During the lull in the action, General Howard reinforced the sector with fourteen regiments; the infantrymen were backed by twenty-six cannons. Repeated charges were unsuccessful as Walthall lost a third of his division. Without support on his right flank, Walthall decided he must withdraw. Stewart agreed with the decision but ordered Walthall to delay his withdrawal until Loring's Division could deploy in the rear to resist a possible counterattack. Stewart and Loring were wounded shortly thereafter and Walthall, as senior general, assumed command of both divisions. The attacks were not renewed.

161

Lee exceeded his orders from Hood, who had instructed the new corps commander "not to attack unless the enemy exposes himself in attacking us."[21] Lee's disobedience and rashness cost the South dearly. The Northerners lost 632 men on July 28 while the Southerners suffered losses nearly five times that figure. For Hood's army, it was a taste of an even more one-sided affair at Franklin, Tennessee. Though the Battle of Ezra Church ended as a tactical defeat for Lee, it represented a strategic defeat for Sherman since his opponent retained control of the railroads.

The same day that General Howard marched for Ezra Church, Sherman sent his cavalry on a raid. He hoped that the horsemen would meet south of Atlanta at Lovejoy's Station in a pincer movement, cut the Macon and Western Railroad, and then penetrate deep into Georgia and free thousands of prisoners at Andersonville Prison. After capturing a wagon train and tearing up two miles of track, Brigadier General Edward M. McCook's (1833-1909; lawyer) Division reached Lovejoy's Station on July 29 and waited.

Major General George Stoneman (1822-1894; West Point 1846) proceeded directly toward Macon in disregard of orders. On July 29, he attempted to storm Macon but was repelled by convalescents and members of the Georgia Militia. Two days later, while heading for Sherman's army, Stoneman's Division was defeated and dispersed at Sunshine Church, ten miles north of Macon. General Stoneman surrendered a brigade as his other two fled for friendly lines. Only a few hundred Union troopers reached safety.

Early in the afternoon of July 29, after Stoneman failed to show up, McCook left Lovejoy's Station. In a series of running fights that culminated on July 30 with a brawl at Brown's Mill, General McCook lost most of his men. Survivors trickled in for days; the heavy losses nearly crippled Sherman's cavalry corps.

The failure of his cavalry to wreck the railroad convinced Sherman to revert to his successful strategy of flanking movements. By shifting the bulk of his forces toward the railroads southwest of Atlanta, Sherman hoped to draw Hood out of his forts. Meanwhile, Hood had extended his lines to the vicinity of East Point, Sherman's objective. When the 23rd and the 14th Corps lunged for East Point, Bate and Clayton stopped them at Utoy Creek on August 6 and 7.

Union artillerists lobbed shells into Atlanta for the next two weeks as Sherman contemplated his next move. On August 10, Hood sent Major General Joseph Wheeler (1836-1906; West Point 1859) and half of his cavalry force on a raid against Sherman's supply lines. The foray accomplished little and Wheeler led his troopers into East Tennessee and out of the campaign.

At the end of August, Sherman decided to commit most of his infantry against the Macon and Western Railroad. On the night of August 25, the 4th Corps withdrew from its trenches north of Atlanta while the 20th Corps remained entrenched south of the Chattahoochee to protect a railroad bridge. With the Army of the Ohio as a pivot point, Sherman's armies converged on the East Point area. The 15th and 17th Corps reached the Atlanta and West Point Railroad, nine miles below East Point and began ripping up the rails on August 28. The 4th and 14th Corps joined in the work the next day; more than twelve miles of irreplaceable track was destroyed.

The abrupt cessation of shelling on August 25 caused the citizens and defenders of Atlanta to hope the Yankees had given up and were in retreat. Hood knew that Sherman had undertaken another flanking movement but he did not know his intent. Would the 20th Corps, still north of the city, descend on the inhabitants if the Army of Tennessee left its entrenchments to give battle? Where would Sherman strike the railroad? At Rough and Ready or Jonesboro? On the afternoon of August 30, Major General John A. Logan's (1826-1886; politician) 15th Corps crossed the Flint River and entrenched less than a mile west of Jonesboro. Though Hood did not appreciate the imminent danger to Jonesboro at first, he responded to the news aggressively. That night he ordered Hardee's Corps, then at East Point, to march for the defense of Jonesboro, followed by Lee's Corps.

General Cleburne, who directed Hardee's Corps while his chief assumed over all command of both corps, opened the battle for Jonesboro at 3:00 P.M. with an artillery barrage. Lee's Corps pitched in prematurely and fought with little spirit. The same brigade of Alabamians that broke at Missionary Ridge dashed away again. Despite the pleas of their officers, the Rebel soldiers refused to advance against Logan's works. "Meanwhile Cleburne's attack gets under way and almost immediately degenerates into farcical chaos."[22] On the left flank, Cleburne's own division, under the command of Brigadier General Mark P. Lowrey (1828-1885; minister) chased Union cavalrymen across the river and took themselves out of the battle. Brown's Division, on the right flank, was murdered by artillery fire and musketry. In the center, General Maney halted Cheatham's old division and asked Cleburne for instructions. That night, Maney was relieved, and he subsequently disappeared from the historical record until 1865. As happened at Ezra Church, the entrenched Federals suffered trifling losses: 172 men. Their adversaries suffered over 2,000 casualties and many Confederates allowed themselves to be captured.

North of Jonesboro, Confederate cavalry protecting the railroad were driven off by the 23rd Corps at Rough and Ready. When General Hood learned the distressing news, he ordered Lee's Corps back to Atlanta. Their departure compelled General Hardee to hold his ground with three divisions instead of six.

On September 1, four Federal corps (4th, 14th, 15th, 16th) were poised to crush one Confederate corps. Around 4:00 P.M., two divisions of the 14th Corps attacked Cleburne's four brigades. The first attempt failed and the Union brigades regrouped. A second effort broke through. Success wrecked two Butternut brigades and captured Brigadier General Daniel C. Govan (1829-1911; planter) along with two batteries.

Sherman, a poor tactician, grew excited at the sight of victory. He ordered two divisions of the 17th Corps to cut off Hardee's retreat, but he could not coordinate his divisions to smother the ragged Rebels with one massive blow. Hardee shifted several brigades from his left flank to support Cleburne's Division and established a new line that resembled the Union fishhook line at Gettysburg. The 4th Corps approached the new line in Hardee's rear and stopped to erect breastworks in fear of an attack. The 15th and 16th Corps did not engage the enemy but stayed in their works and watched the fight. The 17th Corps did not fulfill its mission and Hardee's Corps retreated south during darkness toward Lovejoy's Station.

Interdiction of the Macon and Western Railroad on August 31 forced General Hood to evacuate Atlanta the next day. Stewart's Corps and the Georgia Militia began to march out of the city that evening. Except for a rear guard of cavalry, the last troops were gone by midnight. On the morning of September 2, Mayor James M. Calhoun surrendered Atlanta to Brigadier General William T. Ward (1808-1878; politician) as the Army of Tennessee concentrated at Lovejoy's Station.

Copy of Telegram.

Head Quarters
Near Love joy's Station, Sep 3/64

Gen'l Braxton Bragg.

On the evening of the 30th August the enemy made a lodg[e]ment across Flint River near Jonesboro. We attacked them there on the evening of the 31st, August with two Corps, but failed to dislodge them. This made it necessary to abandon Atlanta, which was done on the night of Septr 1st. Our loss on the evening of the 31st was so small that it is evident that our effort was not a very vigorous one. On the evening of the first of September, Gen'l Hardee's corps was in position at Jonesboro, was assaulted by a superior force of the enemy, and being outflanked, was compelled to withdraw during the night to this point, with the loss of eight guns. The enemy's prisoners report their loss very severe.

I will send a bearer of dispatches tomorrow morning.

(Signed) J.B. Hood
General.

Official
Robert Strange
Maj & A.D.C
Respectfully submitted to His Excellency the President as information.
[*OR* XXXVIII Series I Pt.5 p.1016]

On September 6, Sherman and his armies retired to Atlanta. Though the city had fallen, he ignored the major goal of the campaign, the Army of Tennessee's destruction. This oversight was all but realized at Franklin, Tennessee, when the Confederates "gave perhaps the greatest exhibition of cold-blooded, mass courage ever seen on a battlefield when, without preparation or [artillery] support, they hurled themselves against the Federal works after a long charge across an open field and clung there in a death grapple which was almost their destruction."[23]

Hd Qrs Army of Tennessee
Sept: 6 1864

His Excellency
Jefferson Davis

Your dispatches of the 5th just received. I ordered Genl Cobb[24] to have these troops returned to Augusta and Columbus as the information through Scouts was that the enemy was about making another raid in that direction, and I could easily bring them up when I was ready to give battle. The enemy have now withdrawn in the direction of Jonesboro, and I think will take position at East Point (Atlanta & Decatur?) & recruit his army and prepare for another campaign. I am making and shall make every possible effort to gather the absentees of this army. Shoes and clothing are very much needed. Detailed men, I think, had better for the present remain in the works shops as they cannot march and fight. I shall continue to interrupt as much as possible the communications of the enemy, and hope that Taylors forces will soon cross the River. I would be glad if yourself or General Bragg would visit the Army

JBHood
Genl

[*OR* XXXVIII Series I Pt.5 p.1023]

General Hood transferred his army to the vicinity of Palmetto, twenty-five miles west of Atlanta, on September 21.

Gen'l Bragg,   Palmetto, Sept 21/64

I have ordered the iron removed from the Macon and Atlanta [Western Rail] Road above Griffen and from the Augusta road, all above Oconee River. It would be better for us if there were no railroad from Atlanta to Augusta. Would it not be well to remove iron from a point even further South than this on the Augusta Road? The army very much inspirited by order to move in this direction.

JBHood
Genl

[*OR* XXXIX Series I Pt.2 p.860]

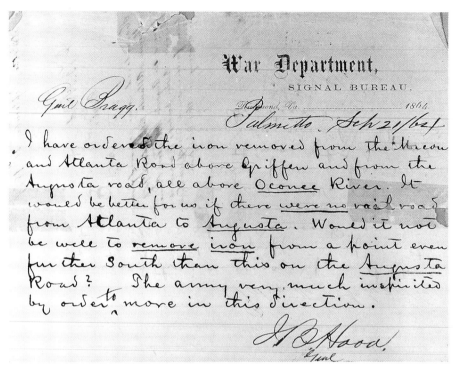

A telegram from General Hood to General Bragg

The following, most unique letter, proved to be prophetic. The last sentence of the above document illustrates concusively that General Hood lied.

Army of Tennessee, Sept 22nd 1864

Hon Jefferson Davis
Prest C.S.

Sir

Prompted by a solemn conviction of duty, I venture in disregard of military etiquette, to tell you Some important truths involving the fortunes of this army, and with it, as I believe, the fate of our confederacy.

History, & knowledge of mankind both teach, that rulers are kept in ignorance of facts which it is of the vastest importance, that they should know. They cannot have personal knowledge of these facts, and those who surround them, and who are their eyes & ears, are unfaithful and uncandid in their duty of giving true reports of facts.

In this respect you share the general fate of other rulers. I am sure that you do not know the condition of this army, and I am also assured that your chief officers of this army will leave you uninformed of the sad truth. I, therefore, having nothing to fear or to hope, from your favor or displeasure, which can deter me from the performance of a solemn duty,_ will take the hazards of this generally unprofitable and unpromising task.

(1)   Army of Tennessee, Sept 3 1864

Hon Jefferson Davis
            Prest C.S.
                        Sir

                                Prompted by a
solemn conviction of duty, I venture in disregard of military etiquette, to tell you
some important, involving the fortunes of
this army, and with it, as I believe, the
fate of our confederacy.

        History, & knowledge of mankind both teach,
that rulers are kept in ignorance of facts
which it is of the vastest importance, that
they should know. They cannot have personal knowledge of these facts, and those
who surround them, and who are their
eyes & ears, are unfaithful and uncandid
in their duty of giving true reports of facts.
In this respect you share the general fate
of other rulers. I am sure that you do not
know the condition of this army, and I
am also assured that your chief officers

The first page of Captain Posey's letter to President Davis

I tell you then, that this army is in a very bad condition,_ a condition that promises no success in the future, but a series of disasters that will complete its ruin, and with its ruin, our subjugation is nearly certain. You know the numerical strength of this army, but you do not, cannot know ["the" lined out] its moral and material condition. Its morale is at the lowest point compatible with it future existence or coherence as an army. Events may happen any day which will dissolve it, like melted snow. You will find an explanation of this condition of the army in a review of its history. That history has been for nearly three years a series of uniform defeats, disasters, & retreats, with only a single exception, in which Chickamauga figures as a dearly=fought, and fruitless victory. Is it strange that an army with such a disastrous career, that has lost every campaign, and every battle but one, from Fishing Creek [Mill Springs] to Jonesboro, is as dispirited, demoralized, & despairing army? A soldier yourself, you know the military value of morale. Let me tell you another fact which you should know and act upon.

This army has no confidence in the skill & capacity of General Hood. It has on the contrary, a fixed, ineradicable distrust of him, in this respect. I cannot be mistaken in this matter. This army will not, cannot make a successful fight under his command. It is immaterial whether this feeling of the army is well founded or not. It is sufficient that it exists as a stubborn fact, and remains to be treated as such. I will not criticise [sic] his conduct in the defence of Atlanta. The result tells its own story. Every movement there was a failure, and he can never again offer battle, with such advantages & chances of success as he then and there had. I only suggest that you inquire specially into the events of that defence, and particularly into the engagement at Jonesboro, & the evacuation of Atlanta. I am informed upon very credible authority that Atlanta was supplied with fifteen days rations, and with a two years supply of ammunition. The waggons [sic] were all sent to the rear, in order to hold Atlanta in any event. This plan was changed in a moment, & a vast supply of ammunition, costing twelve millions of dollars, was destroyed. This was all the reserve ammunition of this army, and we could not now fight two battles, for want of ammunition.

I may state the important but minor fact, that this army is poorly fed & clothed, and deficient generally in the material outfit of an army. As a proof of the morale of this army, let me tell you some facts. When before Atlanta, there were numerous & startling desertions to the enemy. My brigade of Alabamians, deserted largely, & the deserters included men & officers of courage, character & means at home. These were native Alabamians, driven to despair by the apparent prospect before them. Our picquets [pickets] there refused to fight, & were easily captured. At Jonesboro, we ought to have won the fight, and would have done so, had the men fought. Large numbers of men refused to go forward at all, nearly all acted badly, & we were disgracefully repulsed by a handful of men. We lost there about 2000 prisoners, many of whom were captured by being too cowardly to retreat, when ordered to do so, through an open field under fire.

Of that 2000, more than one half took the oath of allegiance or some other oath to the United States, & went north at their own request. We have just effected an exchange of these prisoners, and have thus learned the fact. Three of my Regt were captured there. One has just returned by exchange, & two took the oath.

I leave to your judgment the question are not these grand & startling facts Can you disregard them? What I tell you, I know to be true. I cannot be mistaken. No officer or man in this ["officer" lined out] army has better opportunity of knowing these facts than

8

=cited or dismayed, but I tell you that I can appreciate the military situation and it is perilous in the extreme. But no cause is hopeless, while genius controls, and brave hearts support it.

You have the fortunes of this confederacy in your hands. It depends upon your wisdom, whether we live or die, whether we triumph or fail! You must feel the awful responsibility. I have now done my duty — a rare duty, in telling sad & disagreeable truths to one having the honor a place of a sovereign.

I have the honor to be

Very Respectfully Yr Obt Servt
Ben Lane Posey
Capt commanding 38
Ala Regt Clayton's Div Lee's
Corps, Army of Tenn

The last page of Captain Posey's letter to President Davis

I have. I do not ask you to take my word for it. I implore you to come, & ascertain for yourself. When you come, do not rely upon Lt Generals & Major Generals for information. They are too far removed in intercourse, from the rank & file of this army, to know the opinions and feelings of the soldiers. They cannot tell you the truth if they would, & many of them would not if they could. Call around you the regimental and company officers, and even intelligent & patriotic soldiers in the ranks, & ask them to tell you frankly & fearlessly the truth, the whole truth, & nothing but the truth. Then you will get it. I write this of my own prompting, and not in the interest of any man or officer. I care not who commands, so that he have in him the elements & conditions of success. I have no motive but the interest of our cause. I have as much stake in it, as you, or any of your generals. I have nerves as firm, and a mind and as calm and equal under perils and adversities as you or they. I am not panicked [*sic*] or dismayed, but I tell you that I can appreciate the military situation, and it is perilous in the extreme. But no cause is hopeless, while genius controls, and brave hearts support it.

You have the fortunes of this confederacy in your hands. It depends on your wisdom, whether we live or die, whether we triumph or fail. You must feel the awful responsibility. I have now done my duty _ a rare duty, in telling sad & disagreeable truths to one having the power & place of a sovereign.

> I have the honor to be
> Very Respectfully Yr Obt Servt
> Ben Lane Posey[25] Capt commanding
> 38 AlaRegt. Clayton's Div Lee's
> Corps, Army of Tenn

> Columbus Miss
> May 28th 1878

Major W.L. Walthall

My Dear Sir

Your favor of May 16 received, in which you ask for Mr. Davis _ "That I give my recollections and opinions with regard to the retreat from Dalton to Atlanta and its effect on the "Morale" of the Army _ Whether this was improved or not by the events which immediately followed the fall of Atlanta? What in your opinion would have been the result of the Army had follow'd Sherman on his "March to the Sea," instead of going into Tennessee? What you may know of the decision at Palmetto, as to the future movements of the Army in case of Genl. Sherman's Moving from Atlanta to the Sea?"

I enclose a printed Copy of my report of Hood's Tennessee Campaign in which I speak of the "Morale" of the Army _ I did not serve with the Army of Tennessee till after the battles of July 20 & 22' 1864, fought immediately after Genl Hood assumed Command _ Was with the Army there (except when absent about 6 weeks wounded) till close of the war. From my own observation, Combined with what I learned from others, My opinion was, that the "Morale" of the Army declined from the time Genl Johnston issued his battle order near the Etowah,[26] and then retreated without fighting a general battle _ The Army

170

Columbus Miss
May 28th 1878

Major W. T. Walthall
My Dear Sir

You favor of May 16, received, in which you ask for Mr Davis "That I give my recollections and opinions with regard to the retreat from Dalton to Atlanta and its effect on the "Morale" of the army — Whether this was improved or not by the events which immediately followed the fall of Atlanta? What in your opinion would have been the result if the army had followed Sherman on his "march to the Sea", instead of going into Tennessee? What you may know of the decision at Palmetto, as to the future movements of the army in case of Genl Sherman's moving from Atlanta to the Sea?"

I enclose a printed copy of my report of Hood's Tennessee Campaign in which I speak of the "Morale" of the army — I did not serve with the army of Tennessee till after the battles of July 20 & 22' 1864, fought immediately after Genl Hood assumed Command — Was with the army then (except when absent about 6 weeks wounded) till close of the war.

Letter from S. D. Lee to Major Walthall (4 pages)

from my own observation, combined with
what I learned from others. My opinion
was, That the "Morale" of the army declined
from the time Genl Johnston issued his battle
order near the Etowah, and then retreated
without fighting a general battle - The army
never understood why battle was not delivered
after the issuance of that order, and settled
in a measure into the belief that there would be
no general battle to drive Sherman back -
Being educated in the belief that their entrench
ments could not be carried, the army hesitated
in taking the works of the enemy - This was shown
in the battles around Atlanta, and is in marked
contrast with that same army, on the bloody
and unfortunate field of Franklin, where they
did not hesitate a moment, but displayed
spirit and gallantry unsurpassed by any
army on any field - The spirit of the army
improved from the moment Hood commenced
his forward & aggressive movement on Sherman's
communications - and had the army fought
at Spring Hill instead of Franklin, Hood's
Tennessee Campaign would have been
a brilliant success - The "Morale" of the
Army in the Tennessee Campaign till after
the bloody field of Franklin, was far better
than just preceding and following the

Fall of Atlanta.

After the battles around Atlanta, and the fall of that City the Army was not at all in good spirits. It had fallen steadily back from Dalton to the Chattahoochee, without fighting a general battle. After a change of Commanders a more aggressive policy was pursued in trying to check the flank movements of Sherman. This policy was not successful in the battles of July 20. 22 + 28th July and Aug 30th 1864 - In each instance the Army was partially repulsed. The result was only a more Cautious policy on the part of Genl Sherman, who nevertheless carried his point in each instance. Now, as to what would have been the result had the Army follow'd Sherman on his "March to the Sea" instead of going into Tennessee? Of course, this is a mere matter of Conjecture, Sherman may not have attempted his "March to the Sea", had Hood remained at Palmetto, instead of starting on his aggressive Movement on Sherman's Communications with his whole Army. The probabilities are, that Sherman would have tried to Crush Hood, could he have Caught him, before starting on such a movement. The indications were he would not have tried to keep up his long line of Communications, but would with a Massed Army, Marched to Some point on the Atlantic or Gulf. Had he done this Hood might have delayed him, but not to the extent the

173

Army had done, but could not have prevented
his March in any direction.

As to "What you may know of the decision at
Palmetto as to the future movements of the
Army in case of Genl Sherman moving from
Atlanta to the sea?" I recollect no such deci-
sion - In Council I only recollect discussing the
Condition of the Army, and its Commanders
- Have no recollection of discussing the probable
March of Sherman to the Sea - If there was any
decision arrived at in this contingency, I
do not recollect of having been made aware
of it - Mr Davis and Genl Hood may have
had some understanding on the subject, which
was not Communicated to me, as a Corps Com-
Mander. I do recollect that Genl Hood
claimed the responsibility of the Tennessee
Campaign for himself - I comprehended the movement of the Army from Palmetto to be - A movement on Shermans Communications to compel him
to give up what he had gained in Ga by the
visible insecurity of his line of Communications
at same time by an aggressive or forward
movement to reinspire the Army, and a hope
of being able to strike the enemy divided -
Please inform me if not full enough -
                    Yours Respty
                    S. D. Lee

never understood why battle was not delivered after the issuance of that order, and settled in a measure into the belief that there would be no general battle to drive Sherman back_[27] Being educated in the belief that their entrenchments Could not be Carried, the Army hesitated in taking the works of the enemy _ This was shown in the battles around Atlanta, and is in marked Contrast with the same Army on the bloody and unfortunate feild [*sic*] of Franklin, where they did not hesitate a moment, but displayed spirit and gallantry unsurpassed by any Army on any feild _ The Spirit of the Army improved from the moment Hood Commenced his forward & aggressive movement on Shermans Communications _ and had the Army fought at Spring Hill instead of Franklin, Hoods Tennessee Campaign would have been a brilliant success _ The "Morale" of the Army in the Tennessee Campaign till after the bloody feild of Franklin, was far better than just preceding and following the Fall of Atlanta.

After the battles around Atlanta, and the fall of that city, the Army was not at all in good Spirits. It had fallen steadily back from Dalton to the Chattahoochee, without fighting a general battle _ After a change of Commanders a more aggressive policy was pursued in trying to check the flank movements of Sherman _ This policy was not successful in the battles of July 20, 22 & 28th ["July" lined out] and Aug 30th 1864 _ In each instance the Army was partially repulsed. The result was only a more Cautious policy on the part of Genl. Sherman_ who nevertheless Carried his point in each instance. Now: as to what would have been the result had the Army follow'd Sherman on his "March to the Sea" instead of going into Tennessee? Of course, this is a mere matter of Conjecture, Sherman may not have attempted his "March to the Sea", had Hood remained at Palmetto, instead of starting on his aggressive movement on Shermans Communications with his whole Army _ The probabilities are, that Sherman would have tried to Crush Hood, Could he have Caught him before starting on such a movement. The indications were he would not have tried to keep up his long lines of Communications, but would with a Massed Army, Marched to some point on the Atlantic or Gulf _ Had he done this Hood might have delayed him, but not to this extent this Army had done, but Could not have prevented his March in Any direction.

As to, "What you may have know of the decision at Palmetto as to the future movements of this Army in Case of Genl. Shermans moving from Atlanta to the Sea?" I recollect no such decision _ In Council I only recollect discussing the Condition of the Army, and its Commanders _ Have no recollection of discussing the probable March of Sherman to the Sea _ If there was any decision arrived at in this Contingency, I do not recollect of having been made aware of it _ Mr. Davis and Genl. Hood may have had some understanding on this subject, which was not Communicated to me, as a Corps Commander. I do recollect that Genl. Hood Claimed the responsibility of the Tennessee Campaign for himself _ I comprehended the movement of the Army from Palmetto to be _ A movement on Shermans Communications to Compell [*sic*] him to give up what he had gained in Ga by this visible insecurity of his lines of Communications, at [the] same time by an aggressive or forward movement to reinspire the Army, and a hope of being able to Strike the enemy divided _ Please inform me if not full enough _

Yours Respty
S. D. Lee

President Davis arrived at Palmetto on September 25. Once again he found senior generals at odds. "Hardee had grown attached to Johnston during the early Atlanta campaign, and although he did not fully agree with Johnston's strategy, he believed him to be much better qualified for the position than his successor. Another factor in the matter was that Hood was Hardee's junior in rank and years, and therefore Hood's appointment could be and was interpreted as a lack of confidence in Hardee."[28] Relations between them were not cordial. General Hardee had applied to General Bragg for a transfer two months earlier and after Atlanta fell, he had submitted his resignation, and then withdrew it. General Hood, who blamed Hardee for the failures at the battles of Peachtree Creek, Atlanta, and Jonesboro, desired Taylor or Cheatham to replace Hardee.

Confidence of the army and the people in Hood was another issue that challenged President Davis. During an informal review, the president heard the troops shout for the return of Johnston. The recall of General Johnston did not exist as an option, therefore President Davis created The Military Division of the West and appointed General Beauregard to direct it.

Hood and Davis discussed plans for future operations and decided that the best idea would be to operate on Sherman's communications. If the Federals marched from Atlanta to contend with the Confederates, General Hood could accept battle on advantageous ground. As long as the Rebel army threatened his supply line, Sherman could not operate in large numbers south of Atlanta. Hood, however, had to master the problem of sustaining his own army in the mountains of north Georgia.

On September 27, President Davis left the army for Montgomery, Alabama. The next day General Hardee, relieved from his corps, departed for a new assignment as commander of the Department of South Carolina, Georgia, and Florida. Frank Cheatham took over Hardee's Corps while General Brown assumed the leadership of Cheatham's Division.

The Army of Tennessee crossed the Chattahoochee River at the end of September and by October 3 was located near Lost Mountain, north of Marietta. Stewart's Corps swept east, seized the small garrisons at Big Shanty and Acworth and wrecked miles of track. General French's Division attacked the Federals at Allatoona Pass on October 5. In a stubborn contest that lasted several hours, the Confederates took the colors of the 39th Iowa and 93rd Illinois, but were unable to capture the garrison or the million rations stored there.[29]

Following the failure at Allatoona, Hood's Divisions marched north and were rejoined by General Wheeler's cavalry. On October 9, Beauregard caught up with the army and he learned that Hood had revised his thinking. Instead of withdrawing to Gadsen, Alabama, to fight a decisive battle, as he had discussed with the President, Hood now intended to destroy as much of the railroad as possible north of the Etowah River. Hood believed this action would cause Sherman to either return south or march toward Chattanooga. Should the Federals retire south, Hood would move on Sherman's rear. If the Federals came north, the Confederates would march to the mountains near the Tennessee River in the hope of drawing them into a defensive battle. Beauregard advised Hood to avoid risks to protect the army. He then traveled to Mississippi to confer with General Taylor concerning the problem of organizing a supply line for the Army of Tennessee from Jacksonville, Alabama.

From October 12 to 13, Rebel soldiers north of Resaca tore up the rails that connected Chattanooga with Atlanta. The garrison at Dalton surrendered as Union units reached Resaca on the thirteenth. News of Sherman's approach caused Hood to march his men through the Chattooga Valley toward Alabama. The blue columns followed and reached Gayelsville on October 20. The Army of Tennessee encamped at Gadsen, twenty miles away.

General Hood and his officers believed that their army was in no condition to attack General Sherman. An alternative to entrench and await attack would deliver the initiative to the enemy. Sherman could call up overwhelming numbers of reinforcements which posed an unacceptable risk. To solve this dilemma, Hood "soon arrived at the only logical solution. If he could neither fight nor wait for the Northerners to act, the only alternative was further maneuver...If he moved north, he could threaten Sherman's rail line west of Chattanooga in the Stevenson-Bridgeport area. He might regain the important area between Chattanooga and Nashville. He might even occupy the Tennessee capital, move into Kentucky, reach the Ohio, and threaten Cincinnati."[30]

Should Sherman follow him into Kentucky, Hood reasoned, he would defeat him, then reinforce the Army of Northern Virginia. "It was an entrancing dream—and it was by no means impossible."[31]

Hood's new strategy entailed the abandonment of Georgia to the enemy. President Davis had not agreed to this at Palmetto, and Hood did not tell his superiors of the change in his plans. Beauregard learned of Hood's new strategy at Gadsen; he discussed it with him on the night of October 21. Despite reservations regarding the problem of maintaining a supply line, Beauregard authorized a campaign in Tennessee, with one significant modification. General Wheeler's horsemen would not cross the Tennessee River. Major General Nathan Bedford Forrest's (1821-1877; businessman) cavalry, based in Mississippi, would accompany the army into Tennessee.

Beauregard knew that the real problem with Hood's plan was Hood himself. His administration of the army indicated that he allowed details to take care of themselves. Since the beginning of his military career at West Point and during his service in Virginia, Hood had displayed a tendency toward carelessness. For a successful campaign in Tennessee, attention to such details as recon-

General Nathan Bedford Forrest

naissance, routes to be followed, speed, clear orders, as well as providing supplies, would make more difference than hard fighting.

At the end of October, the Army of Tennessee remained in Alabama because Hood had been unable to locate a suitable point to cross the Tennessee River. Repeated disappointment, first at Guntersville, then at Decatur on October 28 and finally Courtland, resulted in the westward movement of the army. Beauregard's efforts to keep the army supplied were disrupted because Hood neglected to inform him of the latest change in plans. When Hood told his superior that he intended to cross the Tennessee near Tuscumbia, Beauregard agreed. Lee established a bridgehead across the Tennessee River on October 30 to cover the construction of a pontoon bridge. By November 2, his entire corps had passed over the rickety structure.

The strategic situation, however, had changed. The Army of Tennessee, now near Mississippi, was about one hundred miles from Stevenson and Bridgeport, Hood's original objective. Beauregard suggested a modification of plans whereby the army would sprint to Nashville while the cavalry operated against the railroad.

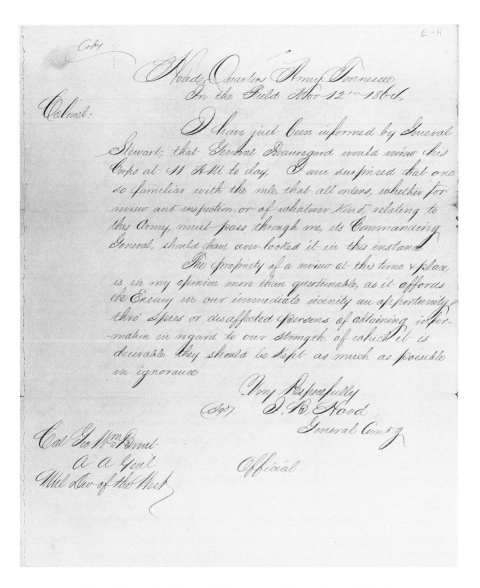

Note directed to General Beauregard from General Hood

By this point, Beauregard recognized "that Hood still had little conception of what his actual operations would be. In a curt note on October 30th, he had his chief of staff ask Hood for a brief summary of past operations and a concise statement of his future plans. Hood remained silent, ignoring this request for three days, while continuing to correspond only with the administration in Richmond about his plans and movements."[32]

Beauregard met his conceited subordinate at Hood's headquarters on November 3. The two generals agreed that the army would march with fifteen days' rations into middle Tennessee on November 5; Hood acknowledged Beauregard's role as his superior and pledged to keep him informed. Hood soon resumed his habit of disregarding Beauregard. Growing friction between them can be measured in the following two documents.

copy

Heade Quarters Army Tennessee
In the Field Nov 12 1864.

Colonel:

I have just been informed by General Stewart, that General Beauregard would review his Corps at 11 AM today. I am surprised that one so familiar with the rule, that all orders, whether for review and inspection, or of whatever kind, relating to this Army, must pass through me, its Commanding General, should have over looked it in this instance.

The propriety of a review at this time & place is in my opinion more than questionable, as it affords the Enemy in our immediate vicinity an opportunity, thro' Spies or disaffected persons of obtaining information in regard to our strength, of which it is desirable they should be kept as much as possible in ignorance

Very Respectfully
(Sgd)   J. B. Hood
General Comdg

Col Geo WmBrent
A Genl   Official
Mil Div of the West

Heade Quarters Military Division of the West
Tuscumbia   November   12th 1864.

General:

In reply to your communication of this date, relative to the review of Stewarts Corps, General Beauregard, directs me to say: that Review was designed by him as an informal one. As he passed, yesterday the Heade Quarters of Lieut Genl Stewart, on his way to "Prospect Hill," he expressed to General Stewart a desire to review his Corps, provided, the weather & the condition of the ground would permit, & he, ["in" lined out] meanwhile,

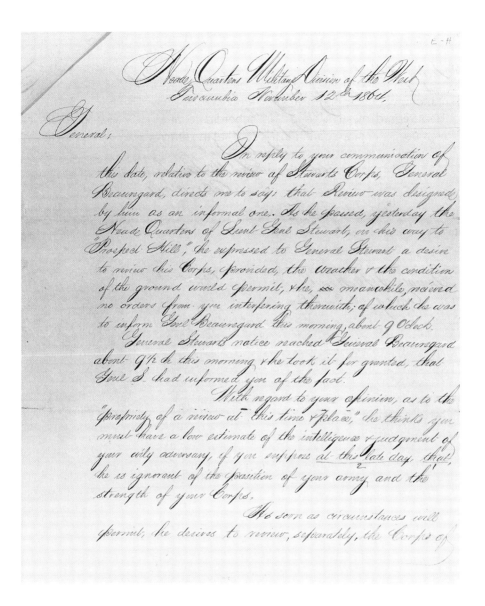

General Beauregard's reply to General Hood's note

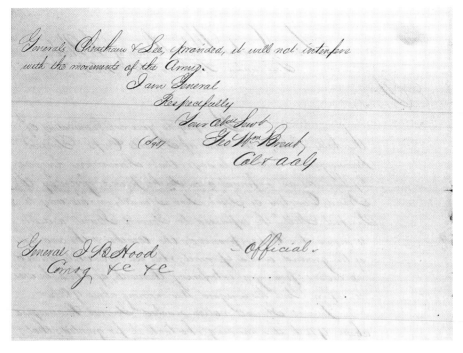

End of General Bearegard's reply

received no orders from you interfering therewith; of which he was to inform Genl Beauregard this morning, about 9 O'clock.

General Stewart's notice reached General Beauregard about 9 1/2 hr this morning & he took it for granted, that Genl S. had informed you of the fact.

With regard to your opinion, as to the "propriety of a review at this time & place," he thinks you must have a low estimate of the intelligence & judgment of your wily adversary, if you suppose at this late day, that, he is ignorant of the position of your army and the strength of your Corps.

As soon as circumstances will permit, he desires to review, separately, the Corps of Generals Cheatham & Lee, provided, it will not interfere with the movements of the Army.

I am General
Respectfully
Your Obdt Servt
(Sgd)   Geo Wm Brent
Col & AAG

General J BHood   Official
Comdg &c &c
[*OR* XXXIX Series I Pt.3 p.913-914]

The following day, without notifying General Beauregard, General Hood relocated his headquarters to Florence, across the Tennessee River from Tuscumbia. Hood's offensive into Tennessee continued to be delayed by bad weather and the slow accumulation of supplies. Good news arrived on November 14 in the form of General Forrest, who had been on a raid in West Tennessee.

Sherman no longer worried about Hood's army, though the threat posed by the Confederates remaining in north Alabama could not be ignored. Before burning Atlanta and embarking on his infamous "March to the Sea," Sherman sent the 4th and 23rd Corps to Tennessee. General Thomas, who commanded the Department of the Cumberland at Nashville, knew that the Confederates were coming, but not their destination.

The last of Hood's army crossed the Tennessee on November 20. Hood possessed little intelligence concerning the enemy's strength, and beyond storming Nashville and marching to the Ohio River, his objectives were ill-defined. Survivors of the hard fought summer battles remained steadfast as they marched along wretched roads through sleet and snow.

General Schofield, who commanded the 4th and 23rd Corps, Thomas' primary body of infantry, fell back from Pulaski to Columbia ahead of General Forrest's cavalry. On November 27, the Army of Tennessee camped before Columbia, but Schofield's formidable force blocked the Columbia Pike, the main route to Nashville, via Spring Hill and Franklin....

The solution to the problem, Hood believed, was to pin Schofield with a vigorous demonstration, then cross the Duck River with seven divisions east of Columbia. Hood hoped to get behind Schofield by rapid movement along a roughly parallel road. "It was [a] bold plan, with its success dependent only on proper execution."[33] And consummate strategy, for John Bell Hood's primary problem as commander of an army was aversion to detail, rather than the inability to comprehend a strategic situation.

On the night of November 27, Schofield evacuated Columbia and entrenched on a ridge north of the river. Two divisions of Lee's Corps, along with most of the army's artillery, occupied the town and its forts. Confederate engineers laid a pontoon bridge across the Duck River the following day. The next morning Hood led his infantry, screened by Forrest's cavalry, toward Spring Hill, twelve miles away. Schofield knew that Hood had outflanked him by crossing the river and as a precaution, he ordered his large artillery and wagon train to Spring Hill along with two divisions of Brigadier General David S. Stanley's (1828-1902; West Point 1852) 4th Corps. By mid-afternoon, Schofield no longer feared he would be assailed on his front. He expected Hood to attack his rear at Rutherford Creek. The sound of gunfire at Spring Hill, however, convinced him that his presence there was necessary. He left Columbia with two brigades; the remainder of his small army would pull out at nightfall.

At 3:00 P.M., the head of Hood's column, General Cleburne's Division, reached Rutherford Creek, two and one-half miles southeast of Spring Hill. General Hood's route had been "a circuitous one, but as Hood neared the village, he had opportunities to attack Stanley or attempt to entrap Schofield. Though Hood could not have known it, both opportunities were destined to slip away during a confused afternoon and evening. The lone fact that cannot be disputed is that Schofield's remaining troops escaped from Columbia along the Spring Hill [Columbia] pike while the Confederate army was within easy striking distance."[34]

The key to an improbable achievement or even a partial success, was control of the Columbia Pike. Hood sent Cleburne's Division toward the town to cooperate with Forrest's horsemen, who had been skirmishing with Union cavalry and infantry since before the forenoon. Cleburne's Brigades advanced into action and the additional pressure broke the blue line, which reformed on the outskirts of Spring Hill. Artillery fire halted Cleburne's progress and his division fell back to regroup. While reorganizing his men, he received orders from Cheatham not to renew the attack. When Bate's Division reached Rutherford Creek, Cheatham was observing the beginning of Cleburne's advance. The corps commander could not direct the deployment of another division. Hood encountered Bate whose division was forming to support Cleburne. He directed the division commander "to move to the turnpike and sweep toward Columbia."[35] This contradicted Hood's previous orders to Cheatham, which had directed him to concentrate his corps for an advance toward Spring Hill.

Bate's Division drove in the direction of the Columbia Pike and encountered the 26th Ohio guarding the road. The Buckeyes were quickly driven off by sharpshooters which left the Rebels within 200 yards of their objective. At this moment, after 5:30 P.M., one of Cheatham's staff officers delivered an order for the division to halt and make contact amid the descending darkness with Cleburne's left flank.

The main Federal defensive perimeter on the outskirts of Spring Hill rested on a ridge that faced south and extended across the Rally Hill Pike which passed east of the high ground. "Like a magnet, the makeshift Federal concentration along the edge of town was drawing large segments of Con-federate troops from all directions. Cheatham's objective was one-dimensional: to attack and overwhelm this apparent enemy bastion."[36]

General Cheatham committed a grave error by focusing his attention on the Federals on Cleburne's front, despite Hood's order to move north. Instead of hammering the Federals before Spring Hill, he might have broken their line by threatening their right flank with Bate's Division. His maneuvering exhibited "a

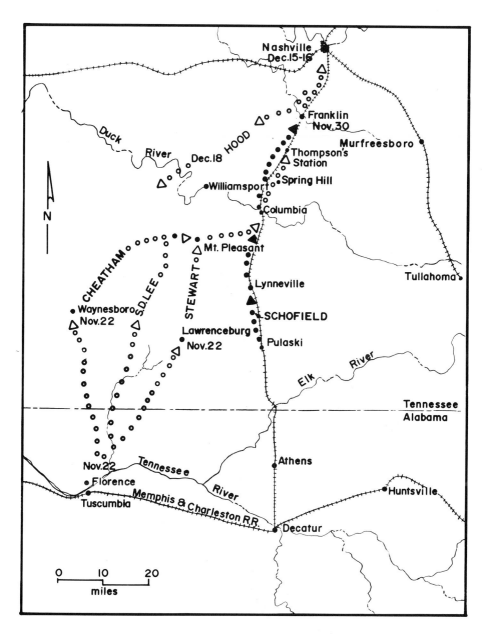

Hood's Tennessee Campaign

strikingly foggy idea of the position of the Confederate troops as well as those of the enemy."[37] Hood and Cheatham share blame for the miscommunication between them, but the responsibility lies with Hood.

Brown's (formerly Cheatham's) Division was deployed at about 5:00 P.M. to the right of Cleburne's command. Cheatham ordered Brown to attack and occupy Spring Hill in concert with Cleburne, and then rode off to find Bate. The general assault would begin when Cleburne's men heard Brown's Brigades going into action.

When General Brown's skirmishers moved forward, they discovered that Union troops outflanked them on the right. Brigadier General Otho F. Strahl (1831-1864; lawyer) reported the situation to Brown, who cancelled the attack, and sent two staff officers in search of General Cheatham.

Around 6:00 P.M., Cheatham learned Brown's reasons for not pressing ahead. Cheatham agreed that an attempt to advance would be too risky. No cavalry covered Brown's exposed flank, it was totally dark, and one of Brown's four brigades, led by Brigadier General States Rights Gist (1831-1864; South Carolina militia), had not reached the field. The temporary corps commander decided that the army commander would know what to do.

Hood assumed that Cheatham's efforts were directed toward the Columbia Pike. At the same time Cheatham set off to find his superior, Stewart arrived at army headquarters. Hood ordered him to push his corps up the Rally Hill Pike and hold a road northeast of Spring Hill to cut off any Federals who might flee east.

Soon after Stewart departed, Cheatham reported to Hood. He demanded to know why the he had not yet occupied the Columbia Pike. Cheatham responded by explaining Brown's problems on the right flank; Hood ordered Stewart to deploy on Brown's right. "There is little doubt that Hood, although perhaps angry with Cheatham for his failure to achieve outright success that day, was not then unduly alarmed by these unlooked-for developments. Throughout the remainder of the day Hood's attitude continued to be firm in the belief that these events were not of great significance; in the morning the Confederate army would bag Schofield's trapped columns with relative ease."[38]

Fortunately for the fleeing Northerners, Hood remained unaware that Brown's Division faced north, instead of west, to monitor the turnpike. Stewart soon discovered the truth, however, and because he was puzzled by his new orders that placed his corps due east of Spring Hill instead of near the Columbia Pike, he returned to Hood for an explanation. Hood failed to recognize the importance of this disclosure and ordered Stewart to bivouac his men. General Forrest received an order to send a division to obstruct the Columbia Pike.

While confusion crippled the concerted efforts of the senior Confederate generals to corner the Federals, General Schofield focused on one fact: his two corps were in grave danger. When he reached Spring Hill at 7:00 P.M., most of his men remained near Columbia. The last division, led by General Woods, did not depart until 10:00 P.M.

During the night, as General Hood and the Army of Tennessee slept, Union soldiers seeking safety at Spring Hill stumbled across Confederate camp fires and trigger happy sentries. Around midnight a barefoot Johnny roused General Hood from his slumber. The unknown, dutiful soldier, reported that enemy infantry and vehicles covered the pike. Hood ordered Cheatham to send out a force toward the pike and fire upon anyone moving along it.

General "Allegheny" Johnson, who had been captured in May with most of his division at Spotsylvania, led T.C. Hindman's former command. Johnson's men had gone into bivouac around 10:00 P.M. south of Bate's Division. Now, to Johnson's dismay, Cheatham ordered him to investigate the reported movement on the pike.

Accompanied by a member of Cheatham's staff, Johnson scouted ahead of his division and found the pike empty. Johnson felt uncomfortable moving his men over unfamiliar ground and feared friendly fire in the dark. He reported his findings and misgivings to Cheatham who agreed the division should sleep where it was, less than half a mile from the Columbia Pike.

General Schofield learned from a captured enemy officer that two corps confronted him at Spring Hill; he realized just how desperate his predicament had become. He worried that the 800 vehicles that accompanied his army would be lost. About the same time that Johnson's Division camped with Cheatham's Corps, Schofield was stunned by the news that enemy cavalry north of Spring Hill had struck the pike and threatened to stall the retreat.

Even though he experienced more stress than Hood, Schofield reacted decisively. He marched with Brigadier General Thomas H. Ruger's (1833-1907; West Point 1854) Division, 23rd Corps, toward Thompson's Station to clear the road. As Ruger's foot soldiers approached, the Rebel horsemen withdrew. Schofield returned to Spring Hill before midnight and an hour later the wagons, ambulances and artillery of his army were rolling toward Franklin, twelve miles away.

At 4:00 A.M., the rear guard arrived from Columbia; by daylight, the last Union troops and vehicles had left Spring Hill. General Schofield rode into Franklin before dawn to discover that the bridges across the Harpeth River had been destroyed. While engineers reconstructed the bridges, dilapidated earthworks, south and west of Franklin, were hastily repaired by the soldiers who would fight behind them. The 4th and 23rd Corps would have to fight a rear guard action.

As commander of the Army of Tennessee, General Hood alone is responsible for the blunder at Spring Hill. General Cheatham, however, who had served with the army since Shiloh, ignored the strategic imperative to close off the Columbia Pike to Federal traffic. Had Cheatham done this, Schofield's fragmented army could have been defeated in detail. Throughout the day, according to his biographer Christopher Losson, Cheatham "displayed a disquieting resemblance to his dead mentor Polk when he failed to keep Hood apprised of the day's events. He was inflexible when Bate reported Yankees on the pike, and may have absented himself from his command during the night."[39]

In the morning, General Brown described General Hood to a staff officer "as wrathy as a rattlesnake...striking at everything."[40] Hood could not comprehend how Schofield had slipped past his lines during the night to escape certain destruction. Around 9:00 A.M., Lee arrived at Spring Hill to find Hood in despair. Hood believed that Schofield's army would get away to Nashville before his own army could catch up and destroy it. Several hours passed before Hood's slender divisions swung onto the pike for the march to Franklin. Lee remained at Spring Hill with most of the artillery because Hood did not believe that the men and additional firepower would be needed.

Half the Union infantry had struggled to within five miles of Franklin by 10:00 A.M. As the afternoon wore on, Schofield became less anxious. His vehicles passed through the perimeter and Woods' Division crossed the Harpeth River along with the 23rd Corps artillery. Though General Thomas desired Franklin to be held for three days until reinforcements from Missouri reached Nashville, Schofield issued orders for his army to cross the river at sundown.

Hood finally sighted Schofield's force from Winstead Hill, some two miles south of Franklin, at about 2:00 P.M. As he viewed the Union defenses through his field glasses, he saw earthworks that covered every approach to the village. A forward line in front of the main works covered the Columbia Pike. Hood probably did not notice the Osage orange hedge that protected the Union left flank near the Lewisburg Pike.

After sizing up the situation, Hood announced to his senior subordinates: "We will make the fight." General Forrest objected to a frontal attack and protested vigorously. He requested a few infantry regiments to assist an effort by his cavalry to cross the river on the east, outflank Schofield and gain possession of the route to Nashville. Hood rejected the suggestion even though General Cleburne supported it. "I don't like the looks of this fight," General Cheatham observed.[41]

Confederate officers and men burned with resolve to close with the enemy who had escaped them the previous day. Hood wanted his army to prove itself because he thought that his soldiers were reluctant to fight out in the open without entrenchments. He could have waited for Schofield to withdraw and then continued on to Nashville, but instead, John Bell Hood, who graduated from West Point just four demerits short of expulsion, taught the Army of Tennessee a lesson in tactics. Ironically, Lee's Corps, which had behaved badly at Jonesboro, played a minor role in the bloodbath known as the Battle of Franklin.

General Stewart's Corps advanced up the Lewisburg Pike and deployed with Loring's Division on the extreme right, Walthall in the center, while French connected with Cleburne's division on the left. Cleburne's three brigades formed to the right of the Columbia Pike and Brown's four brigades formed on their left flank. On the western edge of the field, Bate's small division would try to hit the Federal flank where it curved west, near the Carter Creek Pike. Both Rebel flanks were covered by cavalry.

Chaplain James McNeil of Brigadier General William A. Quarles' (1825-1893; lawyer) Brigade, Walthall's Division, recalled the mood of the soldiers: "The men seemed to realize that our charge on the enemy's works would be attended with heavy slaughter, and several of them came to me bringing watches, jewelry, letters, and photographs, asking me to take charge of them and send them to their families. I had to decline, as I was going with them and would be exposed to the same danger."[42]

Two miles of open field separated the Confederates from their foe. Unlike Pickett's Charge at Gettysburg, no cannonade preceded the Army of Tennessee's advance. Moreover, Robert E. Lee's three divisions charged less than a mile to reach the Federals at Cemetery Ridge. At 4:00 P.M., battle at Franklin began as the proud, ragged regiments "went forward under the declining autumn sun, their bayonets flashing, their tattered battle flags flying in the November breeze. In the whole history of the war there was never such an imposing military spectacle as was here presented—eighteen brigades of infantry [20,000 men], with their cavalry support, marching in a straight line across an open field, in full view of their commanding general and of the entrenched enemy. As they swept on, the watchers from the Federal works could see before them a long line of rabbits, roused from their coverts in the fields and scampering in fright from the menace of the long line of men."[43]

A veteran who wore blue wrote: "It was worth a year of one's lifetime to witness the marshalling and advance of the rebel line of battle...nothing could be more suggestive of strength and discipline, and resistless power than was this long line of gray advancing over the plain."[44]

Eleven members of the brass band in Brigadier General Francis Marion Cockrell's (1834-1915; lawyer) Missouri Brigade provided music for the unfolding tragedy. At first they played the "Bonnie Blue Flag," and as the lines closed the musicians switched to "Dixie."

Two brigades commanded by Brigadier General George D. Wagner (1829-1869; politician), 4th Corps, confronted Brown and Cleburne from the outer works on the Columbia Pike. Wagner disobeyed orders and did not retreat when the unflinching Butternuts began to advance. Outflanked by Stewart's Corps, the Yankees offered brief resistance, and then forced the defenders behind them to hold their fire. A whirling mob of blue and gray soldiers seethed toward the earthworks, when suddenly a volley tore into them at less than 100 yards. Men on both sides fell. In an instant, courage carried the Confederates over the parapet. Three Union regiments in reserve retreated from their position at the main line which left a 200 yard gap around the Columbia Pike.

Brigadier General Jacob D. Cox (1828-1900; lawyer), a 23rd Corps division commander, exercised tactical control of the battle. His ill-advised placement of the two forward brigades allowed the attackers to actually reach the Union line. Here, Hood's poor generalship prevailed. Of the six divisions he employed, none were in reserve to exploit such a breakthrough.[45] If Bate's 1,600 men had supported Brown and Cleburne, the Union army might have broken from the blow of a steel gray hammer. General Bate, who also found a weak spot, was unable to exploit it.

Without orders, Colonel Emerson Opdycke's Reserve Brigade, Wagner's Division, responded to the crisis. Captain Edward P. Bates commanded veterans of Horseshoe Ridge, the 125th Ohio. He described how a punishing volley, delivered at a distance of less than fifty feet, saved General Schofield's army. "Fortunately, the rebels' guns were empty, they having been discharged at our fleeing forces...The essential advantage of volley firing in this instance was to briefly check the onslaught of a horde so great that it might have by force of numbers overwhelmed and by sheer brute force trodden down that comparatively weak line of defense before the two [forward] brigades could reload and fire."[46]

Confederate survivors pushed forward and the two masses of maddened men collided. Savage hand to hand combat surged around the Carter House; each side ordered the other to surrender. Opdycke's men were assisted by those who rallied and their weight of numbers forced the Johnnies back to the main line of works. The Union soldiers retook a second line of works, or retrenched line, before the Carter House. They blasted regiments that pushed toward them from the rear of the Rebel throng. Brigades lost their organization and the Confederate generals lost control of the fight. Uncoordinated charges were repelled with ease. From point blank range, enemy artillery blasted the brave Southerners, who had no such support.[47] By 5:00 P.M., the Union line had stabilized while the Rebels clustered in the ditch outside the main line of works. The future publisher of the *Confederate Veteran*, Sumner A. Cunningham, 41st Tennessee, fired over the parapet as General Strahl handed him loaded muskets. A Yankee volley missed Cunningham but cut down Strahl. As he was carried to the rear, he was struck again and killed.

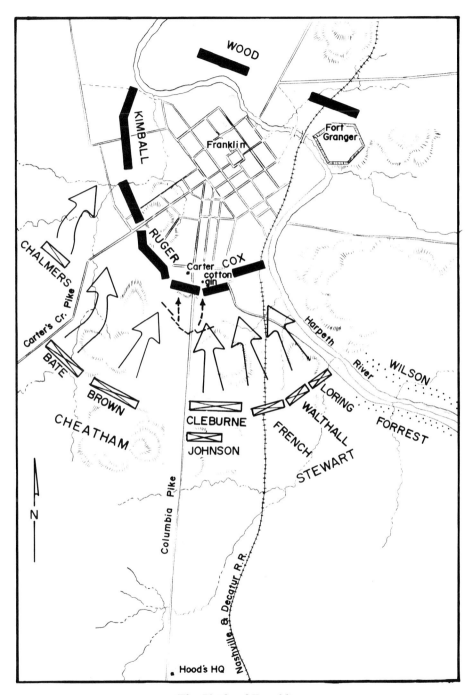

The Battle of Franklin
November 30, 1864

On the right, Loring's Division stumbled into the Osage orange hedge. Halted by the barrier, the Confederates were short range targets for the Northerners. Loring's line was also enfiladed by artillery fire from across the river. Though the 3rd and 22nd Mississippi planted their colors on the parapet near the Lewisburg Pike, Loring's Division was smashed in less than an hour. Walthall's Division was also massacred at the thorny hedge. His reserve brigade (formerly Col. O'Neal's), under Brigadier General Charles M. Shelley (1833-1907; architect), avoided the obstruction. They hit the Union line east of the Columbia Pike, near the Carter Cotton Gin. Part of the brigade poured over the first line of works and joined General Cleburne's men. Cleburne directed his reserve regiments under General Lowrey toward the structure, and went down with a mortal wound in his chest, forty yards from the smoke-shrouded works.

Union reserves rushed to the threatened salient and recaptured a battery. The Confederates were thrown back and brigades foundered in the outer ditch of the earthworks. Enfilade fire cut them down in rows. Even though many desperate Butternuts cried surrender, the 175th Ohio a newly organized regiment in its first fight, continued firing.[48] The Missouri Brigade fought at the Cotton Gin and lost nearly two thirds of its strength. Brigadier General John Adams (1825-1864; West Point 1846) led Loring's reserve brigade against the blood-soaked earthworks. General Adams fell riddled with bullets and his brigade broke up.

A member of Shelley's Brigade, Adjutant R.W. Banks, described the collective experience of the Confederates at Franklin. "When the colors of the twenty-ninth Alabama were planted on the enemy's fortified line, the Confederates were huddled in the ditch like sheep in a shambles. They had not been there long before men were being killed and wounded in more rapid succession than the writer ever saw before or since. They were crowded as closely as it was possible to be and were practically helpless. To go over the works was certain death, or wounds or capture. To run to the rear, aside from the shame of it, was almost of equal hazard. To remain was to accept the most fearful odds imaginable...Death was holding high carnival."[49]

To the west of the Columbia Pike, a lull in the musketry occurred when the Confederates ran low on ammunition. Federals noticed hats and handkerchiefs poked over the parapet on bayonets in token of surrender. Brigadier General George W. Gordon (1835-1911; Western Military Institute 1859) led 300 bewildered soldiers into captivity while other uncaptured survivors staggered to the rear.

Many Southerners continued fighting in the darkness and built breastworks made of corpses. No ground was exchanged during these firefights. Several companies of the 24th South Carolina dashed over the parapet and surprised the 97th Ohio. The daring Carolinians returned with forty prisoners and the 97th's colors. Earlier in the day, First Sergeant Alfred Ransbottom of Company K, 97th Ohio, had captured the colors of the 2nd and 6th Missouri (Consolidated).

The Army of Tennessee's full fury had been expended in less than two hours of heroic combat. After the battle had begun, Lee's Corps came up and deployed in reserve near the forward line of Federal works. General Hood, who remained in the rear, was unable to observe or direct the fight. He sent "Allegheny" Johnson's Division to assist Cheatham's Corps. Night attacks were usually avoided during the Civil War, but Johnson's Division went in around 9:00 P.M. guided by torches. Manigault's Brigade faltered when he was wounded, but the other three brigades reached the outer ditch of the main line. Some of the Rebels fought their way over the parapet to capture the flag of the 73rd Illinois. Their valor only increased the casualty list of an already exhausted army. By 10:30 P.M., the sound of whizzing bullets and exploding shells had been replaced by the moaning wounded.

Around 11:00 P.M., the first Federal units left the earthworks and by 2:00 P.M., the army was safely across the Harpeth River. When morning came, General Cheatham rode over the battlefield in tears. He returned to Franklin in 1883 and recalled that on either side of the Columbia Pike: "The dead were piled up like stacks of wheat or scattered about like sheaves of grain. You could have walked all over the field upon dead bodies without stepping on the ground."[50]

Out of approximately 22,700 Confederate infantry engaged at the Battle of Franklin, Hood lost fully one-third of his force. Estimates of his losses range as high as 8,000 men. In addition to the generals already listed as casualties, the following were wounded: Brown, Cockrell, Scott, Quarles, and Brigadier General Zachariah C. Deas (1819-1882; businessman). Brigadier General John C. Carter (1837-1864; lawyer) suffered a mortal wound; he died on December 10. Brigadier General Hiram B. Granbury (1831-1864; lawyer) and General Gist, both attached to Cleburne's Division, were killed outright. A captain survived to command Quarles' Brigade. The Orphan Brigade of Kentucky suffered no losses at Franklin; it had been destroyed at Jonesboro.

The Federals who slaughtered Hood's soldiers were from three divisions commanded by Brigadier Generals Ruger, Wagner, and James W. Reilly (1828-1905; lawyer), 23rd Corps. The defenders lost 2,326 men. Historian Wiley Sword has offered perhaps the best explanation for the forgotten American tragedy that occurred at Franklin, Tennessee. "Hood on November 30th was angry, overeager, frustrated, and not reasoning well...The tactical battlefield lessons of the past three years had eluded him...John Bell Hood was a sad anachronism, a disabled personality prone to miscalculation and misperception. Unfortunately, he was also a fool with a license to kill his own men."[51]

President Davis also questioned Hood's wisdom.

Copy   Richmond. Nov[em]ber 30 1864.

Gen'l Beauregard
Care of Col Wm Browne.

Yours of 24[th] received. It is probable that the enemy, if short of supplies, may move directly for the coast. When that is made manifest you will be able to concentrate your forces upon the one object, and I hope, if you cannot defeat his attempt, that you may reduce his army to such condition as to be ineffective for further operations. Until Hood reaches the country proper [Ohio River] of the enemy he can scarcely change the plans for Sherman's or Grant's campaigns. They would, I think, regard the occupation of Tennessee and Kentucky of minor importance.

(signed) Jefferson Davis.

The misery and futility of Hood's Tennessee Campaign continued past Christmas.

Head Qrs. Army of Tenn.
Near Nashville, Dec 11 1864

Hon: J. A. Seddon
Secty of War.

Sir:

On the 21st of November, after a delay of three weeks, caused by the bad condition of the Railroad from Okolona to Cherokee, and of the dirt road from the latter point to Florence, and also by the absence of Major General Forrest's command, this Army moved forward from Florence_ Major General Cheatham's Corps taking the road leading towards Waynesboro, and the other two Corps moving on roads somewhat parallel to this, but more to the eastward, with the Cavalry under General Forrest in their advance, and upon their right flank. The enemy's forces were concentrated at Pulaski, with some force also at Lawrenceburg. I hoped to be able to place our Army between these forces of the enemy and Nashville, but they hearing of our advance, evacuated Pulaski upon the 23d, our Cavalry having previously driven off their forces at Lawrenceburg, and moved rapidly by the turnpike and railroad to Columbia.

The want of a good map of the country and the deep mud through which the Army marched, prevented our coming up with the enemy before they reached Columbia, ["Of course_ why did you not place yourself so as to prevent it? G.T.B." *Gen. Beauregard's comment on left margin of page two.*] but on the evening of the 27th of Novr., our Army was placed in position in front of the enemy's works at Columbia. During the night, however, they evacuated the town, taking position on the opposite side of the river, about a mile and a half from the town, which was considered quite strong in front. Therefore late in the evening of the 28th of November, General Forrest with most of his command

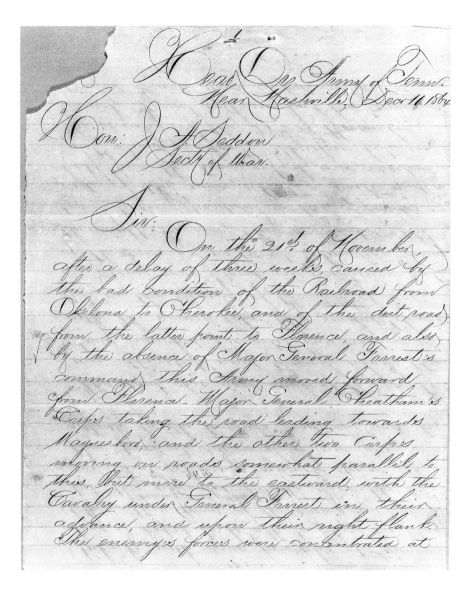

Three pages from General Hood's report on the Battle of Franklin

Pulaski, with some force also at Lawrenceburg. I hoped to be able to place our Army
between these forces of the enemy and Nashville,
but they, hearing of our advance, evacuated Pulaski upon the 23rd,
our Cavalry having previously driven off
their forces at Lawrenceburg, and moved
rapidly by the turnpike and railroad to
Columbia.

The want of a good map of the country,
and the deep mud through which the
Army marched, prevented our coming up
with the enemy before they reached Columbia,
but on the evening of the 27th of Nov.,
our Army was placed in position in front
of the enemy's works at Columbia. During
the night, however, they evacuated the
town, taking position on the opposite
side of the river, about a mile and a
half from the town, which was considered
quite strong in front. Therefore late in
the evening of the 28th of November,
General Forrest with most of his command
crossed Duck river a few miles above

later. We carried the enemy's entire line of temporary works, but failed to carry the interior line. During the night I had our Artillery brought forward and placed in position to open upon them in the morning when the attack should be renewed, but the enemy retreated rapidly during the night on Nashville, leaving their dead and wounded in our hands. We captured about a thousand (1000) prisoners, and several stands of colors. Our loss in officers was severe — the names of the General officers I have already given by telegraph. Our entire loss was four thousand five hundred (4,500). We continued our march towards Nashville, and on the 2nd of December our Army took its present position in front and about two miles from the city.

Lieut. General Lee's Corps, which constitutes our centre, rests upon the Franklin pike with General Cheatham upon his right and General Stewart upon his left. Our line is strongly entrenched and all the

197

crossed Duck river a few miles above Columbia and I followed early in the morning of the 29th, with Stewart's and Cheatham's Corps, and Johnson's division of Lee's Corps, leaving the other divisions of Lee's Corps in the enemy's front at Columbia. The troops moving in light marching order with only one battery to the Corps, my object being to make a rapid march on roads parallel to the Columbia and Franklin Pike, and by placing the troops across this pike, at or near Spring Hill, to cut off that portion of the enemy. The Cavalry engaged the enemy near Spring Hill about mid-day, but their trains were so strongly guarded that they were unable to break through them. About 4 P.M. our Infantry forces, Major General Cheatham in the advance, commenced to come in contact with the enemy, about two miles from Spring Hill, through which the Columbia & Franklin pike passes. The enemy at this time were moving along this pike, with some of their troops formed on the flank of their column to protect it. Major General Cheatham was ordered at once to attack the enemy vigorously and get possession of this pike, and although these orders were frequently and earnestly repeated, he made but a feeble effort and partial attacks, failing to reach the point indicated. Darkness soon came on and to our mortification the enemy continued moving along this road, almost in ear-shot, in hurry and confusion, nearly the entire night. Thus was lost the opportunity for striking the enemy for which we had labored so long, the best which this campaign has offered, and one of the best afforded us during the War. Major Genl. Cheatham has frankly confessed the great error of which he was guilty and attaches all blame to himself. While his error lost so much to the country it has been a severe lesson to him by which he will profit in the future. In consideration of this, and of his previous conduct, I think that it is best that he should retain, for the present, the command he now holds. Before daylight next morning (30th Novr.) the entire column of the enemy had passed us retreating rapidly towards Franklin, burning many of their wagons. We followed as fast as possible, moving by the Columbia & Franklin Pike _ Lieut. Genl. Lee with the two divisions, and trains and artillery, moving from Columbia by the same road. The Enemy made a feint of making a stand on the hills about four (4) miles from Franklin, in the direction of Spring Hill, but as soon as our forces commenced deploying to attack them, and extending to outflank them on their left, they retired slowly to Franklin. This created a delay of some hours. We, however, commenced advancing on Franklin and attacked the place about (4) P.M. _ with the Corps of Generals Stewart & Cheatham _ Johnson's division of Lee's Corps, becoming engaged later. We carried the enemy's entire line of temparary [*sic*] works, but failed to carry the interior line. During the night I had our Artillery brought forward and placed in position to open upon them in the morning ["Why not before?" *Gen. Beauregard's comment on left margin of page six.*] when the attack should be renewed, but the enemy retreated rapidly during the night on Nashville, leaving their dead and wounded in our hands. We captured about a thousand (1000) prisoners, and several stands of colors. Our loss in officers was severe _ the names of the General officers I have already given by telegraph. Our entire loss was four thousand five hundred (4500). We continued our march towards Nashville, and on the 2d of December our Army took its present position in front and about two miles from the city.

Lieut General Lee's Corps, which constitutes our centre, rests upon the Franklin pike with General Cheatham upon his right and General Stewart upon his left. Our line is strongly entrenched and all the available positions upon our flanks and in rear of them, are now being fortified with strong self supporting detached works, so that they may easily be defended should the enemy move out upon us. The enemy still have some (6000) six thousand troops strongly entrenched at Murfreesboro, this force is entirely isolated, and I now have the larger part of the cavalry, under Genl. Forrest, with two brigades of infantry, in observation of these forces, and to prevent their foraging on the country. Should this force attempt to leave Murfreesboro, or should the enemy attempt to reinforce it, I hope to be able to defeat them.

I think the position of this Army is now such as to force the enemy to take the initiative. Middle Tennessee, although much injured by the enemy, will furnish an abundance of commissary stores, but ordnance and certain quartermaster stores will have to come from the rear, and therefore it is very important that the railroad should be repaired, at once, from Cherokee to Decatur [Alabama]. The cars can now ["move" lined out] run from here to Pulaski, on the Tennessee & Alabama [Central Alabama] Rail Road, and we have sufficient rolling Stock, captured from the enemy, to answer our purposes. I will endeavor to put the road in order from Pulaski to Decatur as soon as possible.

As yet, I have not had time to adopt any general system of conscription but hope to do so, and to bring into the Army all men liable to military duty.

Some fifteen (15000) of the enemy's Trans Mississippi troops are reported to be moving to reinforce the enemy here. I hope this will enable us to obtain some of our troops from that side in time for the Spring campaign, if not sooner.

>   Respectfully
>   your obt svt
>   (Sgd)   J B Hood
>   General

"Genl Hood does not seem ["yet" lined out] to understand that he is responsible directly to these Hd. Qrtrs..." *Gen. Beaurgard's comment at the bottom of page eight.* [*Advance and Retreat* p. 355.]

General Hood threatened the Murfreesboro garrison to draw General Thomas out of Nashville. In that event, Hood reasoned, Thomas could be defeated and Nashville occupied. George "Slow Trot" Thomas, however, had no intention to move quickly against his adversary. On November 30, A.J. Smith's 16th Corps divisions arrived to reinforce Thomas' garrison of second-rate troops. With the arrival of the 4th and 23rd Corps on December 1, Thomas was content to rest and reorganize his army. Brigadier General James H. Wilson's (1837-1925; West Point 1860) Cavalry Corps was particularly deficient in mounts and was considered no match for the Confederate cavalry under General Forrest.

Back in Virginia, Grant expected Thomas to move against Hood immediately. Washington dismissed Thomas' insistence that effective cavalry was critical to his operations. As days passed without word of the desired operation against Hood, Grant grew increasingly impatient. On December 7, he recommended to the Secretary of War that Schofield replace Thomas.

At Nashville, on December 8, it began to sleet and snow. Sullen Johnnies, barefoot and hungry, camped out in the open without tents. Blankets were fashioned out of carpet; a scarcity of firewood added to their misery. Hood's supply system barely functioned but the morale in the ranks formed his most important problem. On the picket line, dead soldiers remained unburied and Hood's men could hear enemy activity from within Tennessee's besieged capital.

On December 13, Grant ordered Major General John A. Logan to assume command of Union troops at Nashville if Thomas had not moved by the time he arrived. Harsh weather had forced Thomas to postpone his attack. As the temperature rose on December 14, the countryside thawed. Mud hampered and fog delayed troop movements, but when Thomas finally attacked Hood the next day, only nightfall saved the shards of the once powerful Army of Tennessee from being scattered.

A combined attack of infantry and dismounted cavalry routed remnants of Stewart's Corps on Hood's left flank. Union troops captured sixteen cannon along with hundreds of prisoners. Captain William P. Gale of A.P. Stewart's staff wrote: "The men seemed utterly lethargic and without interest in the battle. I never witnessed such want of enthusiasm, and began to fear for tomorrow, hoping that Gen'l Hood would retreat during the night."[52]

General Hood could not yet admit that his campaign had failed; he fell back and established a new, shorter line. Lee's Corps defended Overton Hill on the right while Stewart's depleted ranks held the center. Cheatham's Corps defended Shy's Hill on the right. The incomparable Forrest and his cavalry remained at Murfreesboro, which weakened Hood's flanks. Bate's two brigades returned to the main army from Murfreesboro and took up a weak defensive position on Shy's Hill at midnight.

The inconclusive fight on December 15 was nearly repeated the next day. General Schofield, commanding the 23rd Corps on Cheathams's front, requested reinforcements from the 16th Corps. General Woods and his 4th Corps advanced in the Union left center. Woods' corps took most of the morning to cover two miles. By noon it began to rain and the second day of the Battle of Nashville was fought beneath a gloomy sky. At 2:45 P.M., General Woods ordered his men forward to take Overton Hill.

Brigadier General James B. Steedman (1817-1883; politican) commanded a scratch unit on the extreme left flank of General Thomas' army. Unattached to the 4th Corps, Steedman's Division of mostly colored troops cooperated aggressively. Heavy artillery against the high ground proved ineffective but one of Steedman's regiments reached the Rebel breastworks. The 13th United States Colored Troops rallied round the flag planted on the parapet and covered themselves with glory. A Southern officer, Brigadier General James

T. Holtzclaw (1833-1893; lawyer) of Clayton's Division commented favorably on the "smoked Yankees," who were unsupported and forced to withdraw. Two white brigades of the 4th Corps achieved less than they did.

Union cavalry, meanwhile, pushed aside the division of Confederate horsemen commanded by Brigadier General James R. Chalmers (1831-1898; lawyer) and a brigade of North Carolina and Texas infantry that protected Hood's left flank. General Wilson's troopers galloped toward the Army of Tennessee's rear. Without Forrest's two cavalry divisions, absent at Murfreesboro, Hood could not stop them. Ohio-born Brigadier General Daniel H. Reynolds (1832-1902; lawyer) commanded a brigade in Walthall's Division. He led his men toward the threatened sector to contain what Hood considered to be a minor problem.

Soon after Reynolds' Arkansans left their place in the line, bursting shells covered Shy's Hill. Hood had reinforced his left flank with the brigades positioned there. Bates' thin division stood alone to defend the northern and western slopes of the hill with little artillery support.

Citizens watched from hills around Nashville as Brigadier General John McArthur's (1826-1906; businessman) Division, 16th Corps, stormed up the hill toward Bate around 3:30 P.M. Brigades on Bate's flank commanded by Brigadier Generals Henry R. Jackson (1820-1898; Mexican War) and Thomas B. Smith (1838-1923; Nashville Military Institute) fought with determination, but in the center of his division, a brigade of Floridians collapsed. Within moments Bate's Division fell apart. A few companies and squads continued to resist as Lieutenant Colonel William M. Shy went down fighting with a bullet through his brain; Generals Reynolds and Smith were captured. The colonel of the 95th Ohio struck Smith repeatedly about the head with his sword. The shameful incident caused injuries to General Smith from which he never fully recovered; the veteran of Shiloh and Chickamauga spent the last forty-seven years of his life in an insane asylum.

Union soldiers broke through the Confederate line from the middle of Shy's Hill to beyond the Granny White Pike toward Overton Hill. Walthall's and Loring's Divisions followed the example of Bate's men and ran to the rear. General Cheatham, who tried to form a line against the enemy cavalry, watched his own corps break up. In less than an hour, Hood's entire left and center dissolved. His panicky soldiers refused to rally on Reynold's Brigade, which joined the stampede. Only Lee's Corps remained intact to cover the Army of Tennessee's flight.

The Granny White Pike, which ran through Hood's line east of Shy's Hill, became a scene of utter confusion as soldiers and wagons scrambled to escape. To the north and west, General McArthur's men and a single 23rd Corps brigade followed the broken divisions unhurriedly, while to the south, General Wilson's dismounted cavalry threatened to encircle the Confederates.

General Stewart tried to rally his men but he was ignored. Terrified Butternuts headed for the Franklin Pike, the only escape route open to them.

In response to McArthur's success, Woods advanced the 4th Corps as did Brigadier General Kenner Garrard's (1827-1879; West Point 1851) Division of the 16th Corps. It was more than "Allegheny" Johnson's and Carter Stevenson's Brigades could endure. The war weary soldiers skipped out to survive. General Clayton's Division on Overton Hill retreated in fragments.

Lee scraped together a few companies along with two guns of the Eufala Light Artillery to defend the Franklin Pike. He appealed to passing soldiers to make a stand. "Rally, men, rally! For God's sake men rally. This is the place for brave men to die!"[53] Too many courageous Southerners had already fallen during the campaign and their surviving comrades knew that weeks of suffering and sacrifice had been in vain. They paid no heed to Hood, Stewart, or Cheatham.

The Battle of Nashville was the most complete victory of the Civil War. Thomas' casualties were 3,000 while Hood's loss of 8,500 prisoners and 53 cannon far surpassed the disaster at Missionary Ridge. By the time Hood's rear guard crossed the Tennessee River into Alabama on December 28, the Army of Tennessee existed in name only, less than 19,000 men remained. As the disheartened survivors marched toward winter quarters, they sang a ditty composed to the tune "Yellow Rose of Texas:"

So now I'm marching southward;
My heart is full of woe.
I'm going back to Georgia
To see my uncle Joe.
You may talk about your Beauregard
And sing of General Lee,
But the gallant Hood of Texas
played hell in Tennessee.[54]

6

SECRET OF THE
LAST CAMPAIGN

Union soldiers entered the capital of the Confederacy on April 3, 1865, after a siege of nearly ten months. Phil Sheridan broke the stalemate before Richmond and Petersburg on April 1 when he turned Robert E. Lee's extreme right flank. At the end of March, Grant had sent Sheridan with a strong strike force west, to force the Rebels out of their trenches and end the war. Following sharp actions at Lewis Farm (March 29), Dinwiddie Court House (March 31), and Gravelly Run (March 31), the Confederates retreated.

General Pickett, who directed five infantry brigades and three cavalry divisions, established a defensive line along White Oak Road in the vicinity of a crossroads known as Five Forks. His position protected the Southside Railroad, the last rail link south from Petersburg. Lee ordered Pickett to hold the line "at all hazards."

Sheridan's afternoon attack on April 1 was a masterful display of tactics. While dismounted cavalry pinned the enemy infantry in front, the 5th Corps advanced on Pickett's left flank across Gravelly Run. As the 5th Corps moved forward, messengers could not locate Pickett to apprise him of the danger. Pickett and Fitzhugh Lee, who commanded the cavalry corps, were enjoying a shad bake more than a mile to the rear. By the time they learned of the impending disaster, it was too late. Two Confederate brigades had been routed and the Federals were headed for the rear of the defensive line.

A spirited charge by a portion of the 3rd Virginia Cavalry enabled Pickett to rejoin his command. He attempted to reorganize the defense of Five Forks but his brigades quickly collapsed. Union cavalrymen supported Sheridan's infantry and thousands of Confederates were captured. The total number of prisoners taken at the Battle of Five Forks numbered 4,500 men. It was the beginning of the end. For the first time in its history, the Army of Northern Virginia had been driven from a battlefield. Sheridan's successful operation had forced Lee to weaken his center to reinforce his right. Early on the morning of April 2, the 6th Corps broke through the portion of the trench line defended by A.P. Hill's Corps. During the Federal advance, General Hill was killed as he attempted to rally his troops. The devoted defenders of Fort Gregg, which protected the inner line of defenses around Petersburg, sacrificed themselves to allow their partners to get away. Lee informed the government that the lines around Richmond and Petersburg could only be held until nightfall.

Lee ordered the Richmond and Petersburg garrisons to concentrate at Amelia Court House. Located on the Richmond and Danville Railroad, thirty-nine miles southwest of Richmond and thirty-six miles northwest of Petersburg, Amelia Court House was a convenient place for the army to receive rations before marching on to North Carolina. During the night of April 2, civilians, government workers, and convalescent soldiers from hospitals streamed out of the city. Ironclads on the James River were blown up and rioting broke out as the Confederacy's capital burned. By daylight, the business district was aflame, mobs looted the stores, and magazines exploded when fire reached the abandoned ammunition. Many people congregated at Capitol Square to avoid the danger.

A brigade of South Carolina cavalry, the Rebel rear guard, clattered across Mayo Bridge as enemy horsemen approached. The span was set on fire and Richmond was occupied by troops under the command of Major General Godfrey Weitzel (1835-1884; West Point 1855). Mrs. Robert E. Lee peered out her window and viewed a Confederate straggler. "He wheeled and fired behind him, rode a short distance, wheeled and fired again; and so on, wheeling and firing as he went until he was out of sight. Coming up the street...rode a body of men in blue uniforms. It was not a very large body. They rode slowly, and passed just beneath my window. Exactly at eight o'clock the Confederate flag that fluttered above the Capitol came down and the Stars and Stripes [guidons of the 4th Massachusetts Cavalry] were run up...We covered our faces and cried aloud. All through the house was the sound of sobbing. It was as the house of mourning."[1] Fifteen minutes later, General Weitzel accepted the formal surrender of Richmond. Union soldiers extinguished the fires and restored order.

Grant expected Lee's army to follow the Richmond and Danville Railroad southwest toward North Carolina. He had no desire to shadow the Rebels but

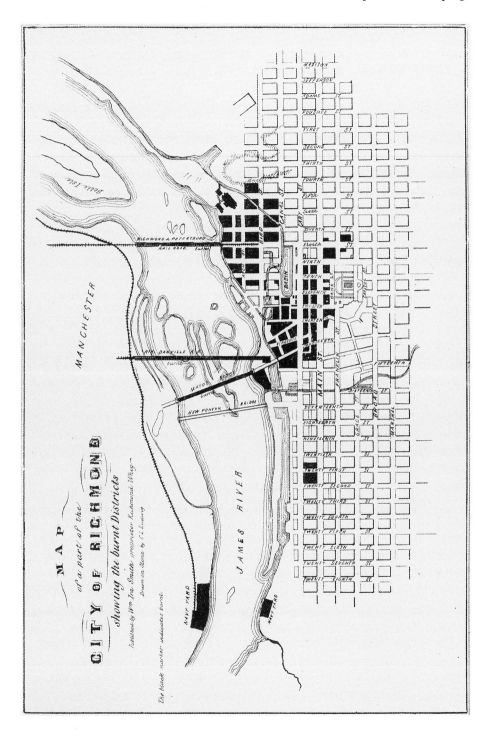

hoped to get ahead of them to cut off their line of retreat. Sheridan set out with his cavalry and the 5th Corps on April 3 to head off Lee's army. The 2nd Corps and 6th Corps followed Sheridan while the Army of the James, under Major General Edward O.C. Ord (1818-1883; West Point 1839), marched along the Southside Railroad. The 9th Corps guarded the wagon train and brought up the rear. The next day at Wilson's Station, new intelligence convinced Grant that Lee had changed his plans. "On the morning of the 4th I learned that Lee had ordered rations up from Danville [Virginia] for his famishing army, and that they were to meet him at Farmville. This showed that Lee had already abandoned the idea of following the railroad down to Danville, but had determined to go farther west, by the way of Farmville. I notified Sheridan of this and directed him to get possession of the road before the supplies could reach Lee."[2]

The conqueror of Vicksburg interpreted the intention of the Gray Fox incorrectly.[3] Lee had arrived at Amelia Court House to discover no rations were available to his army as it began to assemble at its concentration point. "He had ordered rations sent down from Richmond just before he left Petersburg, but in the confusion that lay upon his own headquarters and the Confederate War Department at Richmond these orders were never sent, or if sent were not received, or if received were not executed...."[4]

The Confederates could not resume their southward march without food and wagons were sent out to forage. While the commissary tried to find corn and chickens, the army rested, reorganized, and waited for the rear elements to catch up. Meanwhile, Sheridan's infantry began taking up positions at Jetersville, about seven miles southwest of Amelia Court House on the Richmond and Danville Railroad. Grant maintained his headquarters with the Army of the James.

"That night [April 4] Grant's head-quarters were twenty-seven miles from Petersburg, and [Dennis] Doren's [Superintendent of Construction] men built a loop from the main line on the South Side railroad to head-quarters. The promptness with which the telegraph reached Grant's camp pleased him and he so expressed himself. Messages to Lincoln, Stanton, and probably Sherman, —via—Fort Monroe were soon on their way."[5] Grant could communicate with the War Department in Washington by telegraph from Richmond to City Point, then to Fort Monroe, and Wilmington, Delaware. He telegraphed Secretary of War Stanton: "All of the enemy that retains anything like organization have gone north of the Appomattox & are apparently heading for Lynchburg."[6]

The day's delay robbed the Rebels of their lead in the foot race with the Federals, and the wagons returned nearly empty. Early on the afternoon of April 5, Lee's tired and hungry men advanced toward Jetersville. They hoped to find the desperately needed food at Burkeville, where the railroads from

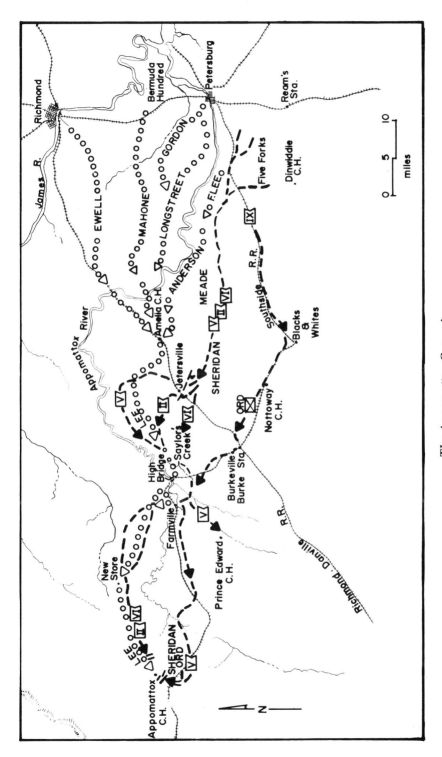

The Appomattox Campaign
March 29 - April 9, 1865

Petersburg and Richmond intersected. General Alexander wrote: "I never saw General Lee seem so anxious to bring on a battle in my life as he seemed this afternoon; but a conference with General W.H.F. Lee[7] in command of the cavalry in our front seemed to disappoint him greatly."[8] Sheridan's strength proved too great for Lee to risk a battle so he decided to outflank Grant with a night march to Farmville, twenty-three miles west. Lee hoped to leave his pursuers behind, provide his men with food at Farmville, and continue the retreat towards North Carolina. Major General William Mahone's[9] Division of Hill's Corps was ordered to Rice's Station, several miles west of Jetersville, to block the enemy while the rest of the army and its vehicles marched away from the pursuers.

Late in the day on April 5, Grant received the following communication from Sheridan.

> The whole of Lee's army is at or near Amelia Court House, and on this side of it. General Davies,[10] whom I sent out to Painesville on their right flank, has just captured six pieces of artillery and some wagons. We can capture the Army of Northern Virginia if enough force can be thrown to this point, and then advance upon it. My cavalry was at Burkesville yesterday, and six miles beyond, on the Danville Road last night. General Lee is at Amelia Court House in person. They are out of rations, or nearly so. They were advancing up the railroad towards Burkesville yesterday, when we intercepted them at this point.[11]

General Edward Porter Alexander

Grant had anticipated his subordinate's request for additional troops. Meade arrived at Jetersville in mid-afternoon followed by the 2nd Corps. The 6th Corps reached the village at 6:00 P.M., too late in the day for an attack, but Meade planned to move against the Confederates at 6:00 A.M. the next morning.

Impressed by Sheridan's plea to finish off Lee's army, Grant left General Ord's column. Accompanied by a tiny escort and a few staff officers, Grant rode sixteen miles cross country. At 10:00 P.M., his party encountered a friendly outpost. The commanding general conferred with Sheridan and issued the following orders to Generals Ord and Meade.

Jetersville Apl. 5th/65 10.10 p.m.

MAJ. GN. ORD, BURKESVILLE

In the absence of further orders move West at 8 a. m tomorrow morning and take position to watch the roads running South between Burkesville and Farmville. I am strongly of the opinion Lee will leave Amelia to-night to go South He will be pursued from here at 6 a.m. if he leaves. Otherwise an advance will be made upon him where he is.

U.S. Grant
Lt. Gn[12]

[April 5, 1865] 10.30 p.m.

MAJ. GN. MEADE,

I have just arrived here leavin [*sic*] having left the Hd of Gn. Ord's Column at about 7.30 p. m some 4 miles West of Nottoway [Court House] He will reach Burkesville to-night after a march of about 28 miles.

Ords orders now are to move West at 8 a. m. and take up a position to watch all the roads leading South crossing between Burkesville and and [*sic*] Farmville.

Your orders for to-morrow morning will hold in the absence of others. It is my impression however that Lee will retreat during the night and if so we will pursue with vigor, I would go over to see you this evening but it is late and I have roade [*sic*] all day.

U.S. Grant
Lt. Gn[13]

Grant's assessment of his opponent's intentions had clearly undergone a change, the reason for which is not revealed in his correspondence, which constitutes the historical record. The Army of Northern Virginia remained the "objective point" for the operations of his two armies. While the Army of the Potomac pursued Lee, the Army of the James would be in position to bar any attempt to reach Danville.

Throughout the night of April 5, the once indomitable Army of Northern Virginia staggered toward Farmville. Fatigue, hunger and despair drove many from the ranks. Discipline broke down in many commands. "By daylight, officers were appalled to find to what a degree Brigades had dwindled. Some regiments had almost dissolved."[14] Unavoidable gaps appeared in the long line of soldiers and vehicles; the trouble began an hour before noon.

Lee and Longstreet were at the head of the column with the still formidable divisions of Mahone and Major General Charles W. Field (1828-1892; West Point 1849). Major General John B. Gordon (1832-1904; enlisted in 1861) brought up the rear with the 2nd Corps. In the center, General Ewell led a force of about 3,000 men that was composed of artillerymen from Richmond, government clerks, sailors, and a sprinkling of veterans under Lieutenant General Anderson.[15] Most of the wagons accompanied the center segment of the column as well. The army was most vulnerable, therefore, in the middle of its line of march.

Around 11:00 A.M., enemy cavalry stabbed at the wagon train, but the Federals were driven off. The vehicles began to roll again as Generals Ewell and Anderson allowed them to pass their commands in order to permit Gordon to close up. A gap developed between the van of the extended column, now approaching Rice's Station, and the remaining foot soldiers and the assorted vehicles. Ewell decided to send the wagons between his command and the 2nd Corps on a different road to avoid the danger, but neglected to inform Gordon of the change. Instead of marching southwest to maintain contact with the main body, Gordon led his men northwest after the wagons. When Anderson resumed the march about 2:00 P.M., he was blocked by Sheridan's cavalry.

Early in the morning Meade had discovered that Lee's army was no longer positioned at Amelia Court House. He quickly wheeled the Army of the Potomac west to follow the still visible Southerners. The 5th Corps moved northwest toward Paineville. The 6th Corps took a route south of the 2nd Corps which marched due west of Jetersville. Amid the confusion between Ewell and Anderson, two divisions of the 6th Corps came up to threaten the rear. Anderson had suggested to Ewell that they combine their small divisions to attack the cavalry, or abandon the wagon train and head for the hills in hopes of finding another road to Farmville. Ewell, however, could not make up his mind and now it was too late. He established a line behind Sayler's Creek to give battle while Anderson organized an attack to clear an escape route, which failed.

The Union soldiers advanced ominously toward Ewell's scratch force, but their center was driven back by the naval battalion's gallant charge. The blueclads enveloped both of Ewell's flanks and a brigade of cavalry hit his right. Resistance crumbled and the Butternut ranks melted away. Gordon's command held off the 2nd Corps and escaped over High Bridge which crossed the Appomattox River. General Ewell and several other generals were captured; Generals Anderson and Pickett escaped. On that black day in the history of the Army of Northern Virginia, Lee lost nearly a third of his army.

Late in the afternoon, Generals Lee and Mahone rode to a hill that overlooked the valley of Sayler's Creek. Mahone described the scene: "...the disaster which had overtaken our army was in full view...hurrying teamsters with their teams and dangling traces (no wagons), retreating infantry without guns, many without hats, a harmless mob, with the massive columns of the enemy moving orderly on. At this spectacle General Lee straightened himself in his saddle, and, looking more the soldier than ever, exclaimed, as if talking to himself: 'My God! has the army dissolved?'"[16]

Lee set up his headquarters in a field north of Rice's Station around sundown. He ordered Longstreet to continue the retreat toward Farmville and dictated the following to his military secretary.

> Confederate States of America
> War Department
> Signal Bureau
> Hd. Qrs Rice's Station
> So-side railroad
> 6 Apl 1865.

His Excy Jeffn Davis,
  I shall be tonight at Farmville. You can communicate by telegraph to Meherrin [Station] & by courier to Lynchburg.

> Very respy
> and truly Yrs
> R.E.Lee

[*OR* XLVI Series I Pt.3 p.1386]

The Army of Northern Virginia suffered a mortal blow at Sayler's Creek. On April 7, Grant initiated an exchange of notes that resulted in the surrender of the Army of Northern Virginia at Appomattox Court House on April 9. The liberal terms he granted Lee began the process of reconciliation between the victorious North and the vanquished South.

The decision to concentrate the Army of the Potomac at Jetersville on April 5 set the stage for the decisive encounter at Sayler's Creek the next day. Grant did not reveal in his memoirs the true reason why he chose to change his strategy of trying to head off Lee's army to prevent its escape to Lynchburg in favor of the concentration at Jetersville. New evidence, presented here for the

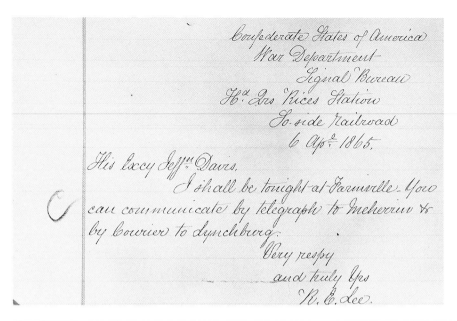

A dispatch from General Lee to President Davis

first time, suggests that Grant learned something heretofore unconfirmed by the historical record. The following letter demonstrates that General Lee himself provided the intelligence that forced him to surrender prematurely.

P.S. Please remember me most kindly to Mr Davis when you have the oppertunity [*sic*] of doing so

    G.W.C.L. [17]

                                              Lexington, Va,
                                              17 June, 1879.

Maj. W. T. Walthall,

Beauvoir (P. O) , Missi.

My Dear Major:

    I have just received your letter of the 11th inst., enclosing a copy of the one of ["the" lined out] 29th Jany. last. I find the original of the latter among a large number of letters handed to me upon my return here, not long since, after nearly a year's absence, and which I have not yet been able to attend to. I don't know why it was not forwarded to me, as I gave the Clerk of the Faculty my P.O. address from time to time with a request to forward my private letters, some of which he did forward, and some he did not & among the latter the letter in question. I am very sorry for the delay, and can attribute it only to the "youth & inexperience of the clerk," who is in most respects a very excellent young man.

    To come to the subject of your letter, however _____ After I was taken prisoner, at Sailor's [*sic*] Creek, with the greater part of the commands of Genl. Ewell, and Genl.

P. S. Please remember me most kindly
to Mr Davis when you have ever
: opportunity. Lexington, Va.,
of doing so.   17 June, 1879.
        GWCL.

Maj. W. T. Walthall,
    Beauvoir (P.O), Miss.
My Dear Major:
                I have just re-
ceived your letter of the 11th inst,
enclosing a copy of one of the
29th Jany. last. I find the origin
of the latter among a large —
number of letters handed to
me upon my return here, not
long since, after nearly a year's
absence, and which I have not
yet been able to attend to. I
don't know why it was not
forwarded to me, as I gave
the Clerk of the Faculty my
P.O. address from time to time
with a request to forward my
private letters, some of which
he did forward, and some

Letter from Custis Lee to Major Walthall (6 pages)

213

he did not a among the latter
the letter in question. I am
very sorry for the delay, and
can attribute it only to the "youth
& inexperience of the clerk", who
is in most respects a very excel-
lent young man.

To come to the subject of
your letter, however —

After I was taken prisoner,
at Sailors Creek, with the greater
part of the commands of
Genl. Ewell, and Genl. "Dick"
Anderson, and was on my
way to Petersburg (between Burkeville & Petersburg, I think) with
the officers of there commands,
we met the U. S. Engineer
Brigade under the command
of Genl. Benham, whom I
had known, prior to the
breaking out of the war,
as one of the Captains of the
Corps of Engineers & my own Corps.

He did not apparently recognize me — and I did not make
myself known to him — but began talking to Genl. Ewell
in a loud tone of voice which
could be distinctly by all around.
I heard Genl. Benham say,
among other things, that "Genl.
Weitzel had found, even
after his entrance into Richmond, a letter from Genl. Lee,
giving the ~~strength army~~
condition of the army of Northern
Va, and what he proposed
to do ~~when~~ if became necessary
to withdraw from the lines
before Richmond & Petersburg —
~~supposing that necessity to exist,
which then seemed not im-
probable~~ and that the letter
was immediately sent to Genl.
Grant". In answer to some
look, or word, of doubt, from
Genl. Ewell, a some one else,

Genl. Benham replied, "oh! there is no doubt about the letter, for, I saw it myself", I think he added. I received the impression at the time, or afterwards, that this letter was a confidential communication to the Secretary of War in answer to a Resolution of the Confed. Congress, asking for the information early in 1865.

When I mentioned, some time afterwards, this statement of Genl. Benham's, to Genl. Lee, the latter said — "This accounts for the energy of the enemy's pursuit. The first day after we left the lines, he seemed to be entirely at

sea with regard to our movements. After that, though
I never worked so hard to
withdraw our army in safety,
he displayed more energy,
skill, and judgment, in his
movements than I ever knew
him to display before".

Of course I do not pretend
to give the exact words of either
Genl. Benham, or of Genl. Lee,
but only the sense of them; but
I think I have quoted the words
themselves quite accurately.

Please excuse the scratched
appearance of this letter; but
I prefer to send it as it is written
than to lose to-day's mail
in rewriting it.

I am very much obliged
to you for your kind interest
in my lawsuit. I have had

two decisions in my favor — in U. S. Courts, and the case now goes to the Supreme Court, where it will be taken up and decided, in course, I am told, in from two to four years.

I am sorry that you have not been able to satisfy yourself in regard to the failure of supplies. I can't see how any one with the most ordinary sense or fairness could presume to blame Mr Davis for the failure. I am disposed to believe now, as heretofore, that it is one of those accidents which are constantly occurring both in peace and war, and which are more noticeable in war in consequence of greater effects, or consequences.

I return the copy of your letter, as I have the original. — Very truly yo.

R E Lee

"Dick" Anderson, and was on my way to Petersburg (between Burkeville & Petersburg, I think) with the officers of these commands, we met the U. S. Engineer Brigade under the command of Genl. Benham,[18] whom I had known, prior to the breaking out of the war, as one of the Captains of the Corps of Engineers __ my own Corps.

He did not apparently recognize __ and I did not make myself known to him __ but began talking to Genl. Ewell in a loud tone of voice which could be distinctly heard by all around. I heard Genl. Benham say, among other things, that "Genl. Weitzel had found, soon after his entrance into Richmond, a letter from Genl. Lee, giving the ["strength and" lined out] condition of the army of Northern Va., and what he proposed to do ["when" lined out] should it ["chance" lined out] become necessary to withdraw from the lines before Richmond & Petersburg, __ ["supposing that necessity to exist, which then seemed not improbable" lined out] and that the letter was immediately sent to Genl. Grant." In answer to some look, or word, of doubt, from Genl. Ewell or some one else, Genl. Benham replied, "Oh! there is no doubt about the letter, for, I saw it myself," I think he added. I received the impression at the time, or afterwards, that this letter was a confidential communication to the Secretary of War in answer to a Resolution of the Confed. Congress, asking for the information early in 1865.

When I mentioned, some time afterwards, this statement of Genl. Benham's, to Genl. Lee, the latter said __ "This accounts for the energy of the enemy's pursuit. The first day after we left the lines, he seemed to be entirely at sea with regard to our movements. After that, though I never worked so hard in my life to withdraw our army in safety, he displayed more energy, boldness, skill, and judgment, in his movements than I ever knew him to display before."[19]

Of course I do not pretend to give the exact words of either Genl. Benham, or of Genl. Lee, but only the sense of them; but I think I have quoted the words themselves quite accurately.

Please excuse the scratched appearance of this letter; but I prefer to send it as it is rather than to lose to_day's mail in rewriting it.

I am very much obliged to you for your kind interest in my lawsuit. I have had two decisions in my favor in U. S. Courts, and the case now goes to the Supreme Court, where it will be taken up and decided, in due course, I am told, in from two to four years.

I am sorry that you have not been able to satisfy yourself in regard to the failure of supplies. I can't see how any one with the most ordinary sense or fairness could presume to blame Mr Davis for the failure. I am disposed to believe now, as heretofore, that it is one of those accidents which are constantly occurring both in peace and war, and which are often more noticeable in war in consequence of greater effects, or consequences.

I return the copy[20] of your letter, as I have the original. _ very truly yrs.

G.W.C. Lee

Douglas Southall Freeman, the premier biographer of Robert E. Lee, considered the salient content of the above letter and concluded that the existence of the document referred to by Generals Benham and Lee was a "fable....In this instance, it is manifest that the alleged letter was confused with a general report [dated March 9, 1865] Lee had made to Secretary Breckinridge on the military outlook. This paper was of interest to the Federals but of no value in shaping the pursuit."[21]

A paper presented to the Massachusetts Historical Society by Thomas L. Livermore in 1906 formed the basis of Mr. Freeman's opinion concerning the veracity of General Benham's statement as recorded by Robert E. Lee's eldest son. In his analysis of Grant's generalship during the Appomattox Campaign, and the possibility of secret intelligence being a factor, Mr. Livermore did not include General Weitzel's testimony.

> I desire to say here in regard to Mr. Dana's[22] visit to Richmond that he stated to me that he had no intention nor wish to give me any instructions and that he was there only to work and report. If my memory serves me correctly he sent daily bulletins to the New York Tribune from Richmond. He wrote a single note to me while I was in command at Richmond. It was in reference to some rebel records which he had heard of. I had made the collection of all these documents a special duty for one of my staff officers. While on this subject I desire to touch upon a letter, the existence or non-existence of which has caused considerable correspondence lately [1879] in the newspapers of the country. Among the documents found in the drawer of Mr. Davis' desk was a confidential letter written by General Lee and laid before the Confederate Senate in secret session. This letter was written in the previous October, if I recollect correctly, and in it Lee frankly and clearly showed that their cause was lost, and, I think, advised them to make the best terms they could. This letter was considered by me so important that I sent it to the Secretary of War by General H.W. Benham who was on that day on a visit to Richmond. It certainly, ought, therefore to be among the archives of the War Department.[23]

General Weitzel's evidence confirms the existence of the letter dismissed by Douglas Freeman and Sir Frederick Maurice, an earlier biographer of Lee. Did Robert E. Lee regard the military situation to be desperate and The Cause hopeless in late 1864? Arthur St. Clair Colyar, a Confederate Congressman from Tennessee, wrote a letter that was published in the *Annals Of The Army Of Tennessee*. The first half of Colyar's letter confirms the fact that Lee knew that the war had been lost.

> I was, as you remember, in the House of Representatives, and on intimate terms with Colonel John. B. Baldwin.[24] Some time in the latter part of the year 1864 (I cannot remember the exact date, but, probably, in November), at the close of a night session, Mr. Baldwin asked me to walk with him, saying, when we got out on the Capitol grounds, that a crisis had come, and something must be done; 'but,' said he, 'for the first time in my life I feel that I lack moral courage to do my duty.' He then went on to say that a determined stand ought to be made for peace, but, knowing Mr. Davis as he did, he feared nothing could be done with him. Said he, 'I have seen General Lee, who gave me to understand

distinctly, that the cause had to fail.' Colonel Baldwin, as you will remember, was during the first year of the war, in the army and under General Lee, and was on most intimate terms with him.

Upon consultation, it was agreed that Mr. Baldwin should, the next day, introduce in the House, in secret session, a resolution for the appointment of a committee to inquire into our resources and ability for carrying on the war. This he did, and the committee was appointed. Mr. B. was chairman, and I was put on the committee. This committee took much proof mainly officers of the army, and, among others, we examined General Lee. I suppose his deposition can be found at Washington. He proved that his army was daily being reduced, and that General Grant's army was daily being strengthened, and that it was only a question of time as to giving up Richmond, and when he did retire, his army could not be sustained for lack of supplies.[25]

A peace conference did take place at Hampton Roads, Virginia, on February 3, 1865, but foundered on the question of slavery and the restoration of the Union.

Based upon the above evidence it is certain that Lee sent a letter to his government in October 1864, as indicated by his son and Generals Benham and Weitzel, which portrayed inevitable defeat. The said letter described a future plan to evacuate the Richmond-Petersburg area and included a pro-jected route (or routes) of retreat, an assembly point (Amelia Court House) and a destination, Danville, Virginia. Further, this letter was discovered at Rich-mond in the Executive Mansion on April 3, 1865. It was seen by the Secretary of War, Edwin M. Stanton, who, after he received Grant's telegram from Wilson's Station, transmitted the contents of Lee's letter, or an abstract thereof, to General Grant. It is, therefore, highly probable that Grant learned of Lee's intentions before he left Wilson's Station on the morning of April 5.

Strategically, before the Battle of Five Forks, Grant believed that his opponent would probably retreat to North Carolina. Tactically, during the course of the last campaign, Grant believed on April 4, that Lee's army was headed west to Lynchburg. This is indisputable. Sheridan believed the same. Available correspondence pertaining to the Army of the Potomac's operations before the afternoon of April 5, cannot explain why Grant revised his estimate of Lee's destination, but the future president provides the clue by quoting the first message Sheridan sent to him on April 5 in his memoir.

Access to the intelligence contained in Lee's October 1864 letter would have caused Grant to reconsider the situation as he then perceived it. On the morning of April 5, Grant sent a message to Sherman that began: "All indications now are that Lee will attempt to reach Danville [move south] with the remnant of his force."[26] Sheridan's message, written at 3:00 P.M., stated that Lee and his army were at Amelia Court House. Grant's quotation of this dispatch in his memoir indicates its importance to him.

Positive news from the reliable Sheridan, the secret intelligence from Stanton, combined with his previous hunch, convinced Grant that Lee would thrust toward Jetersville in an attempt to reach North Carolina by way of Danville. To provide for either contingency, a movement toward Lynchburg or Danville, Grant kept the Army of the James moving west to watch the roads leading south from Farmville. The clarified strategic situation explains Grant's decision to risk his person by riding cross country through hostile territory on the night of April 5. His correct conclusion caused the concentration at Jetersville, since the day before, Grant had directed Sheridan to intercept the enemy at Farmville. Grant's flexibility in the fluid situation resulted in continuous contact with the Confederates, the dismemberment of Lee's army on April 6, and its entrapment and surrender on April 9.

Robert E. Lee, the Confederacy's greatest general (because he won the most battles), entered his family's residence at Richmond on April 15. His former soldiers, Union veterans, and friends competed for his time. Despite his own personal problems and his mental fatigue, Lee found the time to assist those who appealed to him to employ his influence in their affairs.

Richmond

17 Apl '65

Genl

    Allow me to introduce to you Genl Jos. R. Davis,[27] nephew of Pres: Davis, who commanded a brigade in the Army of N.Va_ Genl Davis is on parole & desires to return to his home in Mississippi __ Any facilities you can afford him will be highly appreciated by

your Obt Srvt

R E Lee

Genl Ord

Command at Richmond

With no plans and his military career terminated, Lee expressed to his friends the desire to live as a simple farmer. The question of how he would support his family was answered by Providence. In August, he accepted an unsolicited offer to assume the presidency of Washington College, located in Lexington, Virginia.

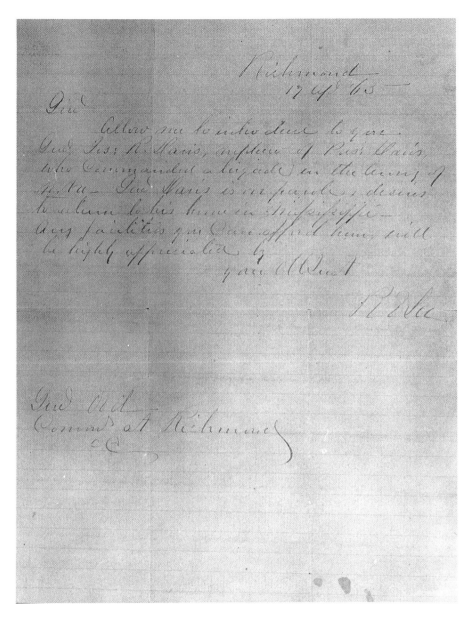

A note from Robert E. Lee to General E.O.C. Ord

Lexington Va: 7 Oct 1869

Dear Sir

I rec'd by Express yesterday a copy of the last order issued to the Army of N. Virginia at Appomattox Ct House, handsomely framed & illustrated, on which it was stated that it had been executed at your Commercial College by yourself; & I presume that I am indebted to you for it. It does great credit to your Institution & Skill, & is a very handsome Specimen of penmanship.

I am very much obliged to you for this token of remembrance & am very resp'y

your ob't serv't
R E Lee

Mr B. B. Euston
Macon, Georgia

A note from Robert E. Lee written less than a year before he died

Lexington Va: 7 Decr 1869

Dear Sir

I recd by Express yesterday a copy of the last order issued to the Army of N. Virginia at Appomattox CtHouse, handsomely framed & illustrated, on which it was stated that it had been executed at your commercial college by yourself; & I presume that I am indebted to you for it. It does great credit to your Institution & Skill, & is a very handsome specimen of penmanship.

I am very much obliged to you for this token of remembrance & am very respt

your Obt Servt
R E Lee

Mr B.B. Euston
Macon, Georgia

As the head of an educational institution, Lee's concern for the welfare of his students was the same as it had been for his soldiers. Many of Washington College's young men had fought with the Army of Northern Virginia. Lee rarely dismissed a student. He considered education to be essential for the future prosperity of the South and admonished individuals who neglected classes and studies by reminding them of the sacrifice their families had made to support their schooling. The following letter from Jubal Early to Jefferson Davis illustrates the depth of Robert E. Lee's Christian concern for the good of his fellow man.

Lynchburg March 28th 1878

My Dear Sir:

Your letter of the 27th ultimo has remained unanswered a good deal longer than I intended, and then ought to have been the case._ When it arrived I was engaged in some writing on which I was very much intent, and as I could give no satisfactory information, in reply to your request for my views and recollections in regard to the failure of the Army of the Potomac under General Johnston, to increase in proportion to the re-enforcements sent it between the 21st of July 1861 and the 20th of October of that year. I laid your letter aside to be answered when I was at leisure, and more time has elapsed without my doing so, than I intended. I am not able to give any views or speculations on the subject, but the most general ones, and they will be of little value to you.__ At that day I was in the habit of attending to my own command, with full reliance upon those above me to do every thing that was proper and necessary for the good of the service and the cause, and I never presumed to question or scan closely any of their proceedings._ In fact that course I prescribed to myself during the whole war, though as my rank and command increased I, of course, knew some of the practical operations of the army, and the experience gained enabled me to form, with more reliance on my capacity to do so, my own views with regard to what was transpiring. __ If in the manuscripts I have furnished you, you find often free expression of my own opinions about measures that were adopted, you must not think that even if these opinions were entertained at the time, I presumed to promulgate them or to offer my opinions to those of the commanders whose business it was to judge for me and all others. My recollection of events was very distinct[ly] known and when, after the war I undertook to commit to paper what I knew, as the effort to "wash our dirty linen" for the public entertainment had begun, I could not refrain from giving my own views in many cases, without however undertaking to critic as a partisan into any of the quarrels that originated from the war. During the war I did not take sides in any of the disputes, but sincerely regretted them; and now I am friendly with all the parties to them though [illegible] ready to give my recollections of the facts as they came within my knowledge_ The same manuscripts furnished you, have been furnished General Johnston & General Beauregard, so far as they affect them respectively; and about the facts and opinions therein expressed I have no concealments._

In regard to the particular points upon which you now want my views, I was really not in a position to enable me to form any opinions that are of any value_ I attended strictly to my own brigade, and had no occasion to know the real strength of the army_ I know that there was a great deal more laxity in granting permissions to be absent in other brigades than in mine, for my officers took occasion to bring it to my notice as a complaint against me_ I believe that mine was the only brigade in that army in which a chain of sentinels was placed around the Camp so as to prevent men from leaving it without permission, and requiring officers [illegible] to report at the guards according to regulations _ But absenteeism to any great extent had not begun I think by the date you last mention (the 20th of October)._ I imagine that you are impressed with the opinion that more troops were really sent to that army than were sent_ I have no exact knowledge on the subject, but I have some general recollections as to Beauregard's part of the army _ In my own brigade there was one regiment the 23rd N.C. which came immediately after_ the others were at the battle, until the 20th Georgia was added to my brigade about the 1st of October_ It had been with the army some time, but came after the battle_ In Rodes' brigade (Ewell's that was) one regiment, the 12th Alabama, came after the battle_ In Bonhams', all I believe were at the battle_ So it was with Longstreet's and Cocke's[28] brigades_ D.R. Jones'[29] brigade, as was organized after the battle, was composed of at least one South Carolina regiment that was at the battle, and perhaps the others were there also_ More brigades were organized into the two divisions of which the 1st Corps of the Army of the Potomac (Beauregard's) was composed, towit Van Dorn's,[30] and Longstreet's _ I think two Louisiana regiments came after the battle, which being united with the two & Wheat's battalion[31] that were at the battle made one of the brigades in Kirby Smith's division of the 2nd Corps_ Elzey's brigade, another brigade of that division, was at the battle, and Trimble's, the third brigade, was composed of some regiments that had been at the battle & some not _ Three brigades constituting the other division of that Corps (G.W. Smith's) were composed of the troops that had come with Johnston from the Valley and new Regiments that came after the battle, the greater part probably being new regiments_ You know Jackson's brigade, that was afterwards, sent to the Valley had been at the battle._ I don't think a third of the army as it existed at the last of October could have come after the battle _ probably not a fourth. ___ I think that it was not until about the last of the Fall, that anything like desertion began, and then to a very limited extent. I recollect to have heard of a case or two in one of my North Carolina regiments about that time ___ I knew of nothing whatever in the management of the army to cause its strength to be really less than it ought to have been_ Of it was not to be expected that raw troops like ours were should be kept as rigidly to their places as experienced and disciplined soldiers _ I was a little more rigid than some others, but that was a matter of particular management by brigade commanders, and I have never had any reason to complain that my efforts to enforce discipline and a rigid compliance with the regulations were not supported at head-quarters.___

After the date of which you speak, I could give some speculations as to the increase of absenteeism in the army, but it would affect the management in Richmond and not at army head-quarters. In the first place, I never thought it judicious to brigade the troops by States.___ In the next place when desertion began, the penalty was not enforced with sufficient vigor_ there being pregnant cases of suspension of sentence, and finally of commutings. So fully was I impressed with the evils [and] effects of the interference that when, afterwards, I had a separate command, and had to pass upon the sentences of courts-martial, I ordered the execution to take place so speedily as to prevent an application being made for suspension_ This was General Jackson's course, and the first execution I saw, was under his orders_ _ General Lee always gave a man ten days to prepare for his latter end, and the consequence generally was that no execution took place._ My idea was that when a man was hurried into eternity with all his sins upon him, the example was more terrible to others, than when he was given time to repent & then was shot with the hope of going to a better place than the army was; and on one occasion I convinced two chaplains of the correctness of my theory, when they came pleading for more time for a man in order that he might repent.___

Of course you will understand that I fully appreciated the humane motives that actuated General Lee and the authorities at Richmond, but I thought that humanity to the suffering women and children and justice to the army required that those who abandoned their colors should suffer the penalty, in order to deter others from following their example

Another source of great mischief and dissatisfaction in the army during the winter of 1861-2, was the granting of permission, by Mr. Benjamin as secretary of war, to officers and some times to privates, to recruit new commands from among the soldiers already serving in the army_ This did great harm, and I ordered every officer who came into my command to recruit for such a purpose, to be put in the guard house_ In one case where an officer had surreptitiously procured an order transferring a man from one of my regiments to his company, that he had permission to insert into an artillery company, I went to Colonel Jordan and peremptorily demanded a revocation of the order, which was done_ it having been issued by his brother who was his assistant._ That officer never came into my camp afterwards.___

The ignoring of such permissions, which was afterwards rendered absolutely necessary, created great dissatisfaction with the men thus recruited; and at Yorktown, there were four companies in [Colonel Roger A.] Pryor's regiment [3rd Virginia], temporarily attached to my command, who laid down their arms and refused to do duty when the conscript act [April 1862] became a law, because they had re-enlisted in a new regiment for which permission had been granted. The surest peremptory measures had to be taken with them, and one of them was not induced to retrimission [?], until I had made it work in the trenches under a provost-guard for two or three days, when the men were brought to their senses._

The interference by State judges under the habeas corpus afterwards became a source of great mischief, and I could give you an instance in which I would have bullied a judge who issued a writ for 19 men in my command at one time, if on his representation, without ascertaining the facts, Mr Seddon had not issued a peremptory order to have the men, all under charges for desertion, discharged the service_

I had an opinion that the State courts had no jurisdiction and wrote to Mr. [Thomas H.] Watts the attorney general, for his opinion, but he declined to give it, because of some precedent set by Mr. [William] Wirt as attorney general [1817-1829] of the United States._

I mention all these things, not because they have any direct bearing on the inquiries you made of me, but to show that when the subject of the cause of absenteeism from our army is broached, a very wide field is opened._ I never supposed, of course, that there was any improper motive or purpose on the part of those in authority in taking the steps I mention, but my own position enabled me to judge of their effects._

You will observe for the return for February 1862, given in a table furnished by [illegible] and copied by me in an article which appears in the July number of the Lee Historical Paper for 1876, that in the Department of Northern Virginia, embracing the Army of the Potomac, the Valley District and the Aquia District there were present 56,396 and present and absent 84,226_ The returns after that time show a much greater proportion absent._ Now, I cannot conceive how, out of the 84,226 present and absent in all the troops that were in the Department of Northern Virginia, supposing all these troops to have been there at the time, there could have been enough men for duty to warrant an advance against McClellan about the 20th of October 1861_ You must have in mind that when General Johnston says "effectives total,"[32] that embraces only the enlisted men for duty, who were given under that head, and excluded officers then on extra duty, sick, & in arrest_ At that time and afterwards we had to take our teamsters from the army, which made the number of extra duty men unusually large_ A stampede of negro teamsters at the first battle of Manassas, had rendered it necessary to detail soldiers__

McClellan's report, page 111, shows that on the 15th of October 1861, the troops under his control, about Washington, & its dependencies, amounted to 133,261 present for duty, and by the 1st of December they had increased to 161,452 present for duty_ Some of them were in Baltimore and some at the Potomac, but all available to resist a forward movement by us._

Since the exceedingly cold spell just after my return, we have had an unusually warm winter and spring, and I fear the consequence will be a general loss of our fruit.__ Instead of March's coming in "like a lamb and going out like a lion", according to the old saying, it has very much the appearance now of going out like a very tame sheep __

Present my best regards to Mrs Davis and believe always

Very truly & faithfully
Yours
Hon. Jefferson Davis   JA Early

An interesting book entitled the *Marble Man*, written by the late Thomas Connelly, delineated the creation of the Lee myth, whereby Southerners interpreted the morality of their war for independence. Douglas Freeman, Clifford Dowdey, Jubal Early, John Esten Cooke, and others depicted their hero as an example of the Christian warrior, who, having discharged his duty under God, accepts the verdict of the battlefield with grace. "Lee's character was almost deified as he became a Christ symbol. If Christ had his Gethsemane, Lee had his Appomattox. Writers turned to Lee as an example of the better man who could lose, and honed his character to perfection."[33]

Lee certainly did not consciously cultivate such an image, nor did he see himself as a saint, but a sinner subject to the will of God. The Southern hero became a device to explain Confederate defeat: good men, with pure motives, do not always succeed. In criticizing Lee the symbol, Connelly also attacked Lee the general. "Lee's aggressive nature bled the Confederacy of manpower. In his first two years as commander of the Virginia army, Lee threw his men into combat in furious assaults. His offensive tactics were dreadfully expensive...."[34] In proportion to Northern manpower this is truth, but as Connelly himself pointed out in his work *Army of the Heartland: The Army of Tennessee*, the war was won in the West, not lost in Virginia. Offensive action compensates for inferiority in numbers, as proven by the success of "Stonewall" Jackson in the Valley Campaign of 1862 and Dick Taylor at Mansfield, Louisiana, in 1864. Richard McMurry, in *Two Great Rebel Armies*, thoroughly refutes charges against Lee's generalship and strategic thinking.[35]

Alan Nolan of Indianapolis carries on Connelly's crusade in an uninspired and legalistic volume entitled *Lee Considered*. Lee customarily referred to the enemy as "those people," a fact that is well known to Civil War students. Following the failure of Pickett's Charge, for example, Captain Robert A. Bright of Pickett's staff, heard Lee tell his downcast division commander: "General Pickett, place your division in rear of this hill and be ready to repel the advance of the enemy should they follow up their advantage."[36] The order surprised Capt. Bright as it was the first time he had ever heard the army commander call the Federals anything but "those people." In a chapter entitled "Those People—The Magnanimous Adversary," Mr. Nolan assails the belief that Lee fought his battles without bitterness because he did not always employ "those people" in conversation or in correspondence.

To prove his point, and to the discredit of his methodology, Mr. Nolan tortures the text of a letter written by Lee on December 8, 1861, to his daughter Ann. He extracts the word "vandals" from Lee's letter to support his case that "Lee constructed a demonic image of the Federals."[37] The full sentence reads: "I am afraid Cousin Julia [Stuart] will not be able to defend her home if attacked by the vandals, for they have little respect for anybody, and if they catch the Doctor

General Robert Edward Lee (seated) with General George Washington Custis Lee (left) and Lieutenant Colonel Walter Taylor

[Richard Stuart] they will certainly send him to Fort Warren or La Fayette."[38] In fact, many Union soldiers were absent from their companies during battle, but returned to the ranks after they had robbed inhabitants who lived in the surrounding area. During the infamous "March to the Sea," Sherman's soldiers looted the possessions of slaves, the people they were supposed to be delivering from evil.

Another curious contention of Mr. Nolan's is that Lee should have unilaterally surrendered his army after his defeat at Gettysburg and the fall of Vicksburg. Even if Lee (and other generals) recognized in the summer of 1863 that the war was lost, his personal sense of duty and honor precluded such an act. Moreover, whether Mr. Nolan agrees or not, an American soldier is required to subordinate his own views to the policy of the civilian government. One wonders what Mr. Nolan would have advised the defenders of the Alamo or the crew of the *Bismarck*, who knew they were on a death ride. What if George Washington had called it quits after Long Island or at Valley Forge? Did Cornwallis request permission from King George III to surrender at Yorktown?

Lee's devotion to "grand offensive strategy" and his "martial qualities," according to Mr. Nolan, inflicted such high losses in 1862 and 1863 that Lee eventually diminished the Army of Northern Virginia's effectiveness. The proper military policy, in Nolan's analysis, for Lee to have followed, should have been positional, defensive warfare, to wear down Northern will with high casualty lists. Fredericksburg is an example, though Mr. Nolan does not cite it as evidence of the merits of his case. "Had Lee adopted this defensive approach [the Seven Days, Chancellorsville?] during the two years that he spent on the offensive, he could have had available a fair proportion of the more than 100,000 of his soldiers and officers who went down during the offensive years. With these additional numbers, he could have maintained mobility and avoided a siege. Maneuvers like Early's 1864 movement could have been undertaken with sufficient numbers."[39]

If "Stonewall" Jackson had recovered from his wounds to command the 2nd Corps in 1864, perhaps he would have captured Washington. Does the same "grand offensive strategy" standard apply to General Bragg's attacks at Murfreesboro and Chickamauga? Would Johnston have used his "fair proportion" to advantage during the Vicksburg or Atlanta Campaigns? Did General A. S. Johnston commit a strategic error when he attacked Grant's army at Shiloh Church? Or was it a missed opportunity, delivered a day too late, to prevent the combination of two opposing armies. The fact that Lee made mistakes, most notably the decision to give battle at Sharpsburg, is clear, and Douglas Freeman lists many other errors in judgment, such as the appointment of General Ewell as a corps commander.[40] However, Mr. Nolan's observations about Lee's generalship constitute a circular argument. In criticizing the symbol Lee became, Mr. Nolan overlooks the nonpareil man Lee was.

On March 30, 1861, Robert E. Lee was promoted to colonel from lieutenant colonel. He refused an offer from the Lincoln administration to command U.S. forces on April 18. Two days later, he resigned his commission as an officer of the U.S. Army and accepted a commission from the state of Virginia as a major general on April 22. Though technically still an officer in the U.S. Army, as far Lee was concerned, his divorce with the North had gone into effect when he mailed his letter of resignation. "In view of Lee's own statements, his conduct, and the timing of his move from loyalty to the United States to making war against it, what may be said about Lee's decision?"[41] Alan Nolan seems to imply that as an American, Lee was a traitor to his country for protecting his family and defending his native state from immoral invasion. The following document answers that question from a different perspective.

Executive Department of Va
Richmond   Nov. 24, 1862

Dear Col,

I have examined the records of the State in reference to your point of enquiry in reference to General Pemberton's tender of service to Virginia

On the 20th of April 1861 the injunction of secrecy having been removed the Governor issued his proclamation inviting officers of the U.S. Army, native or residents in Virginia to take service in her army. In a few days thereafter Genl. (then Major) Pemberton in person tendered his sword to Virginia and on the 28th of the same month he was nominated as Lt. Col. of Active Volunteers, subsequently he was transferred to the Provisional Army of Va on the 9th of May __

I am instructed by his Excellency the Governor to say that he perfectly recollects the pleasure which was afforded him by the prompt & cordial tender made by Maj. Pemberton, who tho' not a native of the South [Philadelphia] was among the first to cast his lot with the state of his adoption, affording an example worthy to be imitated by his iate brethren in arms.

The Governor further bids me say that from what he has learned Major Pemberton reported to him as soon as it was practicable __ The facts referred to are as follows _ When Virginia seceeded [*sic*], 17th April 1861 Major Pemberton was in command of his company at the City of New York __ on the 19th. the ordinance of Secession was made known _ Maj. Pemberton was ordered with his Company to Washington D.C. where he tendered his resignation to U.S. Govt. Eight days elapsed between promulgation of the ordinance of Secession & the appointment of Maj. Pemberton as Lt. Col. in Va Forces and the Gov. is of the opinion that the Maj. had actually tendered his service before his resignation was accepted by the U.S. Govt.

I am very respy
Yr Obt Servt
L. Bassett French
Col & A.D.C.

Col G. W. C. Lee
A.D.C.

On the morning of April 9, 1865, before Lee met with Grant, General Alexander appealed to Lee to not surrender unconditionally. Alexander believed that the army should be ordered to disperse; scattered to continue the struggle. Lee listened "very patiently" until the Georgian had finished his monologue and explained why such a suggestion was impracticable. "And as Christian men, General Alexander, you & I have no right to think for one moment of our personal feelings or affairs. We must consider only the affect which our action will have upon the country at large...But it is still early in the spring, & if the men can be quietly & quickly returned to their homes there is time to plant crops & begin to repair the ravages of the war. That is what I must now try to bring about."

General Lee then assured Alexander that Grant did not expect unconditional surrender but would offer honorable terms. "Then I thought I had never half known before what a big heart & brain our general had...And not only did my own little plan, of running away [to Brazil] if ever I saw a white flag, vanish into thin air, but nothing could now have induced me to miss the opportunity of contributing by presence, example, & every means in my power to carrying out the general's wishes in every respect."[42]

An ardent admirer of the general believed that "to know the real Lee was to watch the old man moving among Lexington's children."[43] The Civil War's most successful general, who graduated from West Point without a demerit and epitomizes devotion to duty, left this world on October 12, 1870.

7

JEFFERSON DAVIS

Jefferson Davis, who served as the chief executive of the Confederate government, demonstrated his insecurity through his unwillingness to listen to the counsel of others, which was compounded by his inability to admit mistakes. He relied on himself to determine military policy and did not delegate authority to subordinates. He concerned himself with minor administrative details such as the promotion of junior officers and their assignments, to the detriment of his fragile health and the well-being of his government.

Davis did not lack talent or determination. Despite his education and years of public service, however, he was unwise. His presidency failed because he "never possessed the temperamental, managerial or interpersonal skills necessary to be a great chief executive."[1] The Mississippi senator was ill-suited to lead a revolution because he was not a man of the people. He disdained advice from their representatives or citizens who called on him at Richmond. Davis' cold and petty exterior created numerous enemies in the press and Congress. Opposition to his seemingly imperious rule grew early in the war yet no one emerged to lead the anti-Davis faction.

One of President Davis' chief critics, Edward A. Pollard, edited the *Richmond Examiner*. Pollard wrote after the war: "In a revolutionary leader, something more is wanted than scholarly and polished intellect. The history of the world shows that, in such circumstances, the plainest men, in point of learning and scholarship, have been the most successful, and that their elements of success have been quick apprehension, practical judgment, knowledge of human nature, and above all, and to increase their stores of judgment, by deigning to learn from every possible source of practical wisdom within their reach."[2]

The future president of the Confederacy was born on June 3, 1808, in a Kentucky log cabin, the youngest of ten children. Before the war of 1812, the Samuel E. Davis family moved to Bayou Teche in Louisiana. Because of the threat posed by British invaders in 1814, the Davises relocated to Woodville, Mississippi. Young Jefferson attended several schools until he reached the age of fifteen, when he enrolled in Transylvania University in Lexington, Kentucky. A year later, he entered West Point and graduated in 1828. The highlight of Lieutenant Davis' career with the 1st Infantry Regiment occurred in the summer of 1832 when he apprehended Black Hawk, chief of the Sauk tribe. Unfortunately, however, harsh duty on the frontier impaired Davis' health and in 1835, tired of army life, he resigned.

Betrothal to Sarah Knox Taylor, daughter of the 1st Infantry's colonel, Zachary Taylor, also influenced Lt. Davis' decision to quit the army. The couple married on June 17, 1835, and moved to Mississippi where they lived at "Hurricane," the plantation of his older brother, Joseph E. Davis. Joseph was one of the richest men in the state, and generously gave his younger brother 800 acres of land. Jefferson began clearing the land he named "Brierfield" to establish himself as a planter. Before the end of summer, both Jefferson and Sarah became deathly ill, and on September 15, Mrs. Davis died. Grief and malaria nearly claimed the life of her husband as well, for Davis did not recover until October, and he spent the winter in Cuba.

Joseph Davis, an enlightened and educated man, treated his slaves with unusual liberality; he did not believe in corporal punishment. A lawyer, Joseph allowed blacks to administer justice in their own courts. Jefferson learned about agriculture from his brother, and during the lonely nights, he spent hours in Hurricane's large library. The widower seldom left his brother's home.

A change in his lifestyle occurred in 1837, when he journeyed to Washington and attempted to revive his miliary career. His unsuccessful effort caused him to return to Brierfield and resume his life as a planter. The plantation gradually prospered, and by 1840 Davis possessed forty slaves; he had also become more outgoing. Politics continued to attract him more than cotton, and in 1845, he was elected to the U.S. House of Representatives. Congressman Davis returned to Washington City in December accompanied by his new wife, Varina Howell Davis.

The couple remained at the capital only a few months. War with Mexico broke out in May 1846, and the following month, Davis was elected colonel of

Confederate President Jefferson Finis Davis

the 1st Mississippi Infantry. He resigned his seat in the House and assumed command of the "Mississippi Rifles." The 1st Mississippi and their colonel distinguished themselves at the Battle of Monterrey (September 21, 1846) when they charged a fort. At the Battle of Buena Vista (February 23, 1847) Col. Davis was wounded in the foot and won national recognition for his brilliant tactics in repelling a cavalry charge. Jefferson Davis emerged from the Mexican War as a hero on crutches with a limitless political future.

Soon after his return to civilian life, Davis received an appointment from the governor of Mississippi to fulfill the unexpired U.S. Senate term of Jesse Speight, who had died May 1. The oath of office was administered to Davis on December 6, 1847. He served on the Military Affairs Committee; in January the Mississippi legislature voted to give him a full term in the U.S. Senate.

Senator Davis supported the extension of slavery into territories such as California and Oregon. This subject was the center of the growing dispute concerning the question of slavery in the United States. Northerners feared the competition between free labor and slave labor. Jefferson Davis avowed that slavery benefited blacks and it served their long term self-interest. He treated his own slaves with kindness and allowed them education, but did not realize that his treatment of them was the exception rather than the rule among his Southern peers. The essence of his pro-slavery views rested on racial superiority. "The slave must be made fit for his freedom by education and discipline and thus made unfit for slavery. And as soon as he becomes unfit for slavery, the master will no longer desire to hold him as a slave."[3] Southerners countered arguments against the immorality of slavery by pointing out the exploitation of Northern laborers by greedy business owners, but did not mention that their slaves lost contact with much of their African culture.

By 1851, the Democratic senator from Mississippi had risen to prominence as a champion of states rights, the principle of state sovereignty that interpreted the Constitution conservatively in regard to Federal interference with local laws. In anticipation of the future, Davis recognized the possibility that the two sections would one day separate. He advocated the development of railroads in the South as well as immigration from the North and Europe. Southern based manufacturing would decrease Southern dependence on the North for consumer goods and provide muskets and munitions.

In September 1851, Davis resigned from the Senate to run for Governor of Mississippi. He lost the election by less than a thousand votes and retired to Brierfield where Varina bore Samuel E. Davis on July 30, 1852. The election of Franklin Pierce to the presidency ended Davis' withdrawal from public service.

President-elect Pierce wrote Davis a letter in mid-December that requested him to visit Washington for consultation on Southern affairs. Davis declined but did not refuse Pierce's invitation that he attend the inauguration. Pierce was inaugurated on March 4, 1853, and the Mexican War hero became Secretary of War in his old friend's cabinet.

Unlike numerous predecessors, Secretary Davis took an active interest in the affairs of his department. Davis antagonized the military establishment by controlling every aspect of an officer's career. The army came to believe that the Secretary of War favored his friends with promotion and preferential assignments. Davis recognized, however, that officers who retained their positions through seniority rather than merit decreased the efficiency of his department. Only death or retirement could remove antiquarians. When two cavalry regiments were organized in 1855, two army associates obtained their colonelcy due to his patronage, not through seniority.

Davis administered the War Department as an autocrat. His desire for reform, as he determined the need, facilitated feuds with senior generals. Davis' most noted antagonist, Lieutenant General Winfield Scott (1786-1866; appointed by Thomas Jefferson), had served in the army since 1808. Before Davis assumed office they had despised each other and Scott resented the authority of anyone but the president. By 1855, Davis concluded that Scott represented a challenge to his domain, an exchange of unsavory letters ensued. Throughout his public career, Davis exhibited a tendency to crush an opponent on paper with organized facts as he perceived them. (At one point in the contest of wills, Davis composed a twenty-seven page letter.) The needless episode with General Scott revealed a serious character flaw within Davis: he could not get along with people who disagreed with him.

During his tenure as Secretary of War, Davis initiated changes that modernized the army. He improved weapons, revised regulations, raised the pay of enlisted men, and built roads and forts along the frontier. Explorers were dispatched to Utah and New Mexico to map the new territories. A scheme to introduce camels into the Southwest was a noted failure, yet when Davis left office, the army's organization was better than before he arrived.

Personal tragedy again stalked Davis while he served at Washington. His beloved son, Samuel, sickened and died on June 13, 1854. President Pierce attended the little boy's funeral. Further heartbreak awaited Varina and her husband at Richmond in 1864, when Joseph E. Davis, born April 18, 1859, fell from a balcony at the back of their Richmond mansion and died from his injuries.

Prior to his departure from President Pierce's cabinet in March 1857, Jefferson Davis had been elected to the Senate. His colleagues chose him to chair the Military Affairs Committee. He also reassumed his role as the foremost Southern spokesman for states rights.

The chief question that troubled the country concerned the admission of Kansas into the Union as a slave or free state. Extension of slavery was vital to the economic survival of the Southern aristocracy, which believed if the territories were organized into free states by law, they would be overpowered in Congress. Jefferson Davis continued to advise fellow Mississippians to be prepared for war. Though he did not advocate secession, Davis knew it seemed inevitable.

Gridlock replaced action in the United States Senate in 1858. Davis became increasingly combative and confrontational with those who disagreed with him on any matter. He avoided a duel with a Louisiana senator only by apologizing for offensive remarks. A violent man, Davis had come to blows with Senator Henry S. Foote of Mississippi during his first term in the Senate.

John Brown, an insane abolitionist, was also a violent man. He led a band of guerrillas in Kansas that ambushed and slaughtered supporters of slavery. In 1859, he seized the arsenal at Harpers Ferry. His aim was to promote the armed insurrection of Southern slaves. Colonel Robert E. Lee thwarted his design with a company of marines. Although he was captured and executed on December 2, Brown lit the fuse of the powder magazine that exploded into civil war. Southerners saw a Northern plot to destroy their institutions by unlawful means. John Brown did receive support from Abolitionists, but a

Senate investigation uncovered no organized conspiracy to bring about a slave revolt.   Many Southern politicians remained unconvinced and "refused to abandon their wild speculations, so useful in inciting passions and congenial to their preconceived notions of northern perfidy. Davis, ever the lawyer at heart, would not let his own prejudices color the facts before him...."[4]

By 1860, politics had become divided in the United States according to geographical location rather than party affiliation. Everyone waited for the presidential election to decide the future of the Union. The Democratic Party split and fielded two candidates, John C. Breckinridge of Kentucky and Stephen A. Douglas of Illinois. Abraham Lincoln, who rejected the extension of slavery into the territories but did not favor abolition, was nominated by the Republican Party. Another group, the Constitutional Party, nominated John Bell of Tennessee.

The election of Abraham Lincoln in November propelled South Carolina into action. On December 20, the Palmetto State withdrew from the Union. To solve the impending crisis, the Senate had created a Committee of Thirteen, that included Davis, to consider compromise. Senator Davis suggested that any agreement accepted by the committee should require a majority vote by both Republicans and Democrats.   He realized that "if the committee's Democratic majority simply overrode the opposition, Republicans at large would condemn their proposals. It was a well-intentioned move, though it crippled the committee at the same time."[5]

President-elect Lincoln, at home in Illinois, refused to consider the extension of slavery into the territories as a basis of agreement. Like most Northerners, Lincoln misread the resolve of Southerners to fight for independence from the Union. The Committee of Thirteen, therefore, could not resolve the question of civil war. Unquestionably, many Southern aristocrats thought that secession was in their long term economic self-interest. This conviction implied armed resistance to Northern invasion. Less affluent non-slaveholders answered the call to arms to protect their homes. Northerners fought to preserve the Union and to defend the Constitution.

William E. Dodd, an early biographer of Jefferson Davis, wrote a fascinating revisionist view of the war's true cause.

The lords of industry and transportation of the year 1906 are as loth to surrender any of their monopoly rights as were those [aristocrats] of 1861; and, according to the view of many acute students, there is as much slavery connected with the later as with the earlier system, and far more hardship and suffering. So that when a great Southern senator, worth a half million dollars, equivalent in power to several millions in our day, threatened to break up the national government, he was doing the same kind of thing, and he afterward assumed the same dictatorial mien, that the great Northern senator does when he defies the power of the nation to fix laws which shall regulate the railway traffic of the country. If there were treason in the extreme demands of privilege in 1861, there is treason in the same demands now presented to the people. Jefferson Davis was the champion of vested rights; the advantage he had over his younger brother of the present time consisted in the then unexploded doctrine of state supremacy.[6]

Mississippi seceded on January 9, 1861, and by the end of the month, Florida, Alabama, Georgia, and Louisiana had left the Union. Before he returned to Mississippi at the end of January, Davis exposed a plot to kidnap President-elect Lincoln. Delegations from the six states that had seceded convened at Montgomery, Alabama, to draft a constitution and choose a president of their confederacy. Texas left the Union on February 1, but its representatives arrived too late to participate. The fifty-five members of the convention who voted, chose the man they believed to be the most qualified. On February 10, while he tended his rose garden at Brierfield, Jefferson Davis received a telegram. It informed him that he had been elected to preside over the provisional government of the Southern Confederacy. Though he preferred to serve the South as a general, the statesman accepted the burden out of a sense of public duty. As events unfolded in the following four years of strife, the nascent Confederacy's choice of chief executive proved unfortunate. Ill-prepared for war, the South required immediate victories before the potential of overwhelming Northern resources could be arrayed to crush its power of resistance.

After the fall of Fort Sumter, the states of Virginia, Arkansas, North Carolina and finally Tennessee seceded. Tens of thousands of men filled camps of instruction and drilled without guns. Only 25,000 muskets, generally of poor quality, were taken from Federal arsenals lying in Southern territory. The firearms that were needed by Confederate governors to arm their recruits could be purchased in Europe, but on April 16, President Lincoln had declared the 3,549 miles of Southern coastline to be under blockade. "Both the Confederates and the European powers doubted the Union's ability to effectively blockade the Confederacy, but the nations of France and England were willing to await the results of the blockade and in May 1861 declared their neutrality, thus giving the North's actions its tacit approval. The Southerners were disappointed by Europe's recognition of the blockade, but still held their belief in the power of cotton."[7]

"King Cotton" provided employment for millions in the European textile industry, but President Davis and his countrymen miscalculated badly. Popular opinion held that without cotton a British fleet would appear off the Southern coast and break the blockade to prevent economic collapse in Britain. Confederates based their belief on faulty logic, for Britain bulged with raw cotton and Egypt had become a new source of supply. "Furthermore, English and

French opposition to slavery ran deep, deeper than Confederates wanted to countenance. Most of all, France was already militarily overextended by recent military adventuring in Mexico, while England was enjoying an era of unexampled peace and prosperity. War with a powerful United States posed a greater threat than the loss of Southern cotton."[8]

Before the blockade went into effect, the Confederate government had the opportunity to import munitions from Europe. Few ships entered Southern ports in 1861 with foreign goods. Prior to the outbreak of hostilities, Jefferson Davis should have appreciated the importance of acquiring arms. Not until Fort Sumter was captured did he send Caleb Huse to Europe, by which time the Confederate agent was forced to compete with Northern arms buyers.

President Davis' delay in sending an agent abroad was unwise because war appeared to be unavoidable before the first shots were fired at Fort Sumter. Davis and his compatriots forgot that the "first" revolution had succeeded when the French government saw an opportunity to back a winner following the smashing American victory over the British at Saratoga in 1777. Moreover, even without a state of belligerency between the North and South, the Confederate nation would need modern weapons for its army. As commander-in-chief, President Davis increased the odds against a successful fight for independence by failing to take the initiative in 1861 to secure war material. During the summer of 1861, the South itself embargoed cotton exports. "It was reasoned that such a policy would soon coerce the British to intervene for Southern cotton. The embargo never had official sanction from the Confederate government, but Jefferson Davis and his advisors gave it their tacit approval, believing in its ultimate success."[9]

Davis was elected to provide leadership, both military and civil, for the Confederacy. He faltered because he did not lead the way. Prior to the war, most necessities for daily life were imported into the South through New York. With the import and distribution of goods from the North prevented by war, it was necessary for the Confederacy to enlarge its merchant fleet and protect its ports with warships. Ten surplus ships of the British East India Company, capable of carrying cargo or being converted into warships, were made available to the Confederacy late in 1861. The cost to Davis' government would have been approximately 40,000 bales of cotton, yet the opportunity was ignored. Instead of enhancing its ability to import both civilian and military goods, the Confederate government encouraged privateers to raid Northern shipping.

In the following letter to Judge William M. Brooks, leader of Alabama's secession convention, President Davis reviewed his military policy in 1861, and uncharacteristically, admitted mistakes.

Richmond Va.
March 15th, 1862

Hon. W. M. Brooks
Marion, Ohio[10]

My dear Sir:

If under other circumstances I might be unwilling to hear criticism of acts, the condition of the country now too fully engrosses all my thoughts and feelings to permit such selfish impatience, and I have read yours of the 25th inst., anxious to gather from it information, and thankful for your friendly remembrance and the confidence your frankness evinces. I acknowledge the error of my attempt to defend all of the frontier, seaboard and inland; but will say in justification that if we had received the arms and munitions which we had good reason to expect, that the attempt would have been successful and the battle-fields would have been on the enemy's soil.[11] You seem to have fallen into the not uncommon mistake of supposing that I have chosen to carry the war upon a "purely defensive" system. The advantage of selecting the time and place of attack was too apparent to have been overlooked, but the means might have been wanting. Without military stores, without the workshops to create them, without the power to import them, necessity not choice has compelled us to occupy strong positions and everywhere to confront the enemy without reserves. The country has supposed our armies more numerous than they were and our munitions of war more extensive than they have been. I have borne reproach in silence because to reply by an exact statement of facts would have exposed our weakness to the enemy. History, when the case is fully understood, will do justice to the men who have most suffered from hasty judgment and unjust censure. Military critics will not say to me, as you do, "your experiment is a failure", but rather wonder at the disproportion between the means and the results. You inform me that "the highest and most reputable authors" say that I "have not had a cabinet-council for more than four months." I read your letter to a member and ex-member of my cabinet today: they were surprised at the extravagance of the falsehood, and did not believe that so much as a week had at any time occurred without a cabinet consultation. I would like to know who the authors of such stories are. Your own estimate of me, I hope, assured you that I would not, as stated, treat the "Secretary of War" as a "mere clerk"; and if you knew Mr. Benjamin you must realize the impossibility of his submitting to the degradation at the hands of anyone. The opposition here complain that I cling too closely to my cabinet, not, as in your section, that they are disregarded, and the only contempt of the sentiments of Congress which is here alleged against me (so far as I have heard) is that their wish for the removal of two or more members of the cabinet has not been yielded to. Perhaps there might be added dissatisfaction on the part of a few at the promotion or appointment of military officers without consulting the members of Congress in relation to them. Against the unfounded story that I keep the Generals of the Army in leading strings may be set the frequent complaint that I do not arraign them for what is regarded their failures or misdeeds, and do not respond to the popular clamor by displacing commanders upon irresponsible statements. You cite the cases of Generals Johnston and Beauregard; but you have heard the story nomine mutata, an[d] though General Johnston was offended because of his relative rank, he certainly never thought of resigning, and General Beauregard, in a portion of his report which I understand the Congress refused to publish, made a statement for which I asked his authority, but it is surely a slander on him to say that he ever considered himself insulted by me. The grossest ignorance of the law and the facts can alone excuse the statement as to the ill-treatment of General Price by me. His letters do not permit me to believe that he is a party to any such complaint. If as you inform me, it is "credibly said" that I "have scarcely a friend and not a defender in Congress or in the Army," yet for the sake of our country and its cause I must hope it is falsely so said, as otherwise our fate must be confided to a multitude of hypocrites. It would be easy to justify the appointments which have been made of Brig. Generals by stating the reasons in each case, but suffice it to say that I have endeavored to avoid bad selections by relying on miliary rather than political recommendations, and upon the evidence of service where the case was one of promotion. It is easy to say that men are proscribed because of their political party. Look for yourself and judge by the men filling the offices whether I have applied party tests. When everything is at stake, and the United power of the south alone can save us, it is sad to know that men can deal in such paltry complaints and tax their ingenuity to slander because they are offended in not getting office. I will not follow the example set me and ascribe to them bad motives, but deem it proper to say that the effect of such assaults, so far as they succeed in destroying the confidence of the people in the administration of their government, must be to diminish our chances of triumph over the enemy, and practically do us more harm than if twice the number of men I can suppose to be engaged in such work were to desert to the standard of Lincoln. You are no doubt correct in your view of the propriety of keeping volunteers in the field, but you will not fail to perceive that when a small force is opposed to a large one the alternative is to retreat or fortify some strong position and, as did General [Andrew] Jackson at New Orleans [in 1815], thus compensate for the want of numbers. But the strength of an army is not merely dependant on numbers; another element is discipline and instruction. The first duty now is to increase our forces by raising troops for the war, and bringing out all the private arms of the country for public defense. If we can achieve our independence, the office-seekers are welcome to the one I hold, and for which possession has brought no additional value to me than that set upon it when before going to Montgomery I announced my preference for the commission of a General in the army. Accept my thanks for the kindness which you have manifested in defending me when so closely surrounded by evil reports. Without knowing what are the many things you have supposed me to have done, and which were disapproved, I venture to say if the supposition was based upon the statements of those "reputable authors" before noticed that I was more worthy of your defence than you believed when making it.

Very respectfully your friend
Jeffn. Davis.

A critical reason for Davis' failure as leader of the Confederacy was his inability to inspire his countrymen. Despite a superior education and training in the classics (he excelled in Greek and Latin), his rhetorical skills were inferior to those of President Lincoln. Whereas Lincoln was a self-educated man who used metaphors to create an image in the mind of the listener, the more literate patrician spoke abstractly. The cold logic of Davis' prose emerged in his speeches, which reinforced his public image. His address to the Mississippi legislature and the people in the Hall of the House of Representatives in December 1862 was an attempt to defend his war policy. John M. Sandige, a pre-war Congressman from the Magnolia State who witnessed the event, wrote an impression of it in the 1890s.

> Expecting to hear from Mr Davis only what might tend to comfort and re assure our people as to the result ["and consequences" lined out] of the movement in which they had engaged ["in" lined out], I was greatly surprised at some of his most earnest declarations ["including, as they did, questions of the most vital character" lined out], _ not that he stated anything incredible ["or unbelievable" lined out], but that he should at such a time, state what his auditors and the South did not want to hear _ much less believe, ["vitally" lined out] true though it might be. ["His courage was underrated!" lined out]
>
> Referring to the War, he said its duration could not be determined, and added, "when the War shall end, as I believe it will, in the separate independence of the Confederate States, the South should look upon it as a hollow Truce only, to be interrupted, at short intervals, for a long period of time to come by ["War" lined out] hostilities; and thus, it would become Southern Statesmen to so legislate as that every boy of the Confederacy, when he attained the age of sixteen or seventeen years, should be required absolutely, to give at least three years of time to a regular military training _ so that, when these ["interruptions" lined out] invasions came, we ["shall" lined out] should have a nation of trained soldiers."
>
> The case so strongly put by Mr. Davis had little of comfort to his hearers, who were already getting somewhat sick of the War ["then on hand" lined out], _ and, who hoped they would never _ through the longest life, _ see another. But they grimly made up their minds to persevere and take whatever may befall them. There was a like determination throughout the South, which carried its soldiers to the last of the battle fields and the surrender of its depleted armies.
>
> Fortunately, as all can now say, the failure of the Secession movement, saved the country from being Mexicanized by internecine struggles ["prescient to" lined out] foreseen by Mr Davis, as was the War then being waged.

Miserable financial policy also played a role in Southern defeat. Like his counterparts in the South, Davis understood little about business or economic affairs. "All his life he had dealt with planters and politicians and occasionally with cotton factors. He had been largely concerned with abstractions, such as states rights and constitutional liberties."[12] Davis did not interfere with the Treasury Department to the degree that he did the War Department but allowed Secretary of the Treasury Memminger to exercise his own judgment. Both men advocated taxation to finance the government but the Congress refused to pass a law that raised revenue from the aristocratic class. Less than two percent of the Richmond government's income was derived from taxes. Bonds sold in Europe and loans became the primary source of funds for government operations.

Without access to a source of gold or silver, relatively little specie circulated in the South. Paper money was issued in its place but after July 1863, its value plummeted. Rampant inflation demoralized soldiers and civilians alike because it crippled the economy. Worthless paper money "weakened not only the purchasing power of the Government but also destroyed economic security among the people."[13]

Richmond, Va., Sept 17th 1863.

J.W. Harrison
Secty. of the "Confederate Society"
Enterprise, Miss.

Sir:___ I have received your letter of the 22d ult. enclosing a copy of an address to the people of the Confederate States, calling upon them to unite in an effort to restore and maintain the par value of the currency with gold by forming societies of citizens who will engage to sell and buy only at reduced prices.

The object of the address is most laudable, and I sincerely hope for it great success in arousing the people to concerted action upon a subject of the deepest importance.

The passion for speculation has become a gigantic evil. It has seemed to take possession of the whole country, and has seduced citizens of all classes from a determined prosecution of the war to a sordid effort to amass money. It destroys enthusiasm and weakens public confidence. It injures the efficiency of every measure which demands the zealous co operation of the people in repelling the public enemy and threatens to bring upon us every calamity that can befall free men struggling for independence.

The united exertions of societies like those you propose should accomplish much towards abating this evil and infusing a new spirit into the community. I trust, therefore, that you will continue you labors until their good effect becomes apparent everywhere.

Please accept my thanks for the comforting tone of your patriotic letter. It is a relief to receive such a communication at this time when earnest effort is demanded and when I am burdened by the complaining and despondent letters of many who have stood all the day idle, and now blame anybody but themselves for reverses which have come and dangers which threaten.

Very respectfully, your fellow citizen,
(Signed) Jeffn. Davis

[This document is reproduced in part in *OR* XXX Series I Pt.1 p.212.]

Richmond   April 2nd 1865

Genl R. E. Lee
Petersburg
Va.

The Secretary of War has shown me your dispatch. To moove [*sic*] to night will involve the loss of many valuables, both for the want of time to pack and of transportation. Arrangements are progressing, and unless you otherwise advise the start will be made.

Jefferson Davis

[*OR* XLVI Series I Pt.3 p.1378]

Near midnight on April 2, 1865, the Confederate government evacuated Richmond. The officials rode the cars on the rickety rails of the Danville Railroad and arrived at Danville the following evening. President Davis still believed that the South could still gain its independence through the continuance of the war. The fall of Richmond had given the advantage to Lee, who could now maneuver against Grant and hold off the Union armies while the government re-established itself in southern Virginia. On April 5, Davis issued a proclamation that breathed defiance. It announced that war against the United States would continue in the mountains until the Northerners were worn out and gave up the struggle. Day after day the president waited anxiously for word about his most important army. Finally, on April 8, a telegram reached President Davis from Secretary of War Breckinridge.[14]

Red House. via Clover Station
'R & D.' R.R.

The Presdt.

Evacuation of Richmond completed in order on morning of third 3. Genl: Lee concentrated pretty well about Amelia C.H. on 5th, but enemy occupied Junction that evening, and our forces moved during the night and morning of the 6th to Rice's Station. During the morning we captured some eight hundred 800 prisoners, but it in afternoon met a serious reverse, & portion of arm[y] placed across Appomattox at High Bridge & other points.

I left Genl: Lee at Farmville yesterday morning where he was passing main body across the River for temporary relief. He will still try to move around towards No. Ca. There was very little firing yesterday, and I hear none today. No definite information as to movements of enemy from Junction towards Danville. Stoneman's[15] advance reported yesterday to be near Libert [*sic*]. Lomax[16] reports enemy in considerable force advancing up Shenandoah Valley. No news from Echols,[17] but he is supposed to be on Stoneman's rear. Genl: Lee has sent orders to Lomax to unite with Echols against Stoneman, and to Colston to make firm defence at Lynchburg.

The straggling has been great, and the situation is not favorable. Genls: Gilmer, Lawton[18] and St. John are with me. We will join you as soon as possible.

J. C. Breckinridge
Secty of War.

[*OR* XLVI Series I Pt.3 p.1389]

On April 10, President Davis and his cabinet learned that the Army of Northern Virginia had surrendered. It was now imperative to abandon Danville. Davis decided to transfer the government to Greensboro, North Carolina where the officials and their clerks would be close to the Army of Tennessee, the last important Rebel army in the field. Davis conferred with his cabinet at Greensboro on April 12 and 13. Postmaster General John H. Reagan described his remembrance of the two sessions in the following letter to his friend Jefferson Davis.

Confederate Postmaster-General John Henninger Reagan

House of Representatives
Washington, D. C., Decr 12th, 1880.

Hon Jefferson Davis,
Beauvoir, Miss,

Respected Sir;

I have had no oppertunity [*sic*] to answer your letter of Oct. 1st. at an earlyer [*sic*] day. You call my attention to page 396 and the following pages of Gen. Johnstons narrative, and ask my remembrance as to his statements. After so long a period of time I find that my recollection is indistinct as to what occurred [*sic*] on the day he refers to, the 12th of April 1865. It is much more distinct as to what occurred the day after that. I do not remember the dates, but take Gen. Johnstons statement of them as correct.

I remember that he and Gen. Beauregard were at Greensboro, and that you conversed with them about the condition and strength of Johnstons army. I do not remember ["the" lined out] that you spoke of being able to have a large army in the field in two or three weeks as mentioned on his page 397. Nor do I remember what was said on that subject, if anything. Nor do I remember what members of the cabinet were togather [*sic*] that day.

I do remember that in the discussion of the strength and condition of Gen Johnstons command that it was stated by General Johns[t]on in substance that he had about fourteen thousand infantry. This is my rememberance what was there said about the number of infantry troops, though I may be mistaken as I see on page 398 of Gen. Johnston's book he puts the number at twenty thousand. That he had five or six thousand cavelry [*sic*], and a good compliment of artil[l]ery. I think these statements were made in response to your enquiries about the strength of his force. In this conversation General Johnston said his force was not strong enough to enable him to fight Gen. Shearman's [*sic*] army; and that if he attempted to retreat he would have to abandon part of his artilery and use the horses for transportation. He also said that he thought a retreat would be disasterous [*sic*] to the country through which the armies would pass. In this, and in relation to the strength of his army Gen. Beauregard concurred with him.

In the evening of that day, in view of the condition of things brought to view by your conversation with Generals Johnston and Beauregard you notified the cabinet to meet you at Col. Woods residence 10 oclock the next morning to consider what course should be adop[t]ed. We met the next morning at the time and place appointed. Mr. Benjamine , Gen. Breckenridge [*sic*], Mr. Mal[l]ory, Mr. George Davis[19] being present with you. Mr. Trenholm[20] was sick and absent. Gen Johnston met with us or came in afterwards. The occasion was a solemn one. Most of those present feeling that we had to meet a condition of things never before calling for cabinet consultation. Common place remarks were made for a time, and it seemed to me no was willing to appro[a]ch the subject we had met to consider.

After some delay I said if no other member was ready to speak I would give my views as to the exigencies before us required us to do. Being told by yourself and others to go on I reviewed our condition referring to the loss of Gen. Lee's army, to the occupation of the Mississippi r[i]ver and much of our ter[r]itory by the federal armies, to the loss of our work-shops, arsenals and depots of supplies, &c, and to the report made by Generals Johnston and Beauregard of the condition of the army in North Carolina. I then advised capitulation, and stated the terms on which I thought we ought to abandon the contest 1st

That we should disband the military forces of the Confederacy. 2nd That we should recognise [*sic*] the constitution and authority of the United States on the followin[g] conditions. 3rd The preservation and continuance of our existing state governments. 4th The preservation of all the political rights of our people, and the rights of person and property secured to them by the Constitution of the United States and of the several states. 5th The Freedom from prosecution or penalties for their participation in the war. 6th That our people should be allowed to march under their own colors and bear their arms to their several states are [and] there turn them over to the federal authorities.

After presenting this view Gen. Breckenridge, Mr. Malory and Mr. George Davis in this order expressed their approval of the position and plan I presented. Mr. Benjamine dissented from it, and thought we should continue the struggle.

Subsequently during this meeting it was agreed General Johnston should on his return to Hillsboro enter on negociations [*sic*] with General Shearman, obtain an armistice and ass[c]ertain what terms could be had.

He left for the army, and we subsequently took up our march for Charlotte North Carolina. About 10 oclock of the night [April 15] we were at Lexington N. C. You sent for Gen. Breckenridge and myself, saying you had a dispatch from Gen Johnston requesting you to send some one, or some persons, I do not remember the expression, to aid in the negociations with Gen Shearman, with whom he was then in communication. You stated that you desired me to go because I had suggested a basis for negociations ["which had been presented to the cabinet" lined out], and that you wished Gen Breckenridge to go because Gen Shearman might be unwilling to recognize one not representing the army. And we went and joined Gen Johnston, reaching him the second night after we left between midnight and daylight.

I fear I have been more tedious on this point than you would wish, but thought it best to give this statement pretty fully as I have seen others which did not give the exact facts.

I ought to add that in the cabinet council at Greensboro N.C. we all agreed that it might be necessary to except the president and members of the cabinet out of the amnesty we proposed to ask for the people, and that this should be done if necessary to the protection of the people.

I had no knowledge, and have no recollection of ever hearing before reading Gen. Johnstons book, of the two papers he speaks, of about the thirty-nine thousand dollars in silver, on page 408 of his book. You seem to suppose I should know because of my being the acting Secretary of the Treasury. You will remember I was not charged with this duty until after we left Charlotte North Carolina.

I did not understooeed [understand] ["there was thirty" lined out] from Mr. Trenholm, the Secretary of the Treasury when his duties devolved on me that there was thirty-nine thousand dollars in silver. I think he said there was thirty-six thousand in ["coin" lined out] silver coin. This was paid out to the troops before they reached Washington Georgia_ I knew nothing of this til told about it at Washington Georgia; at which time he also told me that the troops got it into their heads to take the gold which was also then in their charge, and that the officers along in order to prevent this consented to pay out and did pay out to them about thirty-five thousand in gould [*sic*], this being the equivalent of the amount of silver bullion they had along, which he said in some way they supposed they ought to have_ the gold was given them in lieu of the silver bi[u]llion. You may remember that

I had nothing to do with any of the money except that which reached Washington, Ga.; and never had any knowledge of whey [*sic*] or on whose authority these sums were paid to the troops, except that I have a general recollection that it was thought the best disposition which could be made of the silver was to pay it to the troops, as the government had no means for its safe transportation.

I never had any knowledge of a communication from Gen. Johnston, such as is mentioned on page 409 of his book, urging the payment of the government specie to the army. If there was such a paper it never came to my knowledge. If Gen Johnston supposed the Confederate Executive had a large sum of specie he was much mistaken, and it would seem ought to have known this fact before the time [1874] his book was published.

I never saw Gen Johnston's book until this evening, and have only referred to the pages to which you have called my attention. And I write in a hurried manner not satisfactory to myself.

There is one other matter which occurred between yourself and Gen. Johnston, on the day he and Gen. Beauregard came to Greensboro, to which I will refer, because in one of your letters to me in the past there was some exprssion implying that you did not remember it.

Gen Johnston in speaking of one of his interviews with Gen. Shearman said to you that Gen. Shearman had authorized him to say to you that you could leave the United States on a vessel of the United States and to take whoever and whatever you pleased with you; which in the way it was put looked as if the purpose was to induce you to leave the country. To this you promptly responded that you "would do no["t" lined out] act which would place you under obligations to the federal government, and that you would not leave Confederate soil while the[re] was a Confederate regiment on."

I called up this subject with you in our travels afterwards in May [and] refresh your memory by reminding you that you gave me your reason for voting against the extending of the honors of the American Senate to Gen Kossuth[21] that he abandoned Poland with an army of thirty thousand patriot soldiers in the field. The effect of your expressions showing that you could not do a like thing. I could give you references which would show you that Gen Shearman considered this subject and mentioned it to Gen Johnston, but you have no doubt seen them.

There is a book criticising [*sic*] Gen Shearman's March to the Sea, written by a Mr. Bointon [?] entitled "Shearman's Historical Raid The Memoirs in the Light of the Record," which you have doubtless seen. If not I hope you will obtain it. It contains among other things copies of the written opinions given you by the members of your cabinet at Charlotte, N.C., on the questions you submitted to them [illegible] whether you should agree to the terms agreed to between Generals Johnston and Shearman.

It is right for me to say I have no memoranda or data to aid my memory about these matters, and after so great a lapse of time I am almost afraid to[o] write about them.

My family were all well when I left home. Little Jeff intended to send you his picture if I had written from there. He is now ten years old, and is a bright and good boy. Please remember me kindly to Mrs Davis. If I could have got off from home a little sooner I intended to come by and see you & Mrs Davis. I hope to get to see you this spring or summer.

If you find errors in my statement I will be glad to be advised of them.

Very truly and Sincerely your friend
John H. Reagan

President Davis judged surrender anathema but with his generals and the majority of his cabinet against him, he reluctantly agreed to negotiate with General Sherman. Davis believed talks with the Ohioan would buy time to reorganize the army for continued resistance. General Johnston returned to the Army of Tennessee with a letter addressed to Sherman. On April 17, the army commanders conferred in the farmhouse of James Bennit. Their discussion produced no agreement but Johnston offered to negotiate the surrender of all Confederate armies since the secretary of war was nearby. Sherman considered the idea and they decided to meet again the next day.

After some conversation, Secretary Breckinridge joined the distinguished generals who had opposed each other the year before. They appraised John Reagan's surrender terms but Sherman thought them too vague. Sherman drafted a proposal that called for all Confederate armies to disband. State governments then in existence could maintain their authority if the representatives swore allegiance to the Union. Citizens would enjoy the same political rights as they had before the war; slavery was not mentioned. Johnston and Sherman signed the document and they parted as friends while Breckinridge traveled to Charlotte to relate the details of the agreement.

Secretary Breckinridge reached Charlotte on April 22. President Davis immediately called his cabinet into session to review the terms agreed to by Johnston and Sherman. Johnston had exceeded his instructions by agreeing to surrender all remaining armies, which in effect, finished the Confederacy. President Davis refused to yield to circumstances; he would not make peace. Instead, he requested Breckinridge and the others to explain their views concerning the peace proposal.

Charlotte, N.C. April 23rd 1865

To His Excellency, The President

Sir;

In obedience to your request I have the honor to submit my advice as to the course you should take upon the memorandum or basis of agreement made on the 18th inst by and between Gen J.E. Johnston of the Confederate Army and Maj Gen W.T. Sherman of the United States Army provided that paper shall receive the approval of the United States.

The principal Army of the Confederacy was recently lost in Virginia. Considerable bodies of troops, not attached to that Army, have either disbanded or marched to their homes accompanied by many of their officers. Five days ago, the effective force in Infantry and Artillery of Gen Johnston's Army was but 14,770 men and it continues to diminish. That officer considers it wholly impossible for him to make any head[way] against the overwhelming force [80,000] of the Enemy. Our ports are closed and the sources of foreign supply lost to us. The Enemy occupy all, or the greater part, of Missouri, Kentucky, Tennessee, Virginia and North Carolina and move almost at will through the other states East of the Mississippi. They have already taken Selma, Montgomery,

Columbus, Macon and other important towns depriving us of large depots of supplies and munitions of War. Of the small force still at command many are unarmed and the Ordnance Department cannot furnish five thousand Stand[s] of Small Arms. I do not think it would be possible to assemble equip and maintain an army of thirty thousand men at any point East of the Mississippi River. The Contest if continued after this paper is rejected, will be likely to lose entirely the dignity of regular warfare. Many of the states will make such terms as they may, in others separate and ineffective hostilities may be prosecuted, while the war however waged, will probably degenerate into that irregular and secondary stage out of which greater evils will flow to the South than to the Enemy.

For these and for other reasons, which need not now be stated, I think we can no longer continue with a reasonable hope of success. It seems to me that the time has arrived, in a large and clear view of the situation, prompt steps should be taken to put an end to the war. The terms proposed are not wholly unsuited to the altered state of affairs. The states are preserved, certain essential rights are secured and the Army rescued from degradation.

It may be said that the agreement of the 18th_ inst_ contains certain stipulations which you cannot ["execute" lined out] perform. This is true, and it was well understood by Gen Sherman that only a part could be executed by the Confederate Authorities. In any view of the case grave responsibilities must be met and assumed. If the necessity for peace be conceded, corresponding action must be taken. The modes of negotiation which we deem regular and would prefer are impracticable. The situation is anomalous and cannot be solved upon principles of theoretical Exectitude. In my opinion you are the only person who can meet the present necessities.

I respectfully advise;

1st. That you execute, so far as you can, the 2nd Article in the Agreement of the 18th inst.

2nd. That you recommend to the Several States the acceptance of those parts of the Agreement upon which they alone can act.

3rd Having maintained, with faithful and intrepid purpose, the Cause of the Confederate States while the means of organized resistance remained, that you return to the States and the people, the trust which you are no longer able to defend.

Whatever course you pursue opinions will be divided. Permit me to give mine. Should these or similar views ["not" lined out] accord with your own, I think the better judgment ["of your country and the respect of mankind" lined out] will be that you can have no higher title to the gratitude of your countrymen and the respect of mankind, than will spring from the wisdom to see the path of duty at this time, and courage to follow it regardless alike of praise or blame.

> Respectfully and truly
> Your friend
> (Signed) John C. Breckinridge
> Secretary of War.

A true copy of the original in my possession
Stoddard Johnston

The entire Confederate cabinet advised their President to accept the agreement. Davis went along with their recommendation, but accurately foresaw Washington's rejection of Sherman's terms. Sherman learned on April 24 that the terms were unacceptable to his government. The Union general informed Johnston that hostilities would be resumed in forty-eight hours. Davis hoped the mounted men could get away during an armistice, but General Johnston, eager to end the bloodshed, surrendered the Army of Tennessee to Sherman on April 26. He accepted from Sherman the same terms that Grant had given to Lee.

Davis now led a government committed to peace, yet he refused to acknowledge defeat. Accompanied by a cavalry escort and by Breckinridge, Reagan, and Benjamin, Davis fled Charlotte to join Kirby Smith. At the end of April they entered South Carolina where Davis was warmly received by the state's inhabitants. By May 2, the Confederates had reached the small town of Abbeville, a dozen miles from the Georgia border. That afternoon, Davis called a meeting of his cavalry commanders. They informed him that further talk of resistance was pointless since their men still served not to fight Yankees, but to insure the personal safety of the president. Davis refused to heed their defeatist talk; the war was not over!

Late that night the president departed Abbeville with half of the remaining cavalrymen. The following day the Davis party reached Washington, Georgia. On May 4, he announced his intention to temporarily dissolve his government, which would reassemble west of the Mississippi River. Postmaster General Reagan, three aides, a servant, and four soldiers left Washington with Davis, who continued a journey that would end back in Virginia.

With Yankee patrols searching for them, the president and his men moved quickly. On the night of May 5, Davis overtook his wife and children in central Georgia. Varina Davis still believed in the Cause her husband represented. She advised him to ride unescorted to the Trans-Mississippi where the family would reunite. Jefferson Davis knew that the leisurely pace of his wife's party increased the likelihood of capture and on the morning of May 8 he parted company with his family. Rain, however, slowed Davis' progress and Varina's wagons caught up with him as he dozed in an empty house near Abbeville, Georgia. Davis ordered his wife's party to push on without him, but on the evening of May 9, Jefferson and Varina Davis set up camp near Irwinville. In the following letter, Davis described the circumstances of his capture in response to a distorted account published in the *New York Tribune* on August 3, 1875, and sent to him by a close friend.

Memphis Tenn.
18th Aug. 1875

Rt. Revd. W.M. Green

My dear Bishop & Friend,

Please accept my sincere thanks for your kind letter of the 14th Inst. and for the slip enclosed which had not and as you suppose probably would not have been seen by me. The writer is remembered as a drunken thief distinguished even among his fellows for both vices. His story of conversations with my Wife are false and to any one who ever knew her must be absurd. Even a weaker woman would not have entered into explanations of her conduct to a subaltern of the Guard, and he a man whose conduct had necessarily created a feeling of contemptuous disgust. He did ask Mrs. Davis to let him take a little negro orphan who she had in pity rescued from ill treatment of a negro woman in Richmond who claimed that the boy's mother had left him to her. This application Mrs. Davis refused not considering Hudson[22] worthy of trust. We afterwards heard of his threatening to take the boy when we reached Fortress Monroe, and to save the child from such a fate, when we were at the harbor of Port Royal, he was sent with a note to Genl. Saxton[23] who we learned was at that station, and who we considered a man on whose integrity and humanity we could rely. He was an officer of the Regular Army, and I had known him before the War. Hudson states that he was not the first to see me, my first view of him was when Secty. Reagan pointed him out to me as the man who had stolen his saddle-bags. This was perhaps an hour after our capture. Enclosed I send to you a slip cut from a newspaper, and which is the statement of one unknown by me, but who is shown by his published letter to have integrity and truth, and who after the branding the story, that I was captured in the disguise of woman's clothes as a lie, he in forgetfulness of Hudson assumes that no Officer or Soldier can be found who will testify so falsely. You no doubt observed that want of coherence in Hudson's story which usually attends falsehood. He says I was dressed in female attire, and ["said" lined out] that Mrs Davis in her own justification told him "she did dress Mr. Davis in her attire and would not deny it." But that attire appears by his own statement to have been a water proof cloak and a shawl; now where is the hoop skirt and the petticoat and sun-bonnet, which has been the staple of so many malignant diatribes and pictorials. This Hudson did go to the transport ship in Hampton Roads where my Wife and children were detained after my removal to the Fort, and he and others with him broke open my Wifes trunks and pillaged from them articles of her clothing and the clothing of her children, also various little articles ["among others" lined out] such as an Album of Family & Friends photographic likenesses which had been recently found by a friend of mine in Iowa, the papepor [sic] to ["improve" lined out] enhance its value having stated where and when it was procured; also a medal, a photograph of which was sent to me through the mail from New York, with a modest request for its history. Among the articles of female attire ["so" lined out] stolen ["was a hoop skirt which had (illegible) and was packed in a trunk which had not been" lined out] ["from" lined out] when my Wife's trunks were pillaged, just at the Camp and afterwards on the Ship, there may have been all of those since [illegible] as worn by me for purpose of disguise ["since it was packed until opened after our capture until it was

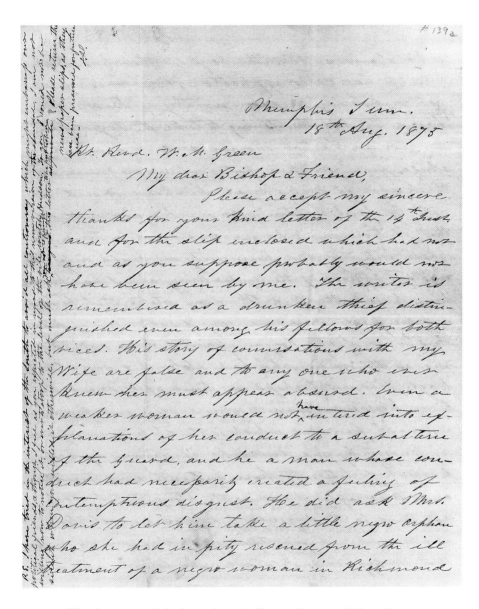

Memphis Tenn.
18th Aug. 1875

Rt. Revd. W. M. Green

My dear Bishop & Friend,

Please accept my sincere
thanks for your kind letter of the 14th Inst.
and for the slip enclosed which had not
and as you suppose probably would not
have been seen by me. The writer is
remembered as a drunken thief distinguished even among his fellows for both
vices. His story of conversations with my
Wife are false and to any one who ever
knew her must appear absurd. Even a
weaker woman would not have entered into explanations of her conduct to a subaltern
of the Guard, and he a man whose conduct had necessarily created a feeling of
contemptuous disgust. He did ask Mrs.
Davis to let him take a little negro orphan
who she had in pity rescued from the ill
treatment of a negro woman in Richmond

The first page of the letter from Jefferson Davis to Bishop Green

opened by those missionaries of civilization" lined out]. I had no trunk there, had gone on horseback, to protect my Wife and children from robbers who it was reported were in pursuit of them; and thus was diverted from the course I was pursuing to join the army in the South West. Having travelled with ["them" lined out] my family for several days and seen them as was supposed beyond ["the infested region" lined out] danger, I had notified my little party consisting of a Secty, three staff officers, four Soldiers & a Servant that after my family and the paroled Soldiers who had volunteered to escort them, had gone into camp for the night, ["that (illegible)" lined out] we would leave them and resume our route to the west; but just at night fall Col. [Preston] Johnston of my staff came to me with the information that he had heard in the village near by, that a party of robbers were to attack the camp that night. My horse was saddled to start and my pistols were in their holsters, but I countermanded the order to leave and remained to protect my Wife and young children. A short time before day I went to sleep in my travelling dress, grey frock coat and trousers, the latter were worn inside of heavy cavalry boots on which remained a pair of conspicuous boot spurs of unusual size. In the grey of the morning my coachman [James Jones] who had remained faithful ["and followed my family" lined out], came to my Wife's tent and aroused me with the announcement that there "was firing over the creek." I stepped out and by the dim light saw Cavalry deployed around our Camp, then turning back told my Wife that we were surrounded by the Enemy's cavalry. She entreated me to leave, and to a water proof "Raglan" which I threw over my shoulders ["added one of her shawls" lined out] as I stepped out of the tent, she followed and put on me one of her Shawls. The water proof was afterwards found to be her's [*sic*] but it was so like my own there being little light in the tent and every thing in confusion within it that it was ["picked up" lined out] taken by mistake. She told the servant woman to ["go with me" lined out] follow me to the stream near by and bring a bucket of water. The Coachman [had] been previously directed to take my horse to a fringe of wood Skirting the Stream towards which I was going. I had gone but a short distance when I was ordered to surrender, and I replied "I will never surrender to a band of thieves," the man dropped his carbine on me as I approached him simultaneously throwing off the cloak & shawl, ["as" lined out] my intent[24] was not executed it is therefore needless to state it. Just then my Wife who had been intently watching, ran up behind me and threw her arms round me. There was nothing more to be attempted. The Soldier showed then no disposition to fire. I said to my Wife "God's will be done", and we turned back to her tent. I then walked on to a fire in rear of it and sat down. After a short time, say half an hour, a man came round to get the names of the Captives, he did not or at least seemed not to know who I was and after the Indian custom I left him to find that out from some body else. Col. Pritchard[25] the comdg officer subsequently told me that he did not learn for three hours after the capture of the camp that I was present. He also claimed credit for the [illegible] shown by the men in not shooting me when I refused to surrender. The "firing over the creek" was between the two ["wings" lined out] Regts[26] of the Enemy's Brigade and we remained for some time waiting for the burial of those killed. There is an irrepressible conflict between this Hudson and truth, so he claimed to have led the charge although a camp of say twenty persons nearly all of them non combattants [*sic*], and by whom not one shot was fired could be the object of a charge by a Brigade of Cavalry. I hope to make the record you suggest, but ["never" lined out] not in it to notice the drunkard, thief, liar, whose statement has found place in the newspapers. The truth has been told many times by men who were with me, but for political ends the "lie" continues to be circulated and tests the adage that when well stuck to it is as good as the truth. As ever I am faithfully

>your friend
>Jefferson Davis

The last page of the letter from Jefferson Davis to Bishop Green

At the left of the first page, the ex-President wrote in the following postscript, vertically.

P.S. I have tried in the interest of the South to avoid all controversy which might embarrass our political friends, & though I feel as you expected in regard to this version of the scandal, I am not willing now to notice it, or ever to stoop to the level of the vile wretch Hudson. To you I could not be silent when you willed it otherwise, but must ask ["to regard" lined out] you not to permit this letter ["as private" lined out] to be published. Please return the news paper slips, as they have been preserved for future use_

J.D.

If Robert E. Lee became the symbol of the Lost Cause, then Jefferson Davis became the living martyr to the Confederacy. Following his capture, the hated Rebel was imprisoned at Fort Monroe, Virginia, in a damp, dark casemate. To prevent his escape, incredibly, the prize prisoner was for a time chained to the wall. Visitors and books, except the Bible, were denied Davis. Brigadier General Nelson A. Miles (1839-1925; commissioned lieutenant 1861) intercepted Mrs. Davis' letters to her husband and he perused them before they were passed on to Mr. Davis, who enjoyed no privacy. A lamp illuminated his cell twenty-four hours a day and his poor health deteriorated. He lost his appetite and had trouble walking, but gradually the harsh conditions imposed upon him improved.

In October of 1865, Davis was transferred to quarters within the fort called Carroll Hall. A long time friend, Reverend Charles Minnegrode visited the Mississippian in December, but it was not until May 3, 1866, that Mrs. Davis was permitted to see the state prisoner. Varina Davis visited her husband daily until the end of July and brought to him a variety of fresh food that restored his health. During this period Davis received permission to walk around the grounds during daylight hours but it was not until May 1867 that Federal authorities released him from prison.

At first, Secretary of War Stanton tried to connect the leader of the Confederacy with the assassination of President Lincoln. When no evidence surfaced to connect Davis to the foul act, Stanton moved on to a charge of treason. President Andrew Johnson and General Grant opposed this action while the Chief Justice of the Supreme Court, Salmon P. Chase, feared acquittal and an embarrassment to the government. The public mood had also grown more forgiving and influential Northerners spoke or wrote on the prisoner's behalf. Persuaded that public opinion was against him, Stanton agreed to allow Jefferson Davis to be turned over to the civil authorities in Virginia. If he had petitioned President Johnson, a fellow Southerner from Tennessee, Davis probably would have received a pardon, but his pride prevailed over pragmatism.

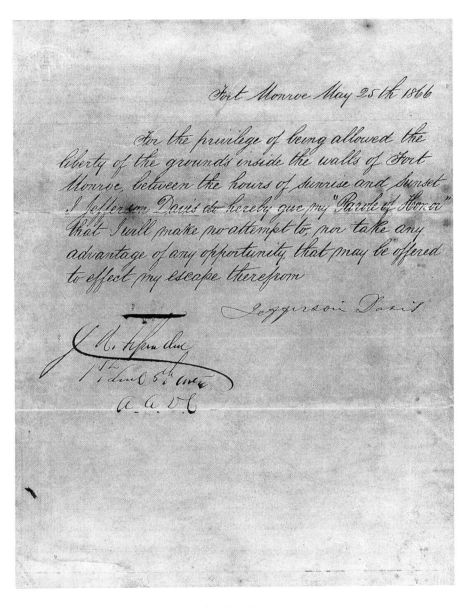

Fort Monroe May 25th 1866

For the privilege of being allowed the liberty of the grounds inside the walls of Fort Monroe, between the hours of sunrise and sunset I Jefferson Davis do hereby give my "Parole of Honor" that I will make no attempt to, nor take any advantage of any opportunity, that may be offered to effect my escape therefrom

Jefferson Davis

The parole of Jefferson Davis

259

On May 13, 1867, Judge John Underwood granted bail to Jefferson Davis, who never stood trial. A year and a half later the government dropped its case against him. Life, however, remained unkind to the tired statesman. Like many other Confederate leaders, Davis failed at business. A steady source of income eluded him, and in October 1871 his son Willie died from diphtheria. In 1875, Mississippians requested their favorite son to represent them in the Senate, but without a formal pardon, he could not participate in Federal government. The following year the nearly penniless former public servant agreed to write his memoirs with the help of Major W.T. Walthall. A wealthy admirer, Sarah Anne Dorsey, furnished Davis a cottage at Beauvoir, Mississippi, on the Gulf Shore.

Work began on *The Rise and Fall of the Confederate Government* in February 1877. Davis provided an outline while Walthall attended to the writing. The arrangement was a mater of economic necessity as the younger man could accomplish the task more quickly. Davis' poor health impeded progress, however, and he visited Varina who lived in Europe due to her psychosomatic illnesses. In July 1877, Mrs. Davis returned to the United States and eventually assisted her husband with his literary project. Her positive attitude relieved the strain on their relationship. Shortly thereafter, yellow fever claimed their last son, Jefferson Jr.

Major Walthall proved to be unreliable. According to the agreement with publisher D. Appleton of New York, the Davis memoir was to be ready July 1, 1878. Walthall did not complete the first volume of the eventual 1500 page work until May 1, 1879. He was not associated with the second volume; an experienced writer from New York finished the work. Finally in mid-1881, the opus was shipped to book stores. "By every measure but one, it was a terrible book. Rambling, disjointed, discursive, and forever disputatious, it spoke for all the personality quirks that had made Davis himself so disliked by many who knew him...throughout the work the logic of his arguments was the same as it had always been which is to say almost none at all other than the automatic assumption that his opinion, whatever it might be, was the right one."[27]

Davis exonerated favorites such as Braxton Bragg but remained hostile to adversaries like Joseph Johnston; he accepted no blame for ultimate defeat. Enemy superiority in numbers and equipment brought about the destruction of the Confederacy. His personal recollection of events is the only redeeming quality of *The Rise and Fall of the Confederate Government*. Due to its high cost, sales were few and Northerners overlooked it. It is unlikely that Davis realized any profits from his work and he adhered to his general policy of avoiding controversy in response to critics.

To his credit, Jefferson Davis respected reconciliation between the Northerners and Southerners. He accepted the verdict of the battlefield even though

Reconstruction troubled him deeply. As any man of advanced age, he enjoyed the company of old friends and attended Confederate reunions. Though never loved like Robert E. Lee, Davis' countrymen grew to respect him. In 1886, he toured Mississippi, Alabama, and Georgia with his youngest child, Varina Anne. Born June 27, 1864, "Winnie" became known as the "daughter of the Confederacy." In the following letter, Davis declined an invitation to speak on the one hundredth anniversary of North Carolina's ratification of the Constitution.

Beauvoir, Miss
25th April 1889

My Dear Friend,

Your very gratifying letter of the 18th inst. has been received. After reading your article in the magazine you sent to me I handed ["the magazine" lined out] it to my daughter ["and she" lined out] who is temporarily absent, therefore I have not been able to find it, when she returns I will as you request send it to you.

You are [at] liberty to use my letter in regard to statements about the treatment of prisoners, as you may think best either as a whole or by extracts.

As to the centennary [*sic*] celebration, let me say to you, for yourself only, that I am too time worn and heart sore, to be equal to the distinguished part to which you would assign me, and I ["wish" lined out] entreat you ["would" lined out] to prevent the proposed invitation.

I feel as in my younger days, ["especial" lined out] but could not satisfactorily express my ["especial" lined out] admiration for the conduct of North Carolina, as well in ["the war" lined out] battles of the Revolution, as in the caution which she displayed in gra[n]ting the larger powers delegated the compact of ["the" lined out] Union.

Even with the Amendments, for which she waited, we have seen how ["fully" lined out] ineffectual paper barriers have resisted usurpation, and can now justly appreciate the wisdom and devotion to inalienable rights, manifested in her confronting isolation in their behalf.

Fraternally yours
Jefferson Davis

Col. W.J. Green
Tokay N.C.

After years of litigation following Joseph Davis' death in 1870, Jefferson Davis recovered Brierfield in 1881; his property never prospered to his satisfaction. During a trip to Brierfield in November 1889, he developed a serious illness. He was conveyed to New Orleans and his wife nursed him on his death bed. A few days before he passed away, Davis confided to her "I am not afraid to die."[28] Davis fell into a coma and succumbed to pneumonia on December 6, 1889.

Jefferson Davis, an honorable, just, querulous man, was not a "fire-eater," but a "Secessionist per se." The former supported secession as policy while the latter favored disunion only as a last resort. Davis answered the public call in 1861 out of a sense of obligation, not of ambition. His capture while trying to discharge a duty that had lost its meaning was consistent with his character. Perhaps it is too simplistic to presume that Davis' decisions alone were responsible for the ruin of the Confederacy, yet the serious military mistakes he committed draws one to that conclusion. The South lost the war in the West, on the battlefield, where the consequences of Davis' misjudgment and mismanagement impacted the most. General Davis may have served the South with distinction and died "in the last ditch," but if he was the best presidential choice available to his section, the Confederate States of America had no future from the beginning.[29]

Following the fall of Vicksburg, Abraham Lincoln prolonged the war when he chose to conquer the Gulf Coast of Texas rather than attacking Mobile. In violation of the Monroe Doctrine, Napoleon III installed a puppet regime in Mexico City which distracted the Lincoln Administration's attention towards an unimportant area. Though Paris never recognized Southern independence, France aided the Confederate cause indirectly by attracting troops to a tertiary theater of operations. Mobile's capture in August 1863 would have permitted Grant to penetrate into central Alabama by mid-September. Confronted by the Army of the Cumberland in north Georgia, the Army of Tennessee would have been powerless to prevent an advance into middle Georgia. It is difficult to comprehend a set of circumstances whereby Generals Johnston and Bragg could have overcome a confident and efficient Army of the Tennessee with a force drawn from the Deep South. Even if Bragg had retreated to defend Atlanta, the strategic point would certainly have fallen that winter. The war could not have continued for long because the North could have concentrated powerful armies to crush Confederate power in Virginia and the Carolinas, which is what happened in 1865.

President Davis was not an evil man. He displayed Christian charity in meeting the physical needs of strangers, but he never seemed to understand the emotional needs of the people he served. John Reagan concluded "that he had two characters—one for social and domestic life and the other for official life. In the first he was one of the most pleasant and genial men I ever knew, a remarkable agreeable conversationalist....In the second he was wholly given to duty. When a subject came up for consideration as important, his habit was to exhaust all available sources of information before reaching a conclusion. The conclusion once reached, that ended it."[30] Whatever sins he may have committed against the Constitution, Jefferson Davis atoned through the endless misfortune and personal suffering that afflicted his tragic life. His last written words were: "May all your paths be peaceful and pleasant, charged with the best fruit, the doing good to others."[31]

APPENDIX

Congressman Colyar drew up a set of resolutions that established a peace commission and designated its members; he then forwarded the proposals to Vice-president Alexander H. Stephens. A secret session of the House of Representatives debated them and President Davis agreed to appoint the commissioners: Stephens, Assistant Secretary of War John A. Campbell, and Senator Robert M. T. Hunter of Virginia. The maneuvering of another Southerner, Francis P. Blair, propelled Davis into action.

Francis Blair had been an intimate friend of President Andrew Jackson and edited the *Washington Globe*, an influential Democratic newspaper. Though he owned slaves, Blair believed that the preservation of the Union superseded sectional interests. By 1860, Blair supported the Republican Party and its candidate, Abraham Lincoln, and he became the President's confidant. Blair's sons, Preston Jr. and Montgomery served as a major general and postmaster general, respectively.

In December 1864, Horace Greeley, editor and founder of the *New York Tribune*, encouraged Blair to approach Lincoln with a peace proposal the presidential advisor had suggested to him some months earlier. The President discussed the idea with Blair in mid-December and responded positively. He told his visitor to return when Savannah, Georgia fell. Savannah was evacuated on December 21 and occupied by Gen. Sherman's army. Three days later Lincoln signed a card that permitted Blair to pass through Union lines and travel south. Francis Blair composed the following note from Grant's headquarters.

Head-Quarters Armies of the United States,

30 December 1864

Jefferson Davis
President &c &c

My Dear Sir:

The loss of Some papers of importance (title papers) which I suppose may have been taken by some persons who had access to my House when Gen Earlys army came in possession of my place induces me to ask the privilege of visiting Richmond. I beg the favor of you to facilitate my enquiries in regard to them

youre obst
F.P.Blair

#121

Head-Quarters Armies of the United States,

_____30. December 1864_

Jefferson Davis

President &c &c

My Dear Sir.

The loss of some papers of importance (little papers) which I suppose may have been taken by some persons who had access to my House when Gen Earlys army were in possession of my place induces me to ask the privilege of visiting Richmond. I beg the favor of you to facilitate my enquiries in regard to them

Yours obt

F. P. Blair

Note from Preston Blair to Jefferson Davis

264

President Davis drafted the following memorandum at the conclusion of his interview with Francis Blair.[1]

Richmond Va

12 Jany 65.

Memo. of a confidential conversation held this day with F.P. Blair of Montgomery County Md.

Mr. Blair stated that not receiving an answer to his application for permission to visit Richmond, which had been sent from the Hd. Qrs. of Genl. Grants army, he returned to Washington and there received the reply which had been made to his application, but by some means had been witheld from him and been forwarded after having been opened.

That he had originally obtained permission to visit Richmond from Mr. Lincoln after stating to him that he (Mr.B.) had for many years held friendly relations with myself, that ["his feeling for me were unchanged" lined out] Mr. Lincoln stopped him _ though he afterwards gave him permission to visit me. He stated in explanation of his position that he being a man of southern blood felt very desirous to see the war between the states terminated and hoped by an interview with me to be able to effect something to that end.

That after receiving the pass which had been sent to him by my direction, he sought before returning, to have a conversation with Mr. Lincoln, had two appointments for that purpose but on each occasion was disappointed and from the circumstances concluded that Mr. Lincoln avoided the interview and therefore came not only without credentials but without such instructions from Mr. Lincoln as enabled him to speak for him. His views therefore were to be regarded merely as his own, and said they were perhaps merely the dreams of an old man &c.

He said despairing of being able to see me he had determined to write to me and had the rough draft of a letter which he had prepared, and asked permission to mail it. Soon after commencing to do so he said (pleasantly) that he found his style was marked by his old pursuit and that the paper appeared too much like an editorial_ He omitted therefore portions of it reading what he considered the main points of his proposition. He had recognized the difference of our positions as not entitling him to a response from me, to to [sic] the arguments and suggestions which he desired to offer. I therefore allowed him to read without comment on my part. When he had finished I inquired as to his main proposition the cessation of hostilities and the union of the military forces for the common purpose of maintaining the "Monroe Doctrine" [and] how that object was to be reached. He said that both the political parties of the U.S. asserted the Monroe doctrine as a cardinal point of their creed. That there was a general desire to apply it the case of Mexico. For that purpose a secret treaty might be made &c.

I called his attention to my past efforts for negociation [sic] and my inability to su[cceed] unless Mr. Lincoln's course in that regard should be changed, how we were to take the first step. He expressed the belief that Mr. Lincoln would now receive commissioners, but subsequently said he could not give any assurance on that point and proposed to return to Washington to explain his project to Mr. Lincoln and notify me if his hope proved well founded that Mr. Lincoln would now agree to a conference for the purpose of entering into negociations.

He affirmed that Mr. Lincoln did not sympathize with the radical men who desired the devastation and subjugation of the Southern states; but that he was unable to control the extreme party which now had great power in the Congress and would at the next session have still more. Referred to the existence of two parties in the cabinet to the ["cursed" lined out] reluctant nomination of Mr. [Salmon P.] Chase to be chief justice &c. &c. &c.

For himself avowed an earnest desire to stop the further effusion of blood, as one every drop of whose blood was Southern he expressed the hope that the pride the power and the honor of the Southern states should suffer no shock. Looked to the extension of Southern territory even to the Isthmus of Darien, and hoped if his views found favor that his wishes would be realized. Reiterated the idea of state sovereignty with illustrations and accepted the reference I made to explanation given in the "Globe" when he edited it of the Proclamation of Genl. Jackson.

When his attention was called to the brutal atrocities of their armies, especially the fiendish cruelty shown to helpless women and children as the cause of a deep seated hostility on the part of our people and an insurmountable obstacle to an early restoration of fraternal relations he admitted the necessity for providing a new channel for the bitter waters, and another bond than that of former memories & interests. This was supposed to be contained in the proposed common effort to maintain the "Monroe doctrine" on the American continent.

It was evident that he counted on the disintegration of the Confederate states if the war continued, and that in any event he regarded the institution of Slavery as doomed to extinction. I thought any remark by me on the first would lead to intimations in connection with public men which I preferred not more distinctly to hear, than as manifested in his general remarks, on the latter point for the reason stated the inequality of his responsibility and mine and preferred to have no discussion.

The only difficulty which he spoke of as insurmountable, was that of existing engagements between European powers and the Confederate States. This point when referred to a second time as the dreaded obstacle to a Secret Treaty which would terminate the war, was met by me with a statement that we had now no such complication, were free to act as to us should seem best, and desired to keep State policy and institutions free from foreign control.

Throughout the conference Mr. Blair appeared to be animated by a sincere desire to promote a pacific solution of existing difficulty, but claimed no other power than that of serving as medium of communications between those who had thus far had no intercourse and were therefore without the cointelligence which might secure an adjustment of this controversy.

To his hopeful anticipation in regard to the restoration of fraternal relations between the sections by the means indicated, I replied that a cessation of hostilities was the first step toward the substitution of reason for passion of sense of justice for a desire to injure and that if the people were subsequently engaged together to maintain a principle recognized by both if together they should bear sacrifices [and] share dangers and gather common renown, that new memories would take the place of those now planted by the events of this war, and might in the course of time restore the feelings which preexisted. But it was for us to deal with the problems before us and leave to posterity questions which they might solve though we could not. That in the struggle for independence ["by the American" lined out] by our Colonial fathers[2] had failure instead of success attended their efforts, Great Britain instead of a Commerce which has largely contributed to her posterity, would have had the heavy expense of numerous garrisons to hold in subjection a people who deserved to be free and had resolved not to be subject.

Our conference ended with no other result than an agreement that he would learn whether Mr. Lincoln would adopt his Mr. Blair's project and send or receive Commissioners to negociate for a peaceful solution of the question at issue, that he would report to him my readiness to enter upon negociation and that I knew of no insurmountable obstacle to such a treaty of peace as would secure advantages to both parties than any result which arms could achieve.

4th Jany. 1865

The foregoing memorandum of conversation was this day read to Mr. Blair and [illegible] altered in so far as he desired in [illegible] respect to change the expressions employed.

Jeffn Davis

OVERLEAF: *Another example of the quality of the material in the Special Collections of the King Library, Miami University — a Lincoln autograph with* **thumbprint.**

Washington Sept 10. 1864

S. N. Holmes Esq

    Dear Sir

I have duly received
yours of Aug 28.

I now send you
the autograph of the
President & will send
you the ———— others
as soon as I have
the leisure to run
to the different Depts

    In haste yours.

      G. E. Matile.

[margin note, written vertically:] The finger marks on the paper are also his. They will do as the often times seals that were made by impressing the thumb on the wax

A. Lincoln.

NOTES

Chapter One

1   Clifford Dowdey, *The Seven Days* (New York: The Fairfax Press, 1978) 37.

2   Brigadier General George Cadwalader 1803-1879; Mexican War.

3   Jackson was promoted on June 17, 1861.

4   William C. Davis, *Battle at Bull Run* (New York: Doubleday & Company, Inc., 1977) 197.

5   Douglas S. Freeman, *Lee's Lieutenant's* (New York: Charles Scribner's Sons, 1944) 74.

6   General Bonham resigned his commission January 29, 1862, and served as governor of South Carolina from December 1862 to December 1864.

7   Brigadier General Thomas Jordan, 1819-1895; West Point 1840. At the Battle of Bull Run he served as General Beauregard's adjutant general with the rank of colonel.

8   Estimates of Union losses range from 2,645-3,334 while estimates of Confederate losses range from 1,752-1,982; Mark M. Boatner, III, *The Civil War Dictionary* (New York: David McKay Company, Inc., 1988) 101.

9   The orders Johnston refers to came from Lee, who commanded all of Virginia's military forces. "The orders themselves were for the most part purely routine, certainly not intended to intrude on Johnston's perquisites as army commander"; Craig L. Symonds, *Joseph E. Johnston: A Civil War Biography* (New York: Norton, 1992) 126.

10 Richard Taylor, *Destruction and Reconstruction: Reminiscences of the Late War*, ed. Richard B. Harwell (New York: Longman's Green and Co., 1955) 44, 45.

11 On December 31, 1862, the 44th Mississippi went into battle armed with sticks; Richard M. McMurry, *Two Great Rebel Armies: An Essay in Confederate Military History* (Chapel Hill: The University of North Carolina Press, 1989) 72.

12 Freeman. *Lee's Lieutenants* 124.

13 Brigadier General Frederick W. Lander 1821-1862; engineer.

14 The Federal Army of the Potomac was created August 15, 1861. Boatner 664. General Johnston's Army of the Shenandoah merged with Beauregard's Army of the Potomac to become known as the Army of the Potomac.

15 Symonds 145.

16 Forts Henry and Donelson were taken February 6 and February 16, 1862, respectively.

17 George W. Randolph replaced Judah Benjamin as Secretary of War on March 22, 1862.

18 Brigadier General Isaac R. Trimble 1802-1888; West Point 1822.

19 Taylor 52.

20   James I. Robertson, Jr., "Stonewall in the Shenandoah: The Valley Campaign of 1862," *Civil War Times Illustrated* 9, (1972): 32.

21   Dowdey 90.

22   Dowdey 102.

23   Edward P. Alexander, *Fighting for the Confederacy: The Personal Recollections of General Edward Porter Alexander*, ed. Gary W. Gallagher (Chapel Hill: The University of North Carolina Press, 1989) 86.

24   Stuart was promoted to brigadier general on September 24, 1861.

25   Alexander 96-98, 107-110. The true reason for "Stonewall" Jackson's disappointing performance during the Seven Days may have been due to ambition. Following the success of his Valley Campaign, he proposed to invade Pennsylvania with 40,000 men. His plan was rejected by Davis and Lee; T. Michael Parrish, *Richard Taylor: Soldier Prince of Dixie*, (Chapel Hill: The University of North Carolina Press, 1992) 223, 224.

26   Boatner 506.

27   William Swinton, *Campaigns of the Army of the Potomac*, Reprint. (New Jersey: The Blue & Gray Press, 1988) 163.

28   Porter was promoted to major general July 1, 1862.

29   Swinton 275.

30   Alexander 205.

31   A.P. Hill was also wounded; Stuart outranked Rodes.

32   Swinton 280.

33   Swinton 307.

34   Emory Thomas, *Bold Dragoon: The Life of J.E.B. Stuart* (New York: Harper & Row Publishers, 1986) 159.

35   Swinton 323.

36   Paul R. Gorman, "J.E.B. Stuart and Gettysburg," *The Gettysburg Magazine*. 1 (1988): 91.

37   Thomas 255.

38   Sheridan was promoted to major general November 14, 1864.

39   Swinton 487.

Chapter Two

1   McMurry. *Two Great Rebel Armies* 105.

2   Stanley F. Horn, *The Army of the Tennessee* (New York: The Bobbs-Merrill Company, 1941) 332.

3   Stephen Woodworth, *Jefferson Davis and His Generals: The Failure of Confederate Command in the West* (Lawrence: University Press of Kansas, 1990) 185.

4   Taylor 117, 118.

5   Horn. *Army of Tennessee* 202.

6   Peter Cozzens, *No better Place To Die: The Battle of Stones River* (Chicago: University of Illinois Press, 1990) 164.

7   William C. Davis, *The Orphan Brigade: The Kentucky Confederates Who Couldn't Go Home* (New York: Doubleday & Company, Inc., 1980) 160.

8   Cozzens. *No Better Place* 199.

9   Joseph E. Johnston, *Narrative of Military Operations During the Civil War.* Reprint (Bloomington: Indiana University Press, 1959) 162.

10 Horn. *Army of Tennessee* 226.

11 Horn. *Army of Tennessee* 226-227.

12 Horn. *Army of Tennessee* 235.

13 Alexander 293.

14 Horn. *Army of Tennessee* 249-250.

15 Hood was promoted to major general October 10, 1862.

16 Glenn Tucker, *Chickamauga: Bloody Battle in the West* (Dayton, OH: Press of Morningside Bookshop, 1984) 249.

17 Nathaniel C. Hughes, Jr. *General William J. Hardee: Old Reliable* (Wilmington, NC: Broadfoot Publishing Company, 1987) 165.

18 Brigadier General William B. Bate commanded a brigade in Stewart's division at Chickamauga. In a note to Davis dated June 16, 1864, Bragg explained he had relieved Hill for: "Having taken active steps to procure my removal in a manner both unmilitary and unofficer like...." U.S. War Department, *The War of the Rebellion: A Compilation of the Official Records of the Union and Confederate Armies.* Vol. 52, Series I, Part 2 (Washington, D.C., 1880-1901) 677. [Hereafter cited as *OR.*]

19 Brigadier General Lucius E. Polk 1833-1892, planter, nephew to Leonidas Polk, commanded Cleburne's old brigade at Chickamauga.

20 Brigadier General Marcellus A. Stovall 1818-1895, merchant, commanded a brigade in Breckinridge's Division at Chickamauga.

21 Brigadier General John C. Brown 1827-1889, lawyer, commanded a brigade in Stewart's Division at Chickamauga.

22 P.D Stephenson, "Missionary Ridge," A Paper Read Before R. E. Lee Camp No.1 of Richmond, Virginia February 21, 1913 (Louisiana Historical Association Collection, Howard-Tilton Memorial Library, Tulane University) 9.

Chapter Three

1   Rodes was promoted to major general on May 7, 1863.

2   Colonel Cullen A. Battle, 1829-1905, lawyer, was promoted to general with date of rank August 20, 1863.

3   Governor Thomas H. Watts, former attorney general of the Confederate government, took office December 1, 1863.

4   Colonel John T. Morgan, 1824-1907, lawyer, 51st Alabama, rejected his commission dated June 6, 1863, on July 14. In November 1863, Morgan accepted his promotion.

5   Colonel O'Neal's military record cannot be questioned since he was wounded twice and commanded his brigade with "unquestioned courage" at the Battle of Chancellorsville; Ezra J. Warner, *Generals in Gray* (Baton Rouge: Louisiana State Press, 1988) 226. General Rodes mentioned Colonel O'Neal for bravery as commander of the 9th Alabama at Gaines Mill. Colonel John B. Gordon, who led Rodes' brigade during the Seven Days, noted Colonel O'Neal's conduct at the

Battle of Malvern Hill; Clement A. Evans, *Confederate Military History* (Atlanta: Confederate Publishing Co., 1899) 139, 140; Douglas S. Freeman, *Robert E. Lee: A Biography* (New York: Charles Scribner's Sons, 1935) 221-222.

6   *OR* XXXIII Series I p. 1133-1134.

7   Freeman. *R.E. Lee* 79.

8   Alexander 234, 235.

9   Capt. Robert E. Lee, *Recollections and Letters of Robert E. Lee*. Reprint (New York: Garden City Publishing Co., 1926) 220.

10   Swinton 340.

11   Boatner 680.

12   Jubal A. Early, *War Memoirs*, ed. Frank E. Vandiver, Reprint (Bloomington: Indiana University Press, 1960) xix.

13   Thomas A. Lewis, *The Guns of Cedar Creek* (New York: Harper & Row, 1988) 59.

14   Lewis 248.

15   Major General Stephen D. Ramseur 1837-1864, West Point 1860, died at General Sheridan's headquarters comforted by pre-war friends on October 20.

16   Brigadier General Armistead Lindsay Long 1825-1891, West Point 1850, was General Lee's military secretary at Gettysburg. Long was promoted to general from colonel on September 21, 1863.

17   Thomas B. Connelly, *The Marble Man: Robert E. Lee and His Image in American Society* (Baton Rouge: Louisiana State University Press, 1977) 73.

18   Connelly 77.

19   "General C.M. Wilcox on the Battle of Gettysburg," *Southern Historical Society Papers*, Volume VI, July-September 1878: 97-124.

20   *Battles and Leaders of the Civil War*, eds. Robert Underwood Johnson and Clarence Clough Buell, vol. III (New York: The Century Co., 1887) 339-356.

21   Warner. *Generals in Gray* 204, 205.

22   *Battles and Leaders* Vol. II, 396-405.

23   *Battles and Leaders* Vol. II, 663-674.

24   Sir Frederick Maurice, *Robert E. Lee The Soldier*, Reprint (New York: Bonanza Books, no date) 163, 289.

25   Glenn Tucker, *Lee and Longstreet at Gettysburg* (Indianapolis: The Bobbs-Merrill Company Inc., 1968) 172.

26   Freeman. *R.E. Lee* 555.

27   Edwin B. Coddington, *The Gettysburg Campaign: A Study in Command*. Reprint (Dayton, OH: Press of Morningside Bookshop, 1983) 360.

28   Harry W. Pfanz, *Gettysburg The Second Day* (Chapel Hill: The University of North Carolina Press, 1987) 112. Hood was promoted to major general on October 10, 1862.

29   "In that fact, which is historically verifiable, much of the criticism of Longstreet evaporates." Freeman. *Lee's Lieutenants* 173, 175.

30   Brigadier General Edward A. Perry 1831-1889, lawyer, had typhoid fever.

31   Richard Moe, *The Last Full Measure: The Life and Death of the First Minnesota Volunteers* (New York: Henry Holt and Company, 1993) 269, 270.

32 Moxley Sorrel, *Recollections of a Confederate Staff Officer*, ed. Bell Irvin Wiley, Reprint (Wilmington, NC: Broadfoot Publishing Company, Wilmington, 1987) 242.

33 Tucker. *Lee and Longstreet* 237.

34 Freeman. *Lee's Lieutenant's* 134.

35 *Battles and Leaders* Vol. III, 313; "Richard H. Anderson...failed to move all of his brigades on the second when he should have, and personally failed to inspire his troops or give adequate orders"; Richard A. Sauers, "Gettysburg Controversies," *The Gettysburg Magazine* January 1991: 118.

36 Tucker. *Lee and Longstreet* 37, 38; "Hill's role in the battle of Gettysburg is an enigma, and none of his actions are more enigmatic than those of the late afternoon of July 2." Pfanz 414.

37 Alexander 242.

38 Lee 102.

39 Larry J. Daniel, *Soldiering in the Army of Tennessee: A Portrait of Life in a Confederate Army* (Chapel Hill: The University of North Carolina Press, 1991) 27, 28.

40 Richardson's guns belonged to Hill's Corps. Alexander intended to support Pickett with them during his advance, but several of the guns were relocated by Gen. Pendleton, chief of artillery. The remainder changed position to avoid Union artillery fire and did not participate in the attack as Alexander planned.

41 Alexander 283.

42 A succinct review of the reasons for Lee's defeat at Gettysburg may be found in Freeman, *Lee's Lieutenants*, 169.

Chapter Four

1 William C. Davis, *Jefferson Davis: The Man And His Hour* (New York: Doubleday & Company, Inc., 1991) 410.

2 Woodworth 180.

3 Woodworth 183. "On October 26, 1862, General Holmes informed the War Department that some 7,000 of the 27,000 men in his army were completely unarmed...'it is only the moral force of numbers, whose condition is carefully concealed that has kept the enemy in check.'" Poorly armed regiments could have been reorganized and armed east of the river for service in Mississippi. Stephen B. Oates, *Confederate Cavalry West Of The River* (Austin: University of Texas Press, 1992) 71, 72.

4 Holmes was promoted to lieutenant general on October 10, 1862.

5 Colonel Lucius B. Northrop, Commissary General.

6 In order to cooperate with Pemberton at Vicksburg, Holmes, as commander of the District of Arkansas, attacked Helena, Arkansas, on July 4, 1863. It was a bloody failure.

7 Parrish 285, 286.

8 Taylor 166.

9 "A glance at a map showing Federal troop dispositions as they were at the beginning of the action makes the Union success seem all the more remarkable. A worse placement of troops for defensive operations could scarcely be envisioned" Ludwell

H. Johnson, *Red River Campaign: Politics and Cotton in the Civil War* (Baltimore: The Johns Hopkins Press, 1958) 166.

10 Parrish 367.

11 Taylor 229, 230.

12 The command structure of Churchill's four brigade division was that of a corps. Brigadier General Mosby M. Parsons, 1822-1865, politician, commanded two brigades from Missouri; Brigadier General James C. Tappan 1825-1906, politician, commanded two brigades from Arkansas. Johnson 149, 159.

13 Parrish 394, 395.

14 Boatner 7, 8.

15 Parrish 375-379.

16 Major General Magruder was assigned to command the District of Texas in October 1862 where he enjoyed moderate success.

17 Brigadier General John M. Thayer, 1820-1906, Indian fighter, commanded the District of the Frontier.

18 Brigadier General Andrew J. Smith, 1815-1897, West Point 1839.

19 Fort De Russy was captured March 14, 1864.

20 This is a misleading figure. Including the unconscripted and men on details, the total strength of the Trans-Mississippi Department was 42,300. The figure given by Smith is accurate regarding the forces available to contend with Banks and Steele. *OR* XXXIV Series I Pt. 2 p. 1075.

21 Major General Edward R.S. Canby 1817-1873, West Point 1839 replaced General Banks.

22 Two divisions of the 16th Corps, referred to as "Detachment, Army of the Tennessee," participated in the Red River Campaign. Two other divisions served with Sherman in the Atlanta Campaign. Six regiments of the 17th Corps were organized into a provisional division under Brigadier General T. Kilby Smith, 1820-1887, lawyer, and served with the 16th Corps. The 13th Corps was broken up in June and reorganized for the Mobile Campaign of 1865.

23 Brigadier General James G. Blunt 1826-1881; abolitionist.

24 Brigadier General John McNeil 1813-1891; businessman.

25 Following his removal by Grant, Rosecrans was assigned to command the Department of Missouri.

26 Brigadier General William L. Cabell 1827-1911; West Point 1850.

27 Oates 153.

28 *OR* XLI Series I Pt. 1 p. 90.

29 Major General Dabney H. Maury 1822-1900, West Point 1846, commanded the District of the Gulf. Encouraged by Beauregard, Buckner, Bragg, and Taylor, among others, he founded the Southern Historical Society.

30 Lee was promoted to brigadier general on November 6, 1862. He commanded the Confederate force at Chickasaw Bayou that defeated Sherman in December. Exchanged after the fall of Vicksburg and promoted to major general on August 3, 1863, Gen. Lee commanded the cavalry in the Department of Mississippi, Alabama, West Tennessee and East Louisiana. He was promoted to lieutenant general on June 23, 1864.

Chapter Five

1   Edwin C. Bearss, *Decision in Mississippi* (Little Rock: Pioneer Press, 1962) 366.
2   Johnston 272, 275.
3   Christopher Losson, *Tennessee's Forgotten Warriors: Frank Cheatham and His Tennessee Division* (Knoxville: The University of Tennessee Press, 1989) 135.
4   General Lee refused to allow Porter Alexander to leave the Army of Northern Virginia; Alexander 335, 336. Porter Alexander was promoted to brigadier general February 26, 1864. General Johnston considered the affair to be an example of President Davis' unfair treatment of him; Johnston 287-289.
5   Wiley Sword, *Embrace An Angry Wind: The Confederacy's Last Hurrah* (New York: Harper Collins Publishers, New York, 1992) 25.
6   Stanley F. Horn, *The Army of the Tennessee* (New York: The Bobbs Merrill Company, 1941) 317.
7   The 20th and 21st Corps were consolidated into the 4th Corps in September 1863. The 20th Corps was organized in April 1864 from the 11th and 12th Corps.
8   Horn. *The Army of Tennessee* 328.
9   Richard M. McMurry, "Cassville." *Civil War Times Illustrated* December 1971: 48.
10 William R. Scaife, *The Campaign For Atlanta* (Atlanta, GA, 1990) 39.
11 Stewart was promoted to lieutenant general on June 23, 1864.
12 Governor Joseph E. Brown of Georgia; Adjutant and Inspector General Robert A. Toombs, Georgia Militia; Vice-president Alexander Stephens; Congressman Louis T. Wigfall of Texas; Major General Gustavus W. Smith, Georgia Militia.
13 See note #2; see also Albert Castel, *Decision in the West: The Atlanta Campaign of 1864* (Lawrence: University Press of Kansas, 1992) 627. Evidence that Gen. Johnston intended to defend Atlanta is suggested by Gen. Schofield. After the war Johnston told him that he planned to resist Sherman by building a series of artillery redoubts connected by trenches in the rear of the city. Johnston believed "that Sherman could not possibly hold all the railroads leading into Atlanta __at the same time__, nor destroy any one of them so thoroughly that it could not be repaired in time to replenish Johnston's supplies in Atlanta." John M. Schofield, *Forty-Six Years in the Army* (New York: The Century Co., 1897) 153; see also Johnston 363, 364.
14 Castel 352, 353.
15 Johnston 349.
16 Sydney C. Kerksis, Margie Riddle Bearss, and Lee A. Wallace, Jr., *The Atlanta Papers* (Dayton, OH: Press of Morningside Bookshop, 1980) 513.
17 Johnston 350.
18 Hughes 228.
19 Castel 394.
20 Horn. *The Army of Tennessee* 357.
21 Castel 431.
22 Castel 502.
23 Horn. *The Army of Tennessee* 361.
24 Major General Howell Cobb (1815-1868; politician) commanded the District of Georgia. He defended Macon against Stoneman.

25 Captain Ben Lane Posey enlisted in 1861 and commanded the "Red Eagles," Company D, 1st Alabama Infantry. In 1864 he commanded Company K, 38th Alabama Infantry; Muster Rolls 1st and 38th Alabama Infantry, State of Alabama Department of Archives and History, Montgomery; Historian Albert Castel describes him as "a knowledgeable and intelligent officer..." Castel 618, 619. At the end of the war, Capt. Posey was under arrest, perhaps for his outspoken nature. Document dated March 14, 1865, furnished by Jack Friend, Mobile, Alabama; Posey survived the war and resumed his law practice at Mobile. In 1874 his business address was: "9 s royal, up stairs, res 82 Government" [Mobile City Directory, 1875]; He became involved in a controversy concerning the fitness of Judge John Elliot of the Alabama Sixth Circuit Court; his name was associated with Republicans James Longstreet and John S. Mosby. "Clarke County Democrat" September 22 and October 27, 1874. This may account for his disappearance from the Mobile City Directory.

26 "Clearly those who claim that Johnston's retreats did not adversely affect morale do so in the face of significant evidence to the contrary" Daniel. *Soldiering* 141, 142.

27 "There was also a widely held belief that trench warfare would not continue and that when Johnston gave the word a large Chickamauga style battle would be fought and decide the campaign" Daniel. *Soldiering* 143.

28 Hughes 244.

29 Kerksis 723-799; Phil Gottschalk, *In Deadly Earnest: The Missouri Brigade* (Columbia: Missouri River Press, Inc., 1991) 414-431.

30 McMurry. "Cassville" 161, 162.

31 Stanley, F. Horn, *Tennessee's War 1861-1865* (Nashville: Tennessee Civil War Centennial Commission, 1990) 379.

32 Sword 65, 66.

33 Sword 97.

34 Losson 203, 204.

35 Sword 126.

36 Sword 131.

37 Horn. *Tennessee's War* 294.

38 Sword 136.

39 Losson 213.

40 Losson 217.

41 Horn. *The Army of Tennessee* 397, 398.

42 Gottschallk 464.

43 Horn. *The Army of Tennessee* 399.

44 McMurry. "Cassville" 175.

45 Bearss. *Decision in Mississippi* 304.

46 Ralsa C. Rice, *Yankee Tigers: Through The Civil War With The 125th Ohio*, eds. Richard A. Baumgartner and Larry M. Strayer (Huntington, WV: Blue Acorn Press, 1992) 194.

47 "...[A]t Franklin only 12 Rebel cannon fired for a very brief time" Gottschalk 493.

48 Isaac Miller, 93rd Ohio, to his brother, December 2, 1864, Ohio Historical Society, Columbus.

49 R.W. Banks, *The Battle of Franklin*. Reprint (Dayton, OH: Morningside Bookshop, 1988) 76-78.

50 Losson 227.

51 Sword 263.

52 Sword 342.

53 Herman Hattaway, *General Stephen D. Lee* (Jackson, MS: University Press of Mississippi, 1976) 144.

54 Horn. *The Army of Tennessee* 418.

Chapter Six

1   Burke Davis, *To Appomattox* (New York: Rinehart & Company, 1959) 130.

2   Ulysses S. Grant, *Personal Memoirs of U.S. Grant*. Reprint (New York: Da Capo Press, 1982) 544.

3   Freeman. *Lee's Lieutenant's* 691, 692.

4   Bruce Catton, *Grant Takes Command* (Boston: Little, Brown and Company, 1968) 450, 451.

5   William R. Plum, *The Military Telegraph During The Civil War In The United States*. Reprint (New York: Arno Press, 1974) 324, 325.

6   John Y., Simon, ed. *The Papers of Ulysses S. Grant*. Volume 14 (Carbondale and Edwardsville: Southern Illinois University Press, 1985) 342.

7   Major General William Henry Fitzhugh "Rooney" Lee 1837-1891, direct commission 1857; son of Robert E. Lee.

8   Alexander 521.

9   Brigadier General Henry E. Davies 1836-1894, lawyer.

10 Mahone was promoted to major general on July 30, 1864.

11 Grant 545.

12 Simon 351, 352.

13 Simon 351.

14 Freeman. *Lee's Lieutenants* 696.

15 Anderson was promoted to lieutenant general on May 31, 1864.

16 Freeman. *Lee's Lieutenant's* 711.

17 Major General George Washington Custis Lee 1832-1913, West Point 1854.

18 Brigadier General Henry W. Benham 1813-1884, West Point 1837, commanded at City Point.

19 Referring to the lost opportunity at Cold Harbor, historian Bruce Catton stated: "...it is perfectly possible that a smashing attack at dawn on June 2 would have succeeded. But the attack was not made on the morning of June 2, or anywhere near there, because this army simply did not have the right kind of reflexes. From the fall of 1861 onward, it [The Army of the Potomac] had never been quite ready. On the battlefield it was heroic but slow...Now the army was twenty four hours late for the offensive that might have won the war..."Catton 259.

20   Beauvoir (P.O.) Harrison Co., Miss.

29 Jan'y 1879.

Dear General:

In a conversation with General St. John [Brigadier General Isaac M. St. John 1827-1880; engineer, replaced Col. Northrop as commissary general] a few weeks ago, he informed me that he had learned__perhaps at second hand, and not directly from yourself;__that when you were made prisoner in 1865, ["that" lined out] you fell into the hands of Gen. Benham of the Federal Army, and that you had learned from him that the Federal commander had obtained important information with regard to General Robert E. Lee's dispositions for the movements of his Army from a paper which fell into the hands of the enemy, either through treachery, or accident, or neglect, on their entrance into Richmond; indeed, that this paper was the means which enabled them to make their arrangements so promptly for intercepting the progress of our troops between Amelia C.H. & Farmville. Gen. St. John seems to have the impression that the paper referred to was a communication from General Lee, either directly to the President or to the Secretary of War __ more probably the former __ which had never reached its proper destination. If there was nothing confidential in the case, will you do me the favor to give me your recollection of it as fully and minutely as possible? Besides its bearing in other respects, it may possibly throw some light upon the yet unexplained failure of General Lee's request for supplies at Amelia C.H. to reach the President or War Department, with regard to which you may remember that I once consulted you. On that subject, by the way, further inquiries has elicited me some incidental information, but nothing sufficiently definite to be satisfactory. All that has been positively ascertained is of a negative character __ if we may so speak without paradox. It seems to be certain that neither the President, Secretary of War, Quartermaster General, nor Commissary General, ever received the requisition. Cols [Walter] Taylor & [Charles] Marshall [staff officers to R.E. Lee] both remember that it was well understood that such a requisition had been made, but cannot state with precision either the channel through which, or the functionary to whom, it was sent. I wrote, at your suggestion, both to Col. [Robert G.] Cole [chief of commissary] and Col. [James L.] Corley [chief quartermaster], but have never received an answer from either. I have never seen any announcement of the result of your lawsuit __ in which there is or ought to be, a more than personal interest felt throughout the South, but hope that by this time your friends have cause to congratulate you on the success of the right, even though it be partial and long-deferred. Very Sincerely Yours, W.L. Walthall Gen'l G.W.C. Lee, Lexington, Va.

21   Freeman. *R.E. Lee* 73.

22   Charles A. Dana was a newspaperman who served as Assistant Secretary of War 1863-1864.

23   Godfrey Weitzel, "Entry of the United States Forces into Richmond, Virginia April 1865. Calling together of the Virginia Legislature and revocation of the same. By Godfrey Weitzel, Major Corps of Engineers and Brevet Major General. United States Army." MSS. VF:W 436E; MSS. qw 436e RMV, (Cincinnati Historical Society) 657, 658. "Entry of the United States Forces into Richmond, Virginia April 1865..."; On April 5 Secretary of War Stanton telegraphed Grant: "It is desirable that all letters & correspondence [p]rivate or public found at Richmond in the Post office or elsewhere should be immediately sent to Mr Seward by Special Messenger I have ordered

Weitzel to do so but if you can spare an intelligent & trusty officer to see that it is done please give the order." Simon 348; Secretary of State Henry Seward.

24 In 1861, Col. Baldwin served as inspector general of the Virginia military and late commanded the 52nd Virginia until the end of the year. Thereafter he served in the Confederate House of Representatives.

25 E.L. Drake, ed., *Annals of the Army of Tennessee and Early Western History*, Vol.I, Num. 4. (July 1878) 162-164.

26 Simon 352; On April 8, Grant wrote Stanton: "The enemy so far have been pushed from the road towards Danville and are now pursued towards Lynchburg. I feel very confidant of receiving the surrender of Lee and what remains of his Army by to-morrow." Simon 367.

27 Brigadier General Joseph R. Davis 1825-1896, lawyer. Davis attended Miami University.

28 Brigadier Philip St. George Cocke 1809-1861, West Point 1832.

29 Brigadier General David Rumph "Neighbor" Jones 1825-1863, West Point 1846.

30 General Van Dorn was assasinated by a jealous husband May 7, 1863.

31 Major Roberdeau C. Wheat commanded the 1st Louisiana Special Battalion (the original "Louisiana Tigers") at First Bull Run. He was mortally wounded June 27, 1862.

32 Johnston 82.

33 Connelly 95.

34 Connelly 208.

35 McMurry. *Two Great Rebel Armies* chapter 9.

36 Tucker. *Lee and Longstreet* 111; Freeman. *Lee's Lieutenants* 711.

37 Alan T. Nolan, *Lee Considered General: Robert E. Lee and Civil War History* (Chapel Hill: The University of North Carolina Press, 1991) 111.

38 To be fair, the next sentence reads: "I fear, too, the Yankees will bear off their pretty daughters." Lee 57.

39 Nolan 101. "Early himself was not greatly concerned over his failure to enter Washington, because he thought that was explicable. When he came to write of the campaign, his pains were spent in answering criticism that on his advance he had lingered too long in the lower part of the Valley. Lee was satisfied with the results..." Freeman. *Lee's Lieutenants* 567, 568.

40 Freeman. *R.E. Lee*, 167, 168.

41 Nolan 42, also chapter 3.

42 Alexander 531-533.

43 Connelly 208.

Chapter Seven

1 Davis. *Jefferson Davis* 455.

2 Edward A. Pollard, *Southern History of the War* (New York: The Fairfax Press, 1977) 271.

3 Clement Eaton, *Jefferson Davis* (New York: The Free Press, A Division of Macmillan Publishing Co., 1977) 69.

4   Davis. *Jefferson Davis* 277.

5   Davis. *Jefferson Davis* 290.

6   William E. Dodd, *Jefferson Davis* (Philadelphia: George W. Jacobs & Company, 1907) 210, 211.

7   Stephen R. Wise, *Lifeline of the Confederacy* (Columbia: University of South Carolina Press, 1988) 25.

8   Davis. *Jefferson Davis* 385.

9   Wise 28.

10 This letter is reproduced as found in the Samuel Richey Collection. It is a typescript on old time rag paper. Even though addressed to an Ohioan, which seemed odd to say the least, the author considered it authentic because of content and style. How it was produced and how it got into the collection is a mystery. Happily, this unique letter can be found on pp. 216-219 "Jefferson Davis, Constitutionalist. His Letters, Papers and Speeches," Volume V, Dunbar Rowland editor, Printed for the Mississippi Department of Archives and History, Jackson, 1923. Minor corrections have been added. It is actually addressed to William H. Brooks of Marion, Alabama, and is dated March 13, 1862. Marion, Ohio, the county seat of Marion County, is north of Columbus.

11 "It was conceded that no decisive success could be gained by attacking General McClellan's army in its position under the guns of a long line of forts. It was agreed, too, that decisive action before the winter was important to us; for it was certain that without it, when the spring campaign opened, the effective strength of the United States army would be much increased by additional numbers and better discipline." Johnston 75.

12 Eaton 197.

13 Douglas B. Ball, *Financial Failure And Confederate Defeat* (Chicago: University of Illinois Press, 1991) 252.

14 General Breckinridge was appointed Secretary of War on February 4, 1865.

15 General Stoneman was exchanged in October. In April 1865 he commanded the District of East Tennessee.

16 Major General Lunsford L. Lomax 1835-1913, West Point 1856.

17 Brigadier General John Echols 1823-1896, lawyer.

18 Major General Jeremy F. Gilmer 1818-1883, West Point 1839; Brigadier General Alexander R. Lawton 1818-1896, West Point 1839.

19 Judah Benjamin was appointed Secretary of State March 18, 1862; Secretary of the Navy Stephen R. Mallory; Attorney General George Davis.

20 Secretary of the Treasury George A. Trenholm.

21 Lajos Kossuth, insurgent governor of Hungary in 1849.

22 Captain Charles T. Hudson, 4th Michigan Cavalry.

23 Brigadier General Rufus Saxton 1824-1908, West Point 1849.

24 A fighter to the bitter end, Jefferson Davis intended to knock Corporal George M. Munger off his horse, then ride away.

25 Lieutenant Colonel Benjamin D. Pritchard commanded the 4th Michigan Cavalry.

26 The camp was surrounded by detachments of the 1st Wisconsin Cavalry and 4th Michigan Cavalry who were unaware of each other's presence. In the pre-dawn darkness, a brief fire fight ensued between the Union soldiers. Two members of the 4th Michigan were killed and one lieutenant was wounded severely. The 1st Wisconsin suffered several casualties but no fatalities. *OR* XLIX Series I Pt. 1 p. 518, 519, 536.

27 Davis. *Jefferson Davis* 676.

28 Davis. *Jefferson Davis* 687.

29 For a discussion on the merits of Robert Toombs and Howell Cobb see Eaton 268-270.

30 Eaton 271.

31 Davis. *Jefferson Davis* 706.

Appendix

1 For a complete account of Francis Blair's mission to Richmond and details on the Hampton Roads Conference, Carl Sandburg, *Abraham Lincoln: The War Years.* Volume Six, The Sangamon Edition (New York: Charles Scribner's Sons, 1941) 28-51.

2 At age twenty three, Samuel E. Davis commanded a militia company in 1779 during the defense of Savannah.

BIBLIOGRAPHY

Alexander, Edward P. *Fighting for the Confederacy: The Personal Recollections of General Edward Porter Alexander.* Ed. Gary W. Gallagher. Chapel Hill: The University of North Carolina Press, 1989.

Ball, Douglas B. *Financial Failure And Confederate Defeat.* Chicago: University of Illinois Press, 1991.

Banks, R.W. *The Battle of Franklin.* Reprint. Dayton, OH: Morningside Bookshop, 1988.

Bearss, Edwin C. *Decision in Mississippi.* Little Rock: Pioneer Press, 1962.

Bearss, Edwin C. and Chris Calkins. *The Battle of Five Forks.* Lynchburg, VA: H.E. Howard, 1985.

Bergeron, Arthur W., Jr. *Confederate Mobile.* Jackson, MS: University Press of Mississippi, 1991.

Bridges, Hal. *Lee's Maverick General.* Lincoln, NE: University of Nebraska Press, 1991 edition.

Boatner, Mark M., III. *The Civil War Dictionary.* New York: David McKay Company, Inc., 1988.

Catton, Bruce. *Grant Takes Command.* Boston: Little, Brown and Company, 1968.

Castel, Albert. *Decision in the West: The Atlanta Campaign of 1864.* Lawrence: University Press of Kansas, 1992.

Coddington, Edwin B. *The Gettysburg Campaign: A Study in Command.* Reprint. Dayton, OH: Press of Morningside Bookshop, 1983.

Connelly, Thomas B. *The Marble Man: Robert E. Lee and His Image in American Society.* Baton Rouge: Louisiana State University Press, 1977.

Cozzens, Peter. *No better Place To Die: The Battle of Stones River.* Chicago: University of Illinois Press, 1990.

—. *This Terrible Sound: The Battle of Chickamauga.* Chicago: University of Illinois Press, 1992.

Daniel, Larry J. *Soldiering in the Army of Tennessee: A Portrait of Life in a Confederate Army.* Chapel Hill: The University of North Carolina Press, 1991.

Davis, Burke. *To Appomattox.* New York: Rinehart & Company, 1959.

Davis, William C. *Battle at Bull Run.* New York: Doubleday & Company, Inc., 1977.

—. *Jefferson Davis: The Man And His Hour.* New York: Doubleday & Company, Inc., 1991.

—. *The Orphan Brigade: The Kentuckians Who Couldn't Go Home.* New York: Doubleday & Company, Inc., 1980.

Dodd, William E. *Jefferson Davis.* Philadelphia: George W. Jacobs & Company, 1907.

Dowdey, Clifford. *The Seven Days.* New York: The Fairfax Press, 1978.

Early, Jubal A. *War Memoirs.* Ed. Frank E. Vandiver. Reprint. Bloomington: Indiana University Press, 1960.

Eaton, Clement. *Jefferson Davis.* New York: The Free Press, A Division of Macmillan Publishing Co., 1977.

Edwards, William B. *Civil War Guns.* Harrisburg, PA: The Stackpole Company, 1962.

Evans, Clement A. *Confederate Military History.* Atlanta: Confederate Publishing Co., 1899.

Faust, Patricia L. ed. *Historical Times Illustrated Encyclopedia of the Civil War.* New York: A Division of Harper Collins Publishers, 1991.

Freeman, Douglas S. *Lee's Lieutenant's.* New York: Charles Scribner's Sons, 1944.

—. *Robert E. Lee: A Biography.* New York: Charles Scribner's Sons, 1935.

Grant, Ulysses S. *Personal Memoirs of U.S. Grant.* Reprint. New York: Da Capo Press, 1982.

Harper, Robert S. *Ohio Handbook of the Civil War.* Columbus: The Ohio Historical Society, 1961.

Hattaway, Herman. *General Stephen D. Lee.* Jackson, MS: University Press of Mississippi, 1976.

Hennessey, John J. *Return to Bull Run: The Campaign and Battle of Second Manassas.* New York: Simon and Schuster, 1993.

Hood, John Bell. *Advance and Retreat.* Kraus Reprint. New York, 1990.

Horn, Stanley, F. *Tennessee's War 1861-1865.* Nashville: Tennessee Civil War Centennial Commission, 1990.

—. *The Army of the Tennessee.* New York: The Bobbs-Merrill Company, 1941.

Hughes, Nathaniel C., Jr. *General William J. Hardee: Old Reliable.* Wilmington, NC: Broadfoot Publishing Company, 1987.

Johnson, Ludwell H. *Red River Campaign: Politics and Cotton in the Civil War.* Baltimore: The Johns Hopkins Press, 1958.

Johnson, Robert Underwood and Clarence Clough Buell eds. *Battles and Leaders of the Civil War.* 4 Volumes. New York: The Century Co., 1887.

Johnston, Joseph E. *Narrative of Military Operations During the Civil War.* Reprint. Bloomington: Indiana University Press, 1959.

Kerksis, Sydney C., Margie Riddle Bearss, and Lee A. Wallace, Jr. *The Atlanta Papers.* Dayton, OH: Press of Morningside Bookshop, 1980.

Lee, Capt. Robert E. *Recollections and Letters of Robert E. Lee.* Reprint. New York: Garden City Publishing Co., 1926.

Lewis, Thomas A. *The Guns of Cedar Creek.* New York: Harper & Row, 1988.

Livermore, Thomas L. "The Appomattox Campaign," Proceedings of the Massachusetts Historical Society, 1906, 1907. Volume XX, Series 2. Boston, 1907.

Losson, Christopher. *Tennessee's Forgotten Warriors: Frank Cheatham and His Tennessee Division.* Knoxville: The University of Tennessee Press, 1989.

Maurice, Sir Frederick. *Robert E. Lee The Soldier.* Reprint. New York: Bonanza Books, no date.

McMurry, Richard M. *Two Great Rebel Armies: An Essay in Confederate Military History.* Chapel Hill: The University of North Carolina Press, 1989.

Mobile City Directory, 1875. Mobile, AL: Henry Farrow & Co., Printers, 1874.

Nolan, Alan T. *Lee Considered General: Robert E. Lee and Civil War History.* Chapel Hill: The University of North Carolina Press, 1991.

Oates, Stephen B. *Confederate Cavalry West Of The River.* Austin: University of Texas Press, 1992.

Parrish, T. Michael. *Richard Taylor: Soldier Prince of Dixie.* Chapel Hill: The University of North Carolina Press, 1992.

Parker, Harold T. *Three Napoleonic Battles.* Durham, NC: Duke University Press, 1983.

Pfanz, Harry W. *Gettysburg The Second Day.* Chapel Hill: The University of North Carolina Press, 1987.

Plum, William R. *The Military Telegraph During The Civil War In The United States.* Reprint. New York: Arno Press, 1974.

Pollard, Edward A. *Southern History of the War.* Reprint. New York: The Fairfax Press, 1977.

Rice, Ralsa C. *Yankee Tigers: Through The Civil War With The 125th Ohio.* Eds. Richard A. Baumgartner and Larry M. Strayers. Huntington, WV: Blue Acorn Press, 1992.

Sandburg, Carl. *Abraham Lincoln: The War Years.* Volume Six, The Sangamon Edition. New York: Charles Scribner's Sons, 1941.

Scaife, William R. *The Campaign For Atlanta.* Atlanta, GA, 1990.

Schofield, John M. *Forty-Six Years in the Army.* New York: The Century Co., 1897.

Sifakis, Stewart. *Compendium of the Confederate Armies.* Alabama, Facts on File Inc., 1992.

Simon, John Y., ed. *The Papers of Ulysses S. Grant.* Volume 14. Carbondale and Edwardsville: Southern Illinois University Press, 1985.

Sorrel, Moxley. *Recollections of a Confederate Staff Officer.* Ed. Bell Irvin Wiley. Reprint. Wilmington, NC: Broadfoot Publishing Company, Wilmington, 1987.

Stewart, George R. *Pickett's Charge.* Cambridge, MA: The Riverside Press, 1959.

Swinton, William. *Campaigns of the Army of the Potomac.* Reprint. New Jersey, The Blue & Gray Press, 1988.

Sword, Wiley. *Embrace An Angry Wind: The Confederacy's Last Hurrah.* New York: Harper Collins Publishers, New York, 1992.

Symonds, Craig L. *Joseph E. Johnston: A Civil War Biography.* New York: Norton, 1992.

Taylor, Richard. *Destruction and Reconstruction: Reminiscences of the Late War.* Richard B. Harwell ed. New York: Longman's Green and Co., 1955.

Thomas, Emory. *Bold Dragoon: The Life of J.E.B. Stuart.* New York: Harper & Row, Publishers, 1986.

Tucker, Glenn. *Chickamauga: Bloody Battle in the West.* Dayton, OH: Press of Morningside Bookshop, 1984.

—. *Lee and Longstreet at Gettysburg.* Indianapolis: The Bobbs-Merrill Company Inc., 1968.

U.S. War Department, *The War of the Rebellion: A Compilation of the Official Records of the Union and Confederate Armies.* 127 Volumes. Washington, D.C., 1880-1901.

Wakleyn, Jon L. *Biographical Dictionary of the Confederacy.* Westport, CT: Greenwood Press, 1977.

Warner, Ezra J. *Generals in Blue.* Baton Rouge: Louisiana State University Press, 1986.

—. *Generals in Gray.* Baton Rouge: Louisiana State Press, 1988.

Wise, Stephen R. *Lifeline of the Confederacy.* Columbia: University of South Carolina Press, 1988.

Woodworth, Stephen. *Jefferson Davis and His Generals: The Failure of Confederate Command in the West.* Lawrence: University Press of Kansas, 1990.

PERIODICALS

Davis, Stephen. "Atlanta Campaign." *Blue & Gray Magazine.* Volume VI, Number 6. August 1989.

Drake, E.L. ed. *Annals of the Army of Tennessee and Early Western History.* Volume I, Number 4. July 1878.

"General C.M. Wilcox on the Battle of Gettysburg." *Southern Historical Society Papers,* Volume VI, July-September 1878: 97-124.

Gorman, Paul R. "J.E.B. Stuart and Gettysburg." *The Gettysburg Magazine.* Issue Number One. July 1988.

Griffin, Massy. "Rodes on Oak Hill: A Study of Rodes' Division on the First Day of Gettysburg." *The Gettysburg Magazine*. Issue Number Four. January 1991.

McMurry, Richard M. "Cassville." *Civil War Times Illustrated*. Volume X, Number 8. December 1971.

McPherson, James. "How Lincoln Won The War With Metaphor"; Taylor, John M. "The Second Surrender." *Military History Quarterly*. Volume 3, Number 3. Spring 1991.

McWhiney, Grady C. "Braxton Bragg." *Civil War Times Illustrated*. Volume XI, Number 1. April 1972.

Robertson, James I., Jr. "Stonewall in the Shenandoah: The Valley Campaign of 1862." *Civil War Times Illustrated*. Volume XI, Number 2. May 1972.

Sauers, Richard A. "Gettysburg Controversies." *The Gettysburg Magazine*. Issue Number 4. January, 1991.

Tucker, Glenn. "Chattanooga." *Civil War Times Illustrated*. Volume X, Number 5. August 1971.

UNIT HISTORIES

Davis, William C. *The Orphan Brigade: The Kentucky Confederates Who Couldn't Go Home*. New York: Doubleday & Company, Inc., 1980.

Gottschalk, Phil. *In Deadly Earnest: The Missouri Brigade*. Columbia: Missouri River Press, Inc., 1991.

Moe, Richard. *The Last Full Measure: The Life and Death of the First Minnesota Volunteers*. New York: Henry Holt and Company, 1993.

OTHER SELECTED SOURCES

Daniel, John W. "Address of Major John W. Daniel Before the Virginia Division of the Army of Northern Virginia, October 28, 1875," Louisiana Historical Association Collection, Howard-Tilton Memorial Library, Tulane University.

Stephenson, P.D. "Missionary Ridge," A Paper Read Before R. E. Lee Camp No.1 of Richmond, Virginia February 21, 1913. Louisiana Historical Association Collection, Howard-Tilton Memorial Library, Tulane University.

Weitzel, Godfrey, "Entry of the United States Forces into Richmond, Virginia April 1865. Calling together of the Virginia Legislature and revocation of the same. By Godfrey Weitzel, Major Corps of Engineers and Brevet Major General. United States Army." MSS. VF:W 436E; MSS. qw 436e RMV, Cincinnati Historical Society.

INDEX

PHOTO CREDITS

Battles and Leaders of the Civil War — 121, 247

King Library, Miami University — vi, 12, 16, 45, 59, 60, 61, 63, 64, 80, 81, 82, 83, 85, 86, 87, 96, 103, 137, 138, 153, 166, 167, 169, 171, 172, 173, 174, 179, 181, 182, 195, 196, 197, 212, 213, 214, 215, 216, 217, 218, 223, 224, 255, 257, 259, 264, 268, 269

Library of Congress — 208

Miller's Photographic History of the Civil War — 69

Karl Sundstrom — 54

Bill Turner — 126

U.S. Army Military History Institute — 3(2), 6, 19, 20, 25, 28, 29, 49 (2), 51, 53, 71, 94, 106, 112, 120, 144, 161, 178, 230, 236